God's Pathway to Eternal Prosperity

God's Pathway to Eternal Prosperity

WENDY ALGERNON ATHERLEY

RESOURCE *Publications* • Eugene, Oregon

GOD'S PATHWAY TO ETERNAL PROSPERITY

Copyright © 2020 Wendy Algernon Atherley. All rights reserved. Except for brief quotations in critical publications or reviews, no part of this book may be reproduced in any manner without prior written permission from the publisher. Write: Permissions, Wipf and Stock Publishers, 199 W. 8th Ave., Suite 3, Eugene, OR 97401.

Resource Publications
An Imprint of Wipf and Stock Publishers
199 W. 8th Ave., Suite 3
Eugene, OR 97401

www.wipfandstock.com

PAPERBACK ISBN: 978-1-7252-6768-8
HARDCOVER ISBN: 978-1-7252-6767-1
EBOOK ISBN: 978-1-7252-6769-5

11/10/20

Contents

Introduction vii

PART ONE: THE CHRISTIAN DEFINED

Chapter 1   We Are Born Sinners 3
Chapter 2   We Need a Savior 10
Chapter 3   Christ Died for Our Sins 20
Chapter 4   Repent 34
Chapter 5   Conversion 58
Chapter 6   We Must Be Holy 62
Chapter 7   Christian Perfection 81

PART TWO: GOD'S PATHWAY TO PROSPERITY

Chapter 8   Prosperity through Wisdom 109
Chapter 9   Prosperity through Obedience 155
Chapter 10   Prosperity through Tithes and Offerings 180
Chapter 11   The Christian Perspective of Wealth 213

Subject Index 229
Scripture Index 251

Introduction

"For I know the plans I have for you, declares the LORD, plans to prosper you and not to harm you, plans to give you hope and a future" (Jer 29:11 NIV). This was a promise of hope to the people of Judah, exiled in Babylon, who were grieved or otherwise discouraged, and who were to be punished for their sins. God would allow the Babylonians to destroy Jerusalem and the temple and enslave some of them. God wanted them to know that they would return to the land after seventy years (v. 10) and he would give them hope and take care of their future. Before the Israelites could be freed from Babylon they were to "seek the peace and prosperity of the city to which I have carried you into exile. Pray to the LORD for it, because if it prospers, you too will prosper" (Jer 29:7 NIV).

God's plan of hope and prosperity for us today includes certain obligations that must be actioned in exchange for his benefits. We know that our future will be properly secured if we trust him with our whole heart. We must not trust in our own abilities, capabilities, and volubility. God has plans for all of us, as nations and individuals, and will execute them if we would love him with our whole heart, soul, mind, and strength. Whatever our needs, vision, problems, or challenges, God has not forgotten us. He has planned a bright future of prosperity, hope, and peace for us, and we can feel safe, secure, and protected from all harm and danger, but we must without deviation or digression follow his pathway in order to be guaranteed the benefits of his promises.

The Bible, which is the pure, unadulterated word of God, is the foundation of this volume. No prophesy of the Scripture is of any private interpretation, for the prophesy did not come at any time by our own will, rather, holy men of God spoke as they were moved by the Holy Ghost. These God-inspired scriptures are profitable for sound doctrine, reproof, correction, and righteous instruction, so that Christians may be completely equipped for every good work. We can trust what is written in the sixty-six books, called the Bible, because God inspired and controlled what was written and our faith and actions should be guided by it.

This book is divided into two parts. The principal purpose of part 1 is to clearly and unequivocally define the Christian, and how the soul prospers, so that readers will understand the expected beneficiaries of God's prosperity. There are so many people who are of the view that they are believers because they go to church often, or that they pay tithes, sing in the choir, teach a Sunday school class or perform some other activity in the church, or that they do good things, or they hold some important office. We will define Christianity and its benefits in part 1 of this book as well as the consequences for not accepting Christ as Lord and Master by living our own selfish lives, without care for others.

Part 1 is also intended help us with our own spiritual growth, to provide the unbeliever with enormous benefits that can be obtained by accepting the God given principles set out herein which are designed to give that hope of eternal salvation with Christ. Basically, then, part 1 is a must-read for all persons who have an interest in an understanding of the principles of Christianity. My first task therefore is to define what is meant when the word *Christian* is used, and also explain what is meant when the word *sinner* is used.

We discuss topics such as sin and its consequences, sinners and their relationship with God, Christ died on the cross for our sins, God's forgives our sins, and offers us eternal life. We also exhort on such topics as holiness, and define Christian perfection. We hope that all of us benefit from part 1 of this book and may its contents draw us closer to our Maker and above all that heaven get the opportunity to rejoice over sinners that repent and become converted to the doctrine of Christ-like living.

Part 2 of this book defines God's pathway to prosperity. The whole earth belongs to God. He owns everything in it. He determines whether the rain falls or the sun shines and who will benefit from these blessings. He determines the harvest and the quality of the harvest. He determines how and when and to whom the harvest is distributed. And it is up to us to determine whether we will put ourselves in the right position to have a share in his prosperity.

When Christians are prosperous, we are able to meet our own needs, share with others who are in need, have enjoyment and help the church and God's people. Jesus taught the very important lesson that Christians should not worry: "Sell your possessions and give to the poor. Provide purses for yourselves that will not wear out, a treasure that will not be exhausted, where no thief comes near and no moth destroys. For where your treasure is, there your heart will be also" (Luke 12:33–34 NIV). Money seen as an end in itself, quickly traps us and cuts us off from God and the needy. We should use our money wisely by using it for God's purposes so that we can build up everlasting treasures in heaven where thieves do not come in and steal and it is not corrupted by moth or any other perishable object.

When we give generously to God's work, we are making an acceptable sacrifice that pleases him who will supply our needs according to his glorious riches in Christ. We should put our hope in God instead of wealth for our security, for it is God who provides us with everything for our enjoyment so that we may: "Take hold of the life that is truly life" (1 Tim 6:17–18).

Prosperity may be defined as blessings from the Lord given to persons who follow in his pathways. It is God's abundant overflow; God's great plan for abundant living for his people. The Bible teaches that we are blessed if we do not walk in the counsel of wicked persons, if we do not take a stand with sinners and when we are not seated with those who make mockery of God. We receive blessings when we delight and meditate in his word every day. Indeed, we will be like an evergreen tree planted by the rivers of water that bears fruits seasonally and as a result, prosper in everything that we do. (Ps 1). God gives us durable riches, honor, and righteousness (Prov 18–21). The blessing of the Lord makes rich and adds no sorrow with it (Prov 10:22).

God's concept of prosperity and abundance is different from how it is viewed by the world and the church. Poverty was viewed by the world as piety. If a Christian was poor, they were holy and if they became rich, they concurrently became unrighteous because their wealth was believed to be obtained by corrupt means.

Here is God's command to Joshua and by extension should be applied to all: "This book of the law shall not depart out of thy mouth, but thou shall meditate therein day and night, that thou mayest observe to do all that is written therein: for then thou shall make thy way prosperous, and then thou shall have good success" (Josh 1:8), including a successful journey through life. Our prosperity and good success depend on our relationship with God. All the ways of prosperity are in God's word. We are to read and meditate on his word every single day so that we may learn from him what we must do in all our circumstances. We are also to delight ourselves in the Lord and we will receive the desires of our hearts from him. If we trust him and unswervingly commit every phase of our life and personality and being to him, he will bring to pass all the desires of our heart (Ps 34:4).

The basic needs of the human race are food, clothing, and shelter, and those who are blessed with more money will own vehicles and have more expensive vacations, entertainment, yachts, private aircrafts, and so on. Generally, we are seeking to satisfy our basic needs and as a result we turn to politicians, who, in order to get elected, promise to satisfy those same basic priorities. They promise to provide jobs, ensure food security, solve our water problems, and you will look so sweet in the finest clothes you will now be able to buy. Our policies will put money in your pockets, they say. The truth is that we serve God so that he supplies all our needs according to his riches in glory. Jesus taught: "Therefore I tell you, do not worry about your life, what you will eat or drink; or about your body, what you will wear. Is not life more important than food and the body more important than clothes?" (Matt 6:25 NIV). Politicians and other civic leaders know that you need food, clothing, shelter and other basic security, and they make you believe that your life is just that and nothing else. You are manipulated because of these needs. They use these needs to influence you. Jesus tells us that these needs are not as important as life. When you lose your job and your ability to earn income; when your government paper is falling apart and your retirement benefits are reduced to nothing, we should not be anxious, Jesus has our backs, because the very government that you put your trust in, is not in a position to help you. To tell you the truth, worrying will build up stress, stress will bring on high blood pressure, with high blood pressure there is the likelihood of a stroke, and a stroke will kill you. All our help comes from God and not from politicians or anyone else. Do not worry if your bank turns you away, or your country experiences economic collapse, or some credit agency gives you or your country a bad credit rating, or if you are retrenched by some government agency or other employer. Do not be dismayed, our heavenly Father knows what you have need of and will take care of you.

We must "seek first his kingdom and his righteousness, and all these things will be given to you as well" (Matt 6:33 NIV). We must seek God and his righteousness first. To seek God means that you must read, mark, and inwardly digest his word; you must desire to know him and the power of his salvation, by your constant prayers and faith in him; you must explore what God has on offer for you by carefully scrutinizing and accepting his promises as written in his Holy Word; and you should get to know him personally by accepting him as your Lord and Savior. Righteousness means that you are in the right position under the proper influence of God's authority by being ready to enter his everlasting kingdom with him. Jesus is telling us once we have received his kingdom and his righteousness all the things that we need will be given to us, and we can trust his promises.

"Therefore, do not worry about tomorrow, for tomorrow will worry about itself. Each day has enough troubles of its own" (Matt 6:34 NIV). The smartest, wisest, and most intellectually capable economist or other societal leader does not have a clue as to whether any government economic plan or other plan will work. They sit together and come with plan A, plan B, and plan C and they cannot say for certain which or if any plan will work. If plan A does not work, they turn to plan B, and if plan B does not work, they turn to plan C, and when plan C does not work, they go back to the drawing board and create another plan or hold town-hall meetings hoping to create that ambitious and exciting plan. And then there is the government that knows that they do not have the answers. They come with their "green paper" because they do not know what to do and want you to tell them what to do. They present their policy statements in "white papers" in which they set out proposals for legislative changes that usually do not work or create new challenges with regard to their implementation. God tells us that we should not worry about tomorrow. Can you take worry to the supermarket and get worry to pay the bill? So why worry when you know that worry does not bring about changes? Why worry when you know for sure that worry will not solve any of your challenges. Worry produces disease and disease kills you.

Tomorrow will worry about itself. God will give us everything we need for each day. Whatever our problems are today, God will solve it today. God provides for our daily needs. We worry too much about things that we do not have. Our needs change every day and God will supply whatever you need for that day. Remember when Israel were miraculously freed from the slavery of Egypt. They started to grumble because they lost faith in God. God provided manna from heaven for them to eat. They were to eat all that they wanted to eat on the day but they were not to store up food for the next day. If anyone stored up any "leftovers" it would have rotted in their tents and of course it would have left an unbearable stench. God does not want us to worry about tomorrow because he will take care of our daily needs.

Prosperity then is that special blessing from God of having sufficient resources and using them to accomplish his will by doing good work and advancing his kingdom: "And God is able to make all grace abound toward you, that ye, always having all sufficiency in all things, may abound to every good work" (2 Cor 9:8). It includes, but is not limited to, power, authority, abundant resources, God's protection and safeguards, opportunities, advancement and growth, completeness, excellent health, contentment, soundness of mind, and goodwill. Prosperity will be examined and explained through the experiences of wisdom, obedience, health, and tithing. Other topics such as the principle of giving, covetousness and greed, the rich young ruler and the rich fool are also covered in part 2 of this volume.

As nations, we must accept the true and living God of Abraham, Isaac and Jacob, as our Savior and Leader. The Bible teaches: "Blessed is the Nation whose God is the LORD: and the people whom he hath chosen for his own inheritance" (Ps 33:12). Our God, who inhabits the heavens, looks down on our nations from his lofty glorious place and observe everything that we do. The sustainable prosperity and success of the nations is therefore in the hands of our leaders who have the responsibility of ensuring that their nations is free to serve him in the best beauty of holiness.

Leadership of our nations includes political leadership. Our political leaders have responsibility for ensuring that the right laws are enacted and followed and that those laws do not run afoul of God's laws. In every country, voters must ensure that those individuals who seek political office have a right relationship with Christ and who will wage war for elevation of the people: socially, culturally, morally, intellectually, and spiritually. When our God is satisfied that we are meeting these challenges, our nations will have prosperity and good success.

The church has the important role of identifying those laws suspected of being contrary to God's holy standard and leading the warfare to ensure that these laws are never enacted or that laws already enacted are repealed. The church must also play an active role in identifying matters that need to be drawn to the attention of lawmakers for the betterment of the nation and improved relationships with God our Father. It is the church's responsibility to pray for the nation and everyone with authority. The church must forcefully speak out, in one accord, on all issues of their country for which God is likely to enforce judgement. Since the church is God's voice in the nation, then it is important to involve the church in all areas of planning and execution of the nation's policies and programs. The church must keep its integrity and must be trustworthy and must do everything within its capability to prevent honorable policies and programs from collapsing, and ensuring that any policies or programs that will be detrimental to the kingdom of God and by extension to the nation will not raise its ugly head by the enactment of statute law.

Most importantly, the church must be the example of being a glorious church without a spot or wrinkle but that it is thoroughly washed in the blood of the Lamb of God that takes away the sins of the world. The church is God's light in the world and that is why she must not roll over and play dead.

The business community and not-for-profit organizations, such as labour unions, also have an important leadership role to play in the life of our nations. They must be proactive leaders with respect to advancing the right causes of their constituents. They must work with each other; governments, churches, and others, in unity, to ensure that the nation is on God's page. And this will guarantee the prosperity and success of our land.

God needed to remind his chosen people, Israel, that it was he who freed them on eagles' wings from the bondage of the Egyptians so that he could be in full control of them. He gave them this advice: "Now therefore, if ye will obey my voice indeed, and keep my covenant, then you shall be a peculiar treasure unto me above all people: for all the earth is mine" (Exod 19:5). God created the earth. All nations of the earth, including Barbados, the entire Caribbean, Europe, and the United States of America, belong to him and so the whole world must claim the promises set out in Exodus 19:5, and all other promises and covenants given throughout the Bible so that we too can be beneficiaries of his many and varied blessings.

Abraham is the father of all nations. The whole world is Abraham's seed. In Galatians 3, Paul writes that there is neither Jew nor Gentile, slave nor free, male nor female, and if we belong to Christ, we are Abraham's seed and heirs according to God's promise. The same writer informs us that we are heirs of God and joint heirs with Christ, with entitlement.

Barbados, my home, has from birth, November 30, 1966, proclaimed that God is the head of our nation, and in the second verse of its national anthem, it has acknowledged that the Lord, God of heaven and earth, guided its people for more than the three hundred years; its complete existence. The anthem declares that God has been supplying our needs and protecting and securing its people, so that we are safe from the hand of the enemy. And with him as captain of our small but wise army, and with him still on the people's side, we will not doubt and we will not fear, because through him, we will conquer all enemies and overcome all our challenges, including our social, economic, financial, and spiritual challenges. These fields and hills which God gave to us are for our peace and prosperity.

PART ONE

The Christian Defined

Chapter 1

We Are Born Sinners

A Christian is a human being, created by God, in the image and likeness of God, who recognizes (1) that he is a sinner; (2) acknowledges that he needs a Savior; (3) recognizes that Christ died for his sins on the cross of Mount Calvary; (4) has repented of his sins; (5) and has turned away or ceased from committing sins. This miraculous act of being saved, with its varying dimensions, occurs all at once, immediately and simultaneously. What this means is that a person who recognizes his sinful state will not have to wait until tomorrow or next week or next year before he requests God's forgiveness, turn from his sins, and ask Jesus Christ to be the Lord and Master of his life. Let us say for example that Rev. Dr. Orlando Seale, president of the Caribbean Nazarene College, Trinidad and Tobago, preached a soul-winning sermon at Kensington Oval in Bridgetown, Barbados. At the conclusion of his sermon he would extend an invitation for persons to accept Christ as their Lord and Savior. A person convicted of sin, who makes the decision to serve Christ, would not accept Christ as Savior in stages. He would recognize that he is a sinner at the same time that he recognizes that he needs a Savior, and that Christ died for his sins. He would repent of his sins and turn from them, and all of this takes place at the same time. The individual makes the important step forward and accepts Christ immediately, and he is immediately a brand new creature in Christ Jesus. A brand new creature because he has surrendered his old carnal life to the cross of Jesus Christ and the new life that he has chosen is a life of surrender to God's will.

There are different stages in the process but the miracle take place immediately and simultaneously and without delay. One of the criminals on the cross, who was to be crucified next to Jesus, our Lord, requested that Jesus grant him mercy when he came into his kingdom. Jesus told him that he would be with him in paradise that same day.

The first step in the process of accepting Christ as Lord and Savior is to acknowledge that we are sinners. The Bible, which is the infallible Word of God, teaches that all have sinned and have become destitute of God's glory (Rom 3:23). In other words, our thoughts, our words and our deeds, have fallen way short of God's righteous requirements. The psalmist put it this way: "Behold, I was shapen in iniquity: and in sin did my mother conceive me" (Ps 51:5). We were all dirty with sin and our righteousness is like filthy rags in God's sight.

In the beginning, God created heaven and earth, over a period of six days. On the sixth and final day of God's work, he created the human race in his own image, after his own likeness. He created mankind in a sinless and pure condition. Man was created emotionally, spiritually, and socially like God with all of its freedoms and privileges. He was created a perfect moral being (upright) (Eccl 7:29). Everything that God created was good (Gen 1:31).

God also created the lovely garden of Eden. Every tree grown in the garden was pleasant to the eye and good for food. Man's principle task was to dress and keep the beautiful garden of Eden that God had created for him. Adam was not alone in the garden. God caused a deep sleep to fall on him, and performed a rib operation. He took the rib from Adam, and made the woman, Eve, and gave her to Adam as a helpmeet.

POWER OF CHOICE

God gave man specific instructions relating to the garden. He could freely eat from every tree grown in the garden except the tree of knowledge of good and evil. There were death consequences for the entire world, if Adam should succumb to the tempter, disobey God, and partake of the smallest taste from the forbidden tree (Gen 2:16–17). God gave man the power to choose. He could have chosen to obey God by not eating from the tree of knowledge of good and evil or he could have chosen disobedience to God by partaking of the fruit that God had ordered him not to eat.

When Eve considered the tree of knowledge of good and evil, she saw that the tree was good for food, that it was a delight to the eyes and a tree to be desired to make one wise. Eve ate of the forbidden fruit and gave some to her husband and he also ate some of the fruit in bold disobedience to God's instruction (Gen 3:6). Man chose to disobey God. He chose to sin against God by disobeying his instructions. As a result of this disobedience, sin entered the world and death by sin, and so death passed upon all men, for that all have sinned (Rom 5:12). Man, immediately died spiritually and stood condemned to eternal death if he should choose to remain and physically die while in that spiritually dead condition.

Adam and Eve were tempted by their physical need for food and chose it above their communion with God. This temptation based on their physical need for food is called the lust of the flesh. They were also tempted because the fruits looked pleasurable. This temptation for pleasure is called the lust of the eyes. They were also tempted by their own desire to become a god. This is the sin of the pride of life. The Bible teaches us that all that is in the world is the lust of the flesh, the lust of the eyes and the pride of life and all of us have fallen to these temptations.

Jesus was tempted in all points as we are tempted, but he refused to yield to the tempter's snare, and committed no sin. He was tempted to pursue worldly things rather than trust in God. When he was hungry, he was tempted to turn stones into bread and eat them. This was the lust of the flesh temptation. He was tempted to do a Hollywood-type stunt by jumping from the temple to be spectacularly rescued by his angels. This is the lust of the eyes-type temptation. Jesus was tempted to worship Satan in order to receive all the kingdoms of this world. Jesus did not yield to this temptation and as born-again Christians we must not submit to the tempter because God have provided a way for us to escape.

The lust of the flesh includes sexual immorality, gossip, and abuse of the body with substances harmful to the body:

> Now the works of the flesh are manifest, which are these; Adultery, fornication, uncleanness, lasciviousness, Idolatry, witchcraft, hatred, variance, emulations, wrath, strife, seditions, heresies, envyings, murders, drunkenness, revellings, and such like: of the which I tell you before, as I have also told you in time past, that they which do such things shall not inherit the Kingdom of God. (Gal 5:19–21)

When we look at things that we should not be looking at, or wish to have things that we should not have; when we look on something with desire in our hearts to have it, or have pleasure from it; when we have a yearning for something that rightfully belongs to someone else and it is contrary to the will of God, we have yielded to the temptation of the lust of the eyes. The story of David and Bathsheba comes to remembrance:

> And it came to past in an eveningtide, that David arose from off his bed, and walked upon the roof of the king's house: and from the roof he saw a woman washing herself; and the woman was very beautiful to look upon. And David sent and enquired after the woman. And one said, Is this not Bathsheba, the daughter of Eliam, the wife of Uriah the Hittite? And David sent messengers and took her; and she came in unto him and he lay with her. (2 Sam 11:2–4)

David succumbed to the temptation of the lust of the eyes by coveting Bathsheba, who rightfully belonged to her husband, Uriah. He succumbed to the temptation of the lust of the flesh by committing the sin of sexual immorality, and the sin of murder followed, and this was followed by the sin of cover-up. Jesus taught that from the moment that we look at a person with the desire to have sex with them, we have committed adultery in our hearts.

The pride of life refers to temptations for power or fame. It means seeking to take credit for something that others or that God did. It is when we are asking others to hold us in higher esteem than we merit. It is trying to feel more important than others around us. It is the desire for power with the intention of using that power for personal honor and glory. The proud person boasts of the cravings of his heart and reviles God. He does not regard God. Satan was thrown out of heaven for the sin of pride:

> For thou [Satan] has said in thine heart, I will ascend into heaven, I will exalt my throne above the stars of God: I will sit also upon the mount of the congregation, in the sides of the north: I will ascend above the heights of the clouds; I will be like the most High. (Isa 14:13–14)

God created Satan as a model of perfection, wisdom and beauty, anointed him the guardian of the cherub, and put him on the holy mount of God. He was blameless from the time he was created until wickedness entered his heart and he became violent, and sinned against God, who expelled him in disgrace from his holy mountain. His heart became proud because of his beauty, and his splendor corrupted him, so God discharged him from heaven, because God cannot be in the presence of sin. Jesus taught that it is men's hearts that produce evil thoughts, slander, arrogance, malice and the like. The Bible teaches that the proud person will be brought low while humility will result in exaltation. God resists the proud but gives grace to the humble.

The Bible teaches that death reigned from the moment of Adam's rebellion against God's authority: "Nevertheless, death reigned from the time of Adam to the time of Moses, even over those who did not sin by breaking a command, as did Adam, who was a pattern of the one to come" (Rom 5:14 NIV). Death resulted from Adam's action of sin, and sin has to be destroyed. Man had to die because God promised that he would die if he ate the fruit from the forbidden tree. God was faithful to that promise. God cannot lie. He must keep his word. He cannot say one thing and do something else. God has exalted his name and his word above all things and his word will not be returned to him void but would fulfill his desires and achieve his purposes. God is obedient to his word.

Power to Choose

God has given the human race the authority to choose; the right to obey him or disobey him. We can follow God's high moral principles or go contrary to them. There are no in-betweens. We are either right or wrong; we are either believers in Christ or we are unbelievers; we are either saved or unsaved. God has given us the authority to choose good and life or choose evil and death. We can choose God's blessings or be cursed. God's blessings include but are in no way limited to him circumcising our hearts and those of our children, and giving us long lives, which we all cherish. The choice is ours and ours alone and God will hold us responsible for all our choices, decisions and actions.

Before the foundation of the world, God had determined to save those who were in Christ:

> According as he hath chosen us in him before the foundation of the world, that we should be holy and without blame before him in love. (Eph 1:4)

> Who verily was foreordained before the foundation of the world but was manifest in these last times for you. (1 Pet 1:20)

> And all that dwell upon the earth shall worship him, whose names are not written in the book of life of the Lamb slain from the foundation of the world. (Rev 13:8)

God determined the conditions for salvation, but not who were to be saved. God knew that man would have sinned, and he made the way for man to be saved by his grace and mercy even before the world began. God made his creation in such a way that man would have to seek and find him by faith.

The problem with sin is that it did not begin when God created Adam in the garden of Eden. Creation was part of the solution for solving the problem of sin. Satan is the author of sin, which commenced with his revolt against God, involving other angels, long before God created the world.

God's chosen people, the Israelites, were miraculously delivered from the slavery of Pharaoh and his oppressive Egyptian army. They journeyed from Egypt through the wilderness for three months before they camped in the Desert Sinai in front of the mountain. They were to become a kingdom of priests and a holy nation. But soon, they returned to their worship of idols that they had left behind in Egypt. They made and worshipped a golden calf. God gave them the power to choose: "I call heaven and earth to record this day against you that I have set before you, life and death, blessing and cursing: therefore, choose life, that both thou and thy seed may live" (Deut 30:19). God gave them the power to choose and then advised them to choose life and live.

God has given humanity specific instructions to obey him and have eternal life. We must be obedient to God's laws. These laws of God include but are not limited to the Ten Commandments, such as the first commandment that God gave to Moses: "Thou shall have no other God before me."

Jesus stated that the greatest and foremost of all God's commandments are these two:

> Thou shalt love the Lord thy God with all thy heart, and with all thy soul, and with all thy mind. . . . Thou shalt love thy neighbor as thyself. On these two commandments hang all the law and the prophets. (Matt 22:37–40)

God's demands are simple. We must love him with every sinew in our mind and bodies. We must love him more than our spouses, children, sports, television, medals, accomplishments, careers, fame, wealth or any other such thing which we may consider important to us. We must dedicate and commit ourselves completely to him.

Israel journeyed through the wilderness for forty years because they doubted God and refused to obey him. The result was that an eleven-day journey on foot took forty years to complete because they had a negative mindset, were an ungrateful people; they were fearful, whiny and adulterous. It took a new generation of Israelites, led by the obedient, faithful, courageous and distinguished leadership of Joshua, for the Israelites to cross Jordan and take possession of the prosperity that they were to inherit when they safely arrived in Canaan land. Joshua's good success and prosperity depended on the character of his strength, courage, and his obedience to God's laws. He was responsible for constantly reading and studying God's word and then teaching the same to the Israelites.

Under Joshua's leadership, the Israelites were given the power to choose whether they would serve the tried, proven and trustworthy God of Abraham, Isaac, Jacob and Moses, or whether they would worship false gods:

> Now therefore fear the LORD, and serve him in sincerity and in truth: and put away the gods which your fathers served on the other side of the flood, and in Egypt; and serve ye the Lord. And if it seem evil unto you to serve the Lord, choose you this day whom ye will serve; whether the gods which your fathers serve that were on the other side of the flood, or the gods of the Amorites, in whose land ye dwell: But as for me and my house, we will serve the Lord. (Josh 24:14–15)

Joshua recognized that his responsibility toward God extended way beyond himself. It included his entire household and the entire nation of Israel.

Let Us Choose Correctly

The whole human race has the power of choice. Our choice should be the same as Joshua's. We will put away idolatry (everything and person which and whom we put before God) and serve the true and living God, and we will lead our household to serve God. We will ensure that we take all opportunities to lead others to the saving Grace and keeping power of the man on the middle cross, Jesus Christ. The Bible teaches that no one can come to Jesus unless the Spirit draws him. We, from our darkened and deceitful understanding, do not have the ability or the power to come to God in our own strength because we are naturally the enemies of God and do not know the things that pertain to God. The Holy Spirit will convict us of sin and draw us to himself. We need to make the right choice and be obedient to the Spirit's call, by refusing to eat of the tree of knowledge of good and evil no matter how desirable that tree appears; being mindful that disobedience to God has death consequences.

And we must begin this process by recognizing that we are sinners in need of a Savior.

Chapter 2

We Need a Savior

SIN DEFINED

Sin is defined as "missing the mark." In other words, man has not reached that high moral standard that befits the character of our Lord and Creator. It is defined in the Bible as a transgression of God's holy law: "Whosoever committeth sin trangresseth also the law: for sin is the transgression of the law" (1 John 3:4). That means we commit sins against the laws of God, the laws of the state and of course we can sin against the laws of organizations. However, laws against the state and organizations, etc., must not be afoul of God's righteous requirements. If the law of the state and of organizations are not in sync with God's laws, we must follow God's laws regardless of the consequences. We must not violate God's laws, and our parliaments must not enact laws that are at variance with God's laws and holy ordinances.

Sin is also defined as lawlessness:

> Everyone who sins breaks the law; in fact, sin is lawlessness. But you know that he appeared so that he might take away our sins. And in him is no sin. (1 John 3:4–5 NIV)

Lawlessness is an act of disobeying God's instructions or commands as exemplified by the disobedience of our foreparents while they were in the garden of Eden. The Bible declares that there is none that doeth good; there are no righteous persons. There is not a just man upon this earth, who doeth good and does not sin (Ps 14:3; Rom 3:10; Eccl 7:20). Sin is conceived in the heart and the heart is deceitful above all things and desperately wicked. God himself examines the heart and try the reins (Jer 17:9–10), and God alone determines the state our relationship with him. No one else has the power or ability to determine our salvation.

Paul stated that he delighted in the law of God according to the inward man. This is the law that compels us to examine ourselves and match our standard of righteousness against that which God requires of us. Paul went on to speak of another law in our members that rages war against our minds and brings us into slavery to the law of sin which is in our members. The mind is controlled by the Spirit of God, and with the flesh, we become the servants of sin. Paul then concludes:

> O wretched man that I am! who shall deliver me from the body of this death? I thank God through Jesus Christ our Lord. So then, with the mind I myself serve the law of God; but with the flesh the law of sin. (Rom 7:24–25; see vv. 7–25 for full context)

Whenever we do something that is not of faith, we commit a sin: "For whatsoever is not of faith is sin" (Rom 14:23). When we have a decision to make, we must make it with a clear conscience being completely satisfied that what we are doing is right and will not displease God. We must be fully persuaded in our own minds what is acceptable to God and we must do it with thanksgiving in our hearts. For example, if we eat pork, we must eat in faith, giving thanks to God. If we do not believe that we should eat pork and knowingly eat it with these doubts in our hearts, our consciences will condemn us and we have breached God's righteous requirements. We must not take any action doubting that what we are doing is right. If we do, we commit sin. When there is doubt, we must leave it out.

We must do good deeds when we know and believe that good deeds must be done: "Therefore to him that knoweth to do good, and doeth it not, to him it is sin" (Jas 4:17). Our consciences make us aware that this is the good that should be done. This is the time when the Holy Spirit speaks to us, and we should obey him. This is not a sin of action but one of inaction because of our failure to do what is right and pleasing to God.

Sin also means that we have fallen short of God's glory: "For all have sinned, and come short of the glory of God" (Rom 3:23). We fall very, very, short of God's holy requirements when we fail to give him the honor, glory and praise, which is due to his matchless name. We fall short of God's glory when we refuse to give him thanks and praise for what he has done for us and for others. We fall short of his glory when we refuse to worship him in spirit and in truth, in the best beauty of holiness and instead cling on to our idolatrous habits.

We sin when we show favoritism. The Apostle James urged believers in Christ not to exhibit favoritism (Jas 2:1). James continued:

> If you really keep the royal law found in Scripture, "Love your neighbor as yourself," you are doing right. But if you show favoritism, you sin and are convicted of the law as lawbreakers. (Jas 2:8–9 NIV)

We must, therefore, as the Apostle Paul prescribed to Timothy, keep God's laws without partiality and nothing that we do should be out of favoritism. God created all people equally and persons must not be treated differently because of wealth, fame, or any other status in our society. To put it differently, we must not judge persons based on their outward appearance nor treat some persons better than others. According to Deut 10:17, the great and awesome God that we serve "shows no partiality and accepts no bribes" (NIV). Jehoshaphat advised his newly appointed judges to

> consider carefully what you do, because you are not judging for mere mortals but for the LORD, who is with you whenever you give a verdict. Now let the fear of the LORD be upon you. Judge carefully, for with the LORD our God there is no injustice or partiality or bribery. (2 Chr 19:6–7 NIV)

If we show preference over another person with equal claim, we commit sin. If we discriminate against another, we sin. Showing partiality and favoritism is sin and we must at all times desist from the practice.

All sin is conceived in the heart. The heart is the wellspring of our physical and our spiritual lives, and we must ensure that sin does not take root there. There are consequences for sin. God warned Adam that if he ate from the tree of knowledge of good and evil he would surely die. The Bible teaches that the wages of sin is death and that the soul that sins shall die (Rom 6:23; Ezek 18:4). We should not only recognize that we are sinners, but that we need a Savior to redeem us from our sins back to God, thus avoiding the consequences of eternal death, while at the same time, receiving the benefits of eternal life.

DEATH AND ITS THREE DISTINCT NATURES

Death is the departure of God's Holy Spirit from the spirit of man. It is the departure of man from the presence of God and it is the departure of man's spirit from his physical body. The day that Adam ate the fruit in disobedience to God, the Holy Spirit left Adam's spirit, and he became dead to God. Adam physically lived for nine hundred and thirty years and produced children after their kind. Children are born spiritually dead to God. They are born with Adam's fallen nature, without the Holy Spirit dwelling in their hearts. Man is born outside a relationship with Christ.

Physical Death

The Bible teaches that there is a time when we will physically die. The breath which God breathed into our nostrils at creation will be withdrawn from us and we will be returned to the dust of the ground from whence we came. Our bodies will have no life. We do not know which day, which hour, which moment in time that death will come knocking at our doors, but we will have to answer that call whenever that call is made. Man born of a woman, has a short time to live and is full of trouble. Life has been shortened for the elect's sake and we should be prepared to meet our Lord as Savior whenever he comes or calls:

> What man is he that liveth and shall not see [physical] death. (Ps 89:48)

> There is "a time to be born and a time to die [physically]." (Eccl 3:2)

> It is appointed unto men once to die [physically]. (Heb 9:27)

> Man that is born of woman is of few days and full of trouble. He cometh forth like a flower, and is cut down: he fleeth also as a shadow, and continueth not. (Job 14:1–2)

The point is that we will one day surrender our physical existence whether we like it or not, and we do not know the moment when we will have to meet face to face, head on, the reality of that fate. The big question is, are we ready to die? Some of us may say yes, we have already paid the undertaker for our funeral expenses. Are we really ready to face eternity? Physical death is a tragedy because of its finality. There is no repentance beyond the grave. When God created us, it was not part of his plan for us to sin, to experience pain, disease and death. Death is our punishment for disobedience to God. It is the last enemy that will be destroyed.

> When the perishable has been clothed with the imperishable, and the mortal with immortality, then the saying that is written will come true: Death is swallowed up in victory. Where, O death, is your victory? Where, O death, is your sting? The sting of death is sin, and the power of sin is the law. But thanks be to God! He gives us the victory through our Lord Jesus Christ. (1 Cor 15:54–57 NIV)

Jesus physically died but is alive forever and ever, and he holds the keys of death and hell.

Spiritual Death

Second, we die spiritually. When God created Adam, he put him in the garden of Eden. God walked in the garden in the cool of the day and had fellowship with him. The Lord instructed Adam that he could eat from every tree in the garden of Eden except the tree of knowledge of good and evil, because the day that he ate form that tree, he would surely die. Adam ate from the forbidden tree, sinned against God, and thus separated himself from him. The very day that Adam rebelled against the will of God, he died spiritually. Adam still had physical life. His body was not physically disintegrated. The Holy Spirit left Adam's spirit and Adam became isolated from God. The lust of the flesh, the lust of the eyes and the pride of life has separated mankind from God. The Bible teaches: "But your iniquities have separated between you and your God, and your sins have hid his face from you, that he will not hear" (Isa 59:2). Man, through the act of disobeying God, died spiritually and faced the further consequences of eternal death. Spiritual death means that we are

> dead in trespasses and sins; Wherein in times past ye walked according to the course of this world, according to the prince of the power of the air, the spirit that now worketh in the children of disobedience: Among whom also we all had our conversation in times past in the lusts of our flesh, fulfilling the desires of the flesh and of the mind; and were by nature the children of wrath, even as others. (Eph 2:1–3)

We were once full of spiritual life, but because we lapsed in our relationship with God, that life was withdrawn from us. We missed the mark, missed the target for which God had created us and were no longer in communion with him. We need to acknowledge and confess that we are spiritually dead, hopeless, and deserve the full penalty of God's righteous judgment. Sin is like a cancer which eats away daily at our relationship with God, until that relationship is totally and completely destroyed, and he no longer communes with us. If we do not have a relationship with Jesus Christ, we are spiritually dead and need a Savior to reestablish our spiritual standing with him:

> But God, who rich in mercy, for his great love wherewith he loved us, Even when we were dead in sins, hath quickened us together with Christ, (by grace ye are saved): And hath raised us up together and made us sit together in heavenly places in Christ Jesus. (Eph 2:4-6)

God's great mercies exhibited through his love and his death on the cross of Mount Calvary has saved us from sin and eternal wrath. He has pardoned and justified us by his grace, and it behooves us to live soberly, righteously, and godly in keeping with our deliverance from the guilt, shame, and penalty of sin. We are saved through God's grace, his free, undeserved goodness and favor, which we receive through our faith in Jesus Christ. One day, coming soon, Christians will be caught up to be forever with the Lord; to live and rein with him in glory but we must reestablish a right relationship with him. If that relationship has not been restored, if we are yet sinners, we are spiritually dead and need Jesus Christ to be our Lord and Savior to save us from eternal death.

Eternal Death

The ultimate aspect of death is the departure of the Holy Spirit of God from man's physical body. Eternal death is the consequence of physically dying, while being spiritually dead, as a result of unconfessed sin to God. When Adam was created, he was expected to have communion with his Creator. God and mankind walked and talked together in the garden of Eden. Adam chose his own obstinate selfishness, which severed the wonderful relationship that existed between them. It was because of Adam's sin of disobedience to God that every man born of a woman is born a sinner, spiritually dead and separated from God. If he physically dies in this spiritually dead state, he will suffer the penalty of being eternally separated from God; in other words, he will reap the wages of sin, which is eternal death.

God will punish those who do not recognize him as Lord, and who do not obey his gospel. He will punish those persons who refuse to confess Jesus as their Lord and who do not believe in their hearts that God raised Jesus from the dead. St. Paul put it this way:

> He will punish those who do not know God and do not obey the gospel of our Lord Jesus. They will be punished with everlasting destruction and shut out from the presence of the Lord and from the glory of his might on the day he comes to be glorified in his holy people and to be marveled at among all those who have believed. This includes you, because you believed our testimony to you. (2 Thess 1:8–10 NIV)

The punishment of which Paul writes is eternal destruction and eternal separation from the presence of his Majesty, the King of kings and Lord of lords.

No person in the Bible spoke more about the reality of judgment and hell than Jesus Christ. Jesus knows about it because he took our judgment when he died on the cross. God judged Christ in our place and only Jesus had the power or ability to do it. When he was dying on the cross, his Father in heaven forsook him, in a way that we will never properly comprehend. Our Lord and his Father in heaven were separated, and it was at that moment, Jesus took the pangs of hell and suffered for us everything that man would have been called on to suffer. He loves us and all he requires of us is to repent and accept him as the Savior of our lives because his desire is that all men, everywhere be saved. The judgment for us was passed on to him.

Christ taught us that there is a time coming soon when believers will be separated from unbelievers. The Son of man will return in all his glory with all his angels. He will summon a conference for all people and will separate us into two groups. His saved people will be on his right and all others will be on his left. His sheep on the right will journey with him into eternal life, while the goats on his left will be destined to eternal damnation (Matt 25:31–46). Furthermore, besides all this, there is a great chasm fixed between the saints of God who have the comfort of Abraham's bosom, and the tormented sinner who is seeking to escape hell's fury. The saints cannot go over to the place of torment to provide comfort to the tormented and the tormented cannot cross over to the comfortable zone of Abraham's bosom to escape their torment (Luke 16:25–26).

Hell is the final destination for those sinners who do not accept the Lord Jesus Christ as Savior of their lives. All peoples and nations who have not repented of their sins and turned from their wicked ways to serve the true and living God will be thrown into hell (Ps 9:17). Hell was prepared for the devil and his demons (Matt 25:41). The Bible teaches that the devil, the beast and the false prophet will eventually be thrown into hell:

> And the beast was taken and with him the false prophet that wrought miracles before him, with which he deceived them

> that had received the mark of the beast, and them that worshipped his image. These both were cast alive into a lake of fire burning with brimstone. And the remnant were slain with the sword of him that sat upon the horse, which sword proceeded out of his mouth: and all the fowls were filled with their flesh. (Rev 19:20–21)
>
> And I saw an angel come down from heaven, having the key of the bottomless pit and a great chain in his hand. And he laid hold on the dragon, that old serpent, which is the Devil, and Satan, and bound him a thousand years, And cast him into the bottomless pit, and shut him up, and set a seal upon him, that he should deceive the nations no more, till the thousand years should be fulfilled: and after that he must be loosed a little season. (Rev 20:1–3)
>
> And the devil that deceived them was cast into the lake of fire and brimstone, where the beast and false prophets are, and shall be tormented day and night for ever and ever. (Rev 20:10)
>
> If any man worship the beast and his image, and receive his mark in his forehead, or in his hand, The same shall drink of the wine of the wrath of God, which is poured out without mixture into the cup of his indignation; and he shall be tormented with fire and brimstone in the presence of the holy angels, and in the presence of the Lamb: And the smoke of their torment ascendeth up forever and ever: and they have no rest day nor night, who worship the beast and his image, and whosoever receiveth the mark of his name. (Rev 14:9–11)

The Bible teaches that hell is a bottomless pit of eternal torment. It is a place of unquenchable fire (Matt 3:12).

> The Son of man shall send forth his angels, and they shall gather out of his kingdom all things that offend, and them which do iniquity; And shall cast them into a furnace of fire: there shall be wailing and gnashing of teeth. (Matt 13:41–42)
>
> So shall it be in the end of the world: the angel shall come forth, and sever the wicked from among the just, and shall cast them into the furnace of fire: there shall be wailing and gnashing of teeth. (Matt 13:49–50)

> But the fearful, and unbelieving, and abominable, and murders, and whoremongers and sorcerers, and idolaters, and all liars, shall have their part in the lake which burneth with fire and brimstone: which is the second death. (Rev 21:8)

Hell is also described as a place of outer darkness. God is light and without him it will be all darkness. Christ himself taught:

> And I say unto you, that many shall come from the east and west, and shall sit down with Abraham, and Isaac, and Jacob, in the kingdom of heaven. But the children of the kingdom shall be cast into outer darkness: there shall be weeping and gnashing of teeth. (Matt 8:11–12)

Outer darkness is separation from God in outer darkness. It will be so dark that persons there will not be able to see one another.

St. Paul teaches us that the heathen is justified through faith and any person who has faith in God is a seed of Abraham and shall receive the blessings of Abraham: "So then they which be of faith are blessed with faithful Abraham" (Gal 3:9). They will enjoy the same glory and happiness as Abraham in heaven. The children of the kingdom are those who knew God as their Lord and were part of the kingdom of believers. These were Christians who returned to their vomit of sin by rebelling against God and did not, like the prodigal son, return to the comfort of their Father's home, and lost their salvation and inheritance with the righteous. They grieved the Holy Spirit out of their lives and will not be in a position to receive the comfort from Abraham and will be cast into outer darkness, the blindness and darkness of the unquenchable fire of hell, where there will be weeping and gnashing of teeth.

Fruitless Christians, who turn away from the work of the kingdom of Christ, will also be cast into outer darkness (Matt 25:30). Those Christians who are not clad in the appropriate wedding garments when the King of kings comes, will be bound by their hands and feet and thrown into outer darkness where there will be weeping and gnashing of teeth (Matt 22:1–14). Persons who do not use their talents and gifts productively will be thrown into outer darkness (Matt 25:14–30). Persons who refuse to do good deeds for others will be cursed into eternal punishment of unquenchable fire, which was prepared for the devil and his angels (Matt 25:31–46).

The eternal separation from God is also referred to, in the Bible, as the second death:

> And I saw a great white throne, and him that sat on it, from whose face the earth and the heaven fled away; and there was

> found no place for them. And I saw the dead, small and great, stand before God; and the books were opened: and another book was opened, which is the book of life: and the dead were judged out of those things which were written in the books, according to their works. And the sea gave up the dead which were in it; and death and hell delivered up the dead which were in them: and they were judged every man according to their works. And death and hell were cast into the lake of fire. This is the second death. And whosoever was not found written in the book of life was cast into the lake of fire. (Rev 20:11–15)

We were all spiritually dead and we are sure that we will all experience physical death, unless we are alive at the time when Christ raptures the church, when those Christians who are alive will be caught up together with those deceased believers, to meet our Lord in the air. We need not experience eternal death. The God of heaven and earth has provided an escape route from eternal damnation. Jesus Christ, God's only begotten son, left the glory of eternal heaven and took the curse of sin within his body, from our shoulders, when he was nailed to the cross, in our place. God has promised us the gift of eternal life if we would only accept him as Lord and Master and serve him only all the days of our lives.

We need someone to save us from our sins and eternal death. We cannot save ourselves. Money, fame and power cannot ensure us eternal life. We need a Savior. We need Christ. The Bible teaches us: "For by grace are ye saved through faith; and that not of yourselves: It is the gift of God" (Eph 2:8). God's grace, his unmerited favor that we do not deserve, rescues us from eternal death. We have wandered so far from God and strayed so far from his righteous requirements that we deserve the death penalty. However, if we trust and believe in him, God will grant us eternal life. Our salvation has already been paid for by the death of Christ on the cross.

Let us recognize that we need a Savior and Jesus is the only one who can save us from our sins and eternal death.

Chapter 3

Christ Died for Our Sins

After Adam's fall from the grace of God, while he was in the garden of Eden, the population of the earth multiplied and so did our sins. The Bible says (Gen 6) that the wickedness of man became great in the earth, and every imagination of the thoughts of his heart was only evil, continually. People ate and drank, got married and were given in marriage. God abhors sin of any kind and it grieved him that he had created the human race. It grieved him at his heart to such an extent that he destroyed the entire world by flood, except for Noah and his family (and a pair of every other living creature that inhabited the earth at that time). Despite God's drastic action, man continued to sin and thus continued to be separated from him.

From among all the nations of the world, God chose the people of Israel to be his own people and entered an everlasting covenant relationship with them to be their God for all generations. God promised Abraham, the Father of all nations, that through him, all the families of the earth will be blessed:

> Now the Lord had said unto Abram, [Abraham], Get thee out of thy country, and from thy kindred, and from thy father's house, unto a land that I will shew thee: And I will make thee a great nation, and I will bless thee, and make thy name great; and thou shall be a blessing: And I will bless them that bless thee, and curse him that curseth thee: and in thee shall all families of the earth be blessed. (Gen 12:1–3)

There are two tremendously important promises in Gen 12:1–3. The remainder of the Scriptures is the record of God fulfilling those promises. God promised to make Abraham a great nation. The Scriptures then show how God made that great nation, Israel, and how he nursed it, provided for it, disciplined it, and fulfilled the second major promise to bless all nations through our Lord and Savior, Jesus Christ. Israel was covenanted to obey and follow the Holy God of their salvation.

Adam, through his disobedience, broke the covenant mankind had with God. Adam's doubt and disobedience were punished by spiritual and physical death and for the unrepentant sinner, eternal death. If we are to return to a right relationship with God, we must demonstrate our faith in him and obey him, and we will be rewarded with eternal life.

Abraham was seventy-five years old and was unfortunate to have no children when God promised him that he would be a father and the father of a great nation. He promised Abraham success and prosperity in the land that he had chosen for him. He promised to make Abraham famous and through him, all the families of the earth would be blessed. Abraham, without hesitation or enquiry, left his home, relatives and country in compliance with the will of God. His act of obedience to God was an outstanding act of faith which God accepted as righteousness. He went on to inherit Canaan land. He became very prosperous and his nephew Lot, whom he took with him, also became rich. They acquired so much wealth that they had to divide the property between them. This resulted in strife between Abraham's employees and Lot's employees. Abraham handled the situation the right way. There was no need for strife. Abraham allowed Lot to choose the sweets of the ever-green Jordan, but that choice included the wicked cities of Sodom and Gomorrah. Abraham chose the godly land of Canaan. God later destroyed Sodom and Gomorrah because the men of Sodom were exceedingly wicked sinners before the Lord. When we sin against God, he is angered and hurt by it. We were created to have fellowship with him and to share in his glory. Despite this grief and anger, he extends his abundant grace, forgiveness and mercy to us.

Israel sunk so deep into depravity and sin that God was required to reestablish that covenant relationship with them, in which he was to be their God, and they were to be his people and which was founded upon the law (Exod 19 and 20).

> Now therefore, if ye will obey my voice indeed, and keep my covenant, then ye shall be a peculiar treasure unto me above all people: for all the earth is mine: And ye shall be unto me a kingdom of priests, and an holy nation. These are the words

which thou [Moses] shalt speak unto the children of Israel. (Exod 19:5–6)

A covenant has obligations and benefits. For their obedience, God would own them, provide for them and protect them. The entire nation of Israel was to be a peculiar treasure, a kingdom of priests, and a holy nation:

> And the Lord said unto Moses, Lo, I come unto thee in a thick cloud, that the people may hear when I speak with thee, and believe thee for ever. And Moses told the words of the people to the Lord. And the Lord said unto Moses, Go unto the people, and sanctify them today and to morrow, and let them wash their clothes. (Exod 19:9–10)

The people of Israel purified themselves as God commanded them to do. God kept his promise and came to the mountain with a thick cloud, lightning, thunder, trumpet, fire, smoke and earthquake. Then God gave the Ten Commandments with his own voice. It was a day of terror for the Israelites who requested that God speak to them in the future through Moses rather than speaking directly to them.

God gave the law through Moses, but man could not keep the law with the perfection that God required. Man needed to be rescued from sin. Since man could not save himself, God provided a remedy of redemption. Man was separated from God and needed to be brought back into a right relationship with him. Shedding of blood was the method that God chose for the redemption of mankind. When Adam opted to disobey God by eating of the tree of knowledge of good and evil, the fig leaves that Adam selected to cover his nakedness could not cover his sins. Blood was shed, to get the skins of the animals to cover the nakedness of Adam and his wife, Eve (Gen 3:21). The shedding of blood is God's method of covering our sins so that he remembers them no more.

SIN OFFERING

After the flood, in order to receive atonement for their sins, God's people, Israel, were required to make a "sin offering" to God as an atonement for specific unintentional sins, and sins committed either accidentally or unknowingly. The people sacrificed unblemished animals such as a young bull, a male goat, a dove or pigeon. Israel confessed their sins to God, and he forgave them their sins and cleansed them of their unrighteousness (Lev 4:1–5; 6:24–30; 8:14–17; 16:3–22). The sin offering eradicated their actual stains of sin and God remembered them no more. It represented Jesus' death on the cross in the place of sinners thus eliminating the need for animal and fowls of the air sacrifices. The Bible teaches that God made Jesus "to be sin for us, who knew no sin; that we may be made the righteousness of God in him" (2 Cor 5:21). The sin offering was an atonement for sinners that restored their right relationship with God. God accepts the sacrifice but takes no pleasure in sin.

GUILT OR TRESPASS OFFERING

The Israelites also sacrificed as a "guilt or trespass offering," an unblemished ram or lamb as mandatory atonement for sin unintentionally committed by desecrating God's sacred property (Lev 5:15). This sacrifice was also made when another person was deliberately injured by such acts as telling lies and dishonesty. Where the act required restitution, the guilty party paid the full compensation and an additional amount of 25 percent. The sinner confessed his sins to God, who in turn forgave the sins of the trespasser (Lev 5:14-19; 6:7; 7:1-16). The guilt offering represented Jesus' ransom on the cross in our place. He took our debt, our punishment, our guilt, so that we can be restored into a righteous relationship with him: "Yet it pleased the Lord to bruise him; he hath put him to grief: when thou shalt make his soul an offering for sin, he shall see his seed, he shall prolong his days, and the pleasure of the Lord shall prosper in his hand" (Isa 53:10).

BURNT OFFERING

The burnt offering was another method of sacrifice that the Holy God of Israel accepted to restore sinful mankind into a right relationship with him. An unblemished bull, ram or male dove or young pigeon was completely burned and the smoke from the sacrifice ascended to God and was for him "an aroma pleasing to the Lord" (Lev 1:9 NIV). The ultimate completion of the burnt-offering sacrifice resulted in Jesus' one-time, once-for-all-time sacrificial death on the cross of Mount Calvary as atonement for the sins of the entire universe. The Bible teaches that God did not require sacrifice and burnt offering and sin offering. God prefers obedience because obedience is better than sacrifice and to heed is better than the fat of rams. It was mission impossible for the blood of birds and animals to take away the sins of the world: "He did not enter by means of the blood of goats and calves; but he entered the Most Holy Place once for all by his own blood, having obtained eternal redemption" (Heb 9:12 NIV). It required our Lord to leave the glorious majesty of heaven to sojourn on earth in bodily form to be our ultimate sacrifice on the cross for all.

JESUS—THE ULTIMATE SACRIFICE

God needed a perfect sacrifice for the sins of the entire world because the sacrifices of animals and birds could not properly reconcile us to him. Man was allowed to select the animal or bird for the sacrifice, but they were required to provide an unblemished atonement. God so loved the world that he gave his only begotten and unblemished son as an atonement for our sins, that whosoever believeth in him should not perish but have everlasting life. Some seven hundred years before the birth of his Majesty, the King of kings and Lord of lords, Isaiah the prophet prophesied that a miraculous event would take place. He told Ahaz, king of Judah, that the Savior of the world would be born of a virgin and he would be named Emanuel, that is to say, "God is with us." Jesus became the body of God, the vessel in which God lived to carry out the blood sacrifice for our sins, the blood of his covenant with us.

The birth of Our Lord and Savior Jesus Christ happened this way. Joseph was engaged to a virgin named Mary. Before they were legally married and before they were involved in a sexual relationship, Mary became pregnant. The beautiful Mary, from an obscure village, was highly favored by God. The Angel of the Lord visited Joseph, to whom Mary was engaged, and informed him that Mary's conception was through the Holy Ghost, through the earthly presence of God, who will bring his own Son into the world and through her would unite himself with human flesh, and that the baby will be called Jesus because he will "save his people from their sins" (Matt 1:21). Mary had found favor with God. The Holy Ghost came upon her and the Power of the Highest overshadowed her so that the Holy Child which she carried in her womb was and is called "The Son of God" (Luke 1:35). We do not have to understand scientifically how this could happen. We are dealing with God, who is the Lord of nature and who is not locked into dimensions and categories. Jesus, who was conceived by divine action, was about to be revealed as the Savior of the world. The Holy Spirit is the presence and power of God. God's presence can produce new life beyond human intervention. The first truth that we have observed about God is that he is the creator. He spoke into nothing and nothing became something. All of nature is subject to him. He can speak to any aspect of nature and get his desired outcome.

He truthfully existed from the beginning:

> In the beginning was the Word, and the Word was with God, and the Word was God. And the Word was made flesh and dwelt among us, (and we beheld his glory, the glory as of the only begotten of the Father,) full of grace and Truth. (John 1:1, 14)

God left his throne of glory and came to this sin-infested earth as a man; the Son of Man, God himself in a human body. The only begotten of God had crossed the line from creator to creature. Omnipotence emptied itself and omniscience learned that there is something called time.

Jesus was truly God because he was conceived by the Holy Ghost and had within him the true nature, titles, attributes and characteristics of the true and Living God. He is eternal. He created all things:

> For in him all things were created: things in heaven and on earth, visible and invisible, whether thrones or powers or rulers or authorities; all things have been created by him and for him. He is before all things, and in him all things hold together. (Col 1:16-17 NIV)

He was truly a man because he was born of a human being, the Virgin Mary. God mysteriously manifested himself in the flesh. He made himself of no reputation, took upon him the form of a servant and was made in the likeness of men (Phil 5:7). Jesus, the Son of man, and also the Son of God: "Is come to seek and to save that which was lost" (Luke 19:1) from the penalty of sin, which is eternal death.

Jesus lived on this earth for thirty-three years, with the final three dedicated to teaching and preaching the good news of the kingdom of God to the whole world, and it was during this period that he healed the sick, restored the sight of the blind, made the crippled walk, restored the hearing of the death, cleansed lepers, cast out devils and demons from possessed persons, walked on water, stilled the storm, and raised Lazarus from the dead. After he completed his ministry on earth and the time was ripe for his imminent return to his Father in heaven, he told his disciples that the time had come for him to eat his final Passover with them while he was here on earth. He announced the date of the Passover feast to his disciples. On Thursday, two days from today, I will feast with you for the final time, after which "the Son of man is betrayed to be crucified" (Matt 26:2).

The Passover is one of the most sacred occasions for the Jews. It is a celebration of their departure from one thousand five hundred years of slavery in Egypt. And Jesus was about to usher in a new kind of freedom and peace to the entire world; freedom of spirit and a peace of mind that surpasses all man's understanding. Jesus was calm when he announced his own death penalty for the sins of the whole world. This announcement about his death was not his first announcement: "From that time on Jesus began to explain to his disciples that he must go to Jerusalem and suffer many things at the hands of the elders, the chief priests and the teachers of the law, and that he must be killed and on the third day be raised to life" (Matt 16:21 NIV). He was now specific about the actual date and time that his execution would take place.

While the Jews were celebrating the Passover, their freedom from bondage in Egypt, Jesus announced to his disciples for the final time that he would be sacrificed for the sins of the whole world. While Jesus was preparing his disciples for this painful moment of suffering and agony, the chief priests, teachers of the law and elders of the people assembled at the palace of the high priest (not the normal meeting place in the temple) to plot Jesus' arrest by trickery and then murder him. Jesus was a threat to the religious leaders of that time because he publicly exposed their hypocrisy and reduced their religious influence over citizens.

The time was now at hand for Judas to betray Jesus. Judas was one of the twelve disciples whom Jesus chose from the beginning of his ministry and it is almost unbelievable that a person who was so close to the bosom of Jesus could be the one to allow Satan to enter his heart and commit the hideous act of betraying Jesus. As Christians, we must know that Satan must not take root in our hearts, and we must stop blaming him for our wrongdoings. Satan will mercilessly destroy us and others through us, if we flirt with his fiery darts. Judas went to the chief priests and entered a covenant with them to betray Jesus for thirty pieces of silver.

At the time our Lord ate his last supper with his disciples in the upper room of a house at Jerusalem, he partook of the bread and the wine, which established the New Testament in his blood and which is now the symbol of communion celebration in memory of his death, burial and resurrection. In 1 Cor 11:20–34, Paul chastised the church for profaning the Lord's Supper by their gluttonous and drunken behavior. The church was divided over the Communion so that each member went ahead and partook of the supper alone. Some members were full while others were hungry and yet others got drunk from the wine. Jesus gave up his body on the cross and when we participate in his supper, we are each individually, recognizing and remembering his suffering for our sins that gives us the hope that we will have a future with him in eternity.

The Lord's Supper is to be taken in a worthy manner. The Lord's Supper is valuable. It is worthy to take it in remembrance of Christ. We are not to participate with complacency without thinking about its significance. As often as we take the Lord's Supper, we are actually asking God to forgive us our trespasses and sins, and must therefore recognize the sacredness and solemnness of this worship: "Whoever eats the bread or drinks the cup of the Lord in an unworthy manner will be guilty of sinning against the body and blood of the Lord" (1 Cor 11:27 NIV). We must carry out a self-examination (1 Cor 11:28) to determine what is the nature of our relationship with Christ before we partake of the body and blood of Christ. We can eat to our own damnation. We can become weak and sick or we can die if we participate in this act of worship in a manner which displeases God. So that there is bad news for church members. Sitting at the Lord's table and participating in the Lord's supper, baptism, leadership roles in the church and the like, is not a guaranteed entry into the portals of heaven. Our righteousness must exceed the righteousness of the teachers of the law and the Pharisees.

After the Passover meal, Christ went on the Mount of Olives, and to the garden of Gethsemane, to prepare himself to be the final Passover Lamb, and he took his disciples with him. Jesus knew that he was going to die and was exceedingly sorrowful. He was in great anguish as he fathomed the physical torture, pain and suffering that he was about to endure. He did not have to go to the cross but this was the purpose for which he came to this earth and he was determined to fulfill this commission.

Jesus went aside a little further away from his disciples, into the garden to pray, and he took three of his most trusted and dependable disciples with him, namely, Peter and the two sons of Zebedee, James and John, and invited them to watch with him. He went yet a little further into the garden alone, fell on his face and requested the Father to allow the cup of suffering and separation to pass from him. This was the cup of bitter agony of the passion of his painful death. If it were at all possible, if there was any other way that man could be saved and God glorified; in any event it is the Father's will that will be done and not Jesus' own will. He cried out to God again; this time accepting that he had to die: "My Father, if it is not possible for this cup to be taken away unless I drink it, may your will be done" (Matt 26:42 NIV). So deeply agonizing and earnest was his prayer that his sweat was as if it was great drops of blood falling to the ground.

After Jesus had prayed, he talked to his disciples about the importance of praying to prevent them from succumbing to temptation, but before he had concluded his conversation with the disciples, the traitor arrived in the garden with a large crowd, who were sent from the chief priests and elders. They were armed with swords and clubs. Judas then betrayed Jesus with a kiss and he was arrested. Jesus was charged and tried in the religious court three times and in the Roman court three times for the offense of blasphemy against God and for announcing that he was the Son of God and Messiah. He was beaten, mocked, and whipped with leather tongs tipped with balls of metal and shards of bone. Jesus' flesh was torn and blood dripped from his head from the long thorns from which they made a crown for his head.

He suffered the humiliation of several illegal mock trials before Annas (John 18:13), Caiaphas and the Sanhedrin council (Matt 26:57–68); and Roman trials before Pontus Pilate, then Herod and then Pilate again (Luke 23:1–25). They spat in his face. They repeatedly and violently battered him. They smote him with the palm of their hands and asked him to identify the culprit who had violently assaulted him. They whipped him. They stripped him of his robe. The soldiers platted a crown from thorns and put it on his head. They mocked him, and said: "Hail, King of the Jews." They hit him on the head with a reed. They gave him a drink of vinegar mingled with gall. Then the ultimate sacrifice for our sins, they crucified him on the cross:

> He is despised and rejected of men; a man of sorrows, and acquainted with grief: and we hid, as it were our faces from him. . . . Surely he has borne our griefs, and carried our sorrows: yet we did esteem him stricken, smitten of God and afflicted. But he was wounded for our transgressions, he was bruised for our iniquities: the chastisement for our peace was upon him, and with his stripes, we are healed. He was oppressed, and he was afflicted, yet he opened not his mouth: he is brought as a lamb to the slaughter, and as a sheep before her shearers is dumb, so he openeth not his mouth. (Isa 53:3–5, 7)

Jesus voluntarily gave his life on the cross for the sins of the whole world. That gift of eternal life is available to us, but we must accept him by faith as Lord and Savior.

BENEFITS OF JESUS' DEATH

Jesus was well aware that wicked men would murder him, but this was the divine purpose for he came to this sin cursed earth. By hanging on the tree, he took this curse for us, to redeem us with his own blood from the curse of the law. He was indeed the ultimate sacrifice, the spotless, unblemished, non-defective, sinless Lamb of God, whose blood purifies and cleanses us from every sin. Jesus died because sin had to be paid for with blood and the blood of birds and animals could not do it. God substituted himself in our place and we rightfully deserved to die for our acts of sin: "But we do see Jesus, who was made a little lower than the angels for a little while, now crowned with glory and honor because he suffered death, so that by the grace of God he might taste death for everyone" (Heb 2:9 NIV).

Jesus is the unblemished Lamb of God that takes away the sins of the world. God is Spirit and spirits do not have flesh and blood and a spirit does not die. Blood had to be shed for the atonement of our sins. God had to take the body of a man with flesh and blood so that he could shed his blood by dying on the cross for the remission of our sins: "Since the children have flesh and blood, he too shared in their humanity so that by his death he might destroy him who holds the power of death—that is, the devil" (Heb 2:14 NIV).

Jesus' death was necessary. God needed to take away our sickness, suffering and pain:

> Surely he took up our pain and bore our suffering, yet we considered him punished by God, stricken by him and afflicted. But he was pierced for our transgressions, he was crushed for our iniquities; the punishment that brought us peace was upon him, and by his wounds we are healed. (Isa 53:4–5 NIV)

Jesus died because:

1. We have redemption through his blood, the forgiveness of our sins, according to the riches of his grace (Eph 1:7).
2. Christ blotted out the record of charges against us and took them away by nailing them to the cross (Col 2:14).
3. Jesus bore our sins in his body on the tree, so that we might die to sin and live to righteousness. By his stripes we are healed (1 Pet 2:24).
4. Christ redeemed us from the curse of the law, being made a curse for us, for it is written, cursed is everyone who hangs on a tree (Gal 3:13).
5. "Therefore, brothers and sisters, since we have confidence to enter the Most Holy Place by the blood of Jesus, by a new and living way opened for us, through the curtain, that is, his body, and since we have a great priest over the house of God, let us draw near to God with a sincere heart with the full assurance that faith brings, having our hearts sprinkled to cleanse us from a guilty conscience and having our bodies washed with pure water" (Heb 10:19–22 NIV).
6. "Now in Christ Jesus we who once were far away have been brought near through the blood of Christ" (Eph 2:13 NIV).
7. "We are bought with a price and are required to glorify God in our body and in our spirit, which are God's" (1 Cor 6:20).

8. "I have been crucified with Christ and I no longer live, but Christ lives in me. The life I live in the body, I live by faith in the Son of God, who loved me and gave himself for me" (Gal 2:20 NIV).

9. "In this was manifested the love of God toward us, because that God sent his only begotten Son into the world, that we might live through him. Herein is love, not that we loved God, but that he loved us, and sent his Son to be the propitiation for our sins" (1 John 4:9–10).

10. "Hereby perceive we the love of God, because he laid down his life for us: and we ought to lay down our lives for the brethren" (1 John 3:16).

11. "My little children, these things write I unto you, that ye sin not. And if any man sin, we have an advocate with the Father, Jesus Christ the righteous: And he is the propitiation for our sins, and not for ours only, but also for the sins of the whole world" (1 John 2:1–2).

12. "But if we walk in the light, as he is in the light, we have fellowship one with another, and the blood of Jesus Christ his Son cleanseth us from all sin" (1 John 1:7).

God substituted himself for us and bore our sins in his body by dying on the tree in our place. We deserved to die, but he took our place so that we might regain his favor and be adopted into the family of God. The cross that Jesus carried and the blood that was spilled thereon is the symbol of our Christian faith, although to many, its message is foolishness or madness. The cross is the very essence of God's wisdom and power. His powerful name is a name above all names, in which we must believe, and be baptized, because there is no other name under heaven, given among men, wherein we must be saved.

The cross is probably the cruelest, most agonizing form of capital punishment ever practiced at anytime in the world because it willfully and deliberately delayed death until the maximum torture had been inflicted. This punishment was reserved for persons convicted of murder, rebellion or armed robbery in some circumstances. Jesus was betrayed, rejected and condemned by his own people, their political leaders and church leaders. He had no sins for which to make sacrifice and the blood spilled on that old rugged cross was not of calves or goats. It was his own precious blood that was spilled once for all, forever.

The blood of Christ justifies (Rom 3:25).
The blood of Christ is the blood of atonement (Rom 3:25).
The blood of Christ redeems us for God (Rev 5:9).
The blood of Christ is the blood of forgiveness (Heb 9:22).

It is through the blood of Christ that Christians will enter the Most Holy place (Heb 10:19).

The blood of Christ cleanses us from all sin (1 John 1:7).

The blood of Christ reconciles us back into a right relationship with God (Eph 2:13).

We make peace through the blood of Christ (Col 1:20).

THE RESURRECTION OF JESUS FROM THE GRAVE

The devil must have thought that he had won a resounding victory. After all, he had our Lord nailed to the cross and heard him breathe his last breath. He knew that the chief priests and Pharisees met with Pilate to discuss how he could secure the dead body to prevent the dead body of our Lord from escaping or prevent the disciples or someone else from stealing him. The devil listened as Pilate ordered maximum security for the body and the grave where our Lord was buried. He watched as they "made the sepulchre sure, sealing the stone, and setting a watch" (Matt 27:66). Certainly, there was no escape; that deceiver, that wandering imposter, was properly sealed in the tomb, the devil must have thought. Yes, these murderers remembered that Jesus said that within three days of his death, God would raise him from the dead.

On that glorious Easter morning, at the rising of the sun, Mary Magdalene, the other Mary (the mother of James and Joses), Salome, Joanna, and others, hurried to the sepulchre to prepare Jesus' body for its final burial with spices that they had bought: "And, behold, there was a great earthquake: for the angel of the Lord descended from heaven, and came and rolled back the stone from the door, and sat upon it" (Matt 28:2). So much for the sealing of the tomb and securing the premises. The Almighty power of God was at work: "Except the Lord build the house, they labor in vain that built it: except the Lord keep the city, the watchman waketh but in vain" (Ps 127:1). Our God did not seal the sepulchre. He did not set watch over Jesus' body or the tomb, and therefore, the tomb was not properly sealed, and the security for the body was severely flawed and compromised, leaving opportunity for the inevitable breach that occurred.

The appearance of the angel was as bright and startling as lightning, and his clothes were white as snow, reminding us of the brilliance of Jesus' appearance at the transfiguration. The guards, as courageous as they were, fainted at the brilliant appearance of the angel. The angel spoke to the women from the tomb. He told them that they must not be afraid because he knew that they were looking for Jesus, who was crucified. The angel continued: "He is not here: for he is risen, as he said. Come, see the place where the Lord lay" (Matt 28:6).

Jesus had informed his disciples that he would die, and within three days, he would be raised from the dead (Matt 16:21; 17:22–23; 20:19; Luke 24:6–7), and his pronouncements concerning the resurrection came to pass. The women were greeted with an empty tomb.

Our Lord is not in the tomb. He is risen and ascended to his Father in heaven and is seated at his right hand, pleading and interceding our cause, with groans that cannot be uttered. And because he rose from the dead:

1. "For if we have been planted together in the likeness of his death, we shall be also in the likeness of his resurrection: Likewise reckon ye also yourselves to be dead indeed unto sin, but alive unto God through Jesus Christ our Lord" (Rom 6:5, 11).

2. "The eyes of your understanding being enlightened; that ye may know what is the hope of his calling, and what is the riches of the glory of his inheritance in the saints, And what is the exceeding greatness of his power to us-ward who believe, according to the working of his mighty power, which he wrought in Christ, when he raised him from the dead, and set him at his own right hand in the heavenly places, far above all principality, and power, and might, and dominion, and every name that is named, not only in this world, but also in that which is to come: And hath put all things under his feet, and gave him to be the head over all things to the church, Which is his body, the fulness of him that filleth all in all" (Eph 1:18–23).

3. "Even when we were dead in trespasses and sins, hath quickened us together with Christ, (by grace ye are saved;) And hath raised us up together, and made us sit together in heavenly places in Christ Jesus: That in the ages to come he might shew the exceeding riches of his grace in his kindness toward us through Jesus Christ" (Eph 2:5–7).

4. "And you, being dead in your sins and the uncircumcision of your flesh, hath he quickened together with him, having forgiven you all trespasses" (Col 2:13).

5. "If ye then be risen with Christ, seek those things which are above, where Christ sitteth on the right hand of God. Set your affection on things above, not on things on the earth. For ye are dead, and your life is hid with Christ in God. When Christ who is our life, shall appear, then shall ye also appear with him in glory" (Col 3:1–4).

6. "Blessed be the God and Father of our Lord Jesus Christ, which according to his abundant mercy hath begotten us again unto a lively hope by the resurrection of Jesus Christ from the dead, To an inheritance incorruptible, and undefiled, and that fadeth not away, reserved in heaven for you, Who are kept by the power of God through faith unto salvation ready to be revealed in the last time" (1 Pet 1:3–5).

7. "The like figure whereunto even baptism doth also now save us (not the putting away of the filth of the flesh, but the answer of a good conscience toward God,) by the resurrection of Jesus Christ: Who is gone into heaven, and is on the right hand of God; angels and authorities and powers being made subject unto him" (1 Pet 3:21–22).

The resurrection was truly God's divine cancellation of the verdict of the Jewish authorities. Christ was returned to his place of supreme honor at the right hand of God our Father, a place where he is glorified and exalted. The crucified and risen Jesus is both Lord and Christ; our Prince and Savior. He has the power and authority to save us from our sins through repentance, forgiveness, and the gift of the Holy Spirit.

Chapter 4

Repent

Having acknowledged that we are sinners, that we need a Savior, and that Christ died on the cross for our sins, we must repent of our sins. Repentance is very deep sorrow and contrition for our sins and separation from God, our Father. God commands all people, everywhere, to repent. None of us were without sin.

> If we say we have no sin, we deceive ourselves, and the truth is not in us. If we confess our sins, he is faithful and just to forgive our sins, and to cleanse us from all unrighteousness. If we say that we have not sinned, we make him a liar, and his word is not in us. (1 John 1:8–10)

Repentance also means that we have changed our hearts and minds about our attitude to committing sins against our Lord and Savior Jesus Christ. We no longer reject him, but accept that he is the only Savior of the world from sin and eternal death. Repentance is for sinners. Jesus taught us that the healthy do not need a physician but only they that are sick (Luke 5:31–32). So why is it important to repent?

REPENT THAT WE MAY BE FORGIVEN OF OUR SINS

We need to repent so that we can be forgiven of our sins and so that we receive the gift of the Holy Spirit: "Then Peter said unto them, Repent, and be baptized every one of you in the name of Jesus Christ, for the remission of sins, and ye shall receive the gift of the Holy Ghost" (Acts 2:38). Repentance results in God's forgiveness of our sins. Forgiveness or pardon from sin is God's conscious, deliberate, intentional and voluntary decision not to hold us accountable for our sinful actions. He buries our sins in the sea of his forgetfulness and gives us a new creation in him. We are declared just or righteous and acquitted from the penalty of sin, which is eternal death, and made righteous by faith in him.

REPENT TO RECEIVE THE GIFT OF THE HOLY GHOST

When we repent of our sins, we also receive the gift of the Holy Ghost. Jesus told his disciples that it was important that he return to his Father and that he would send the Comforter (Holy Ghost) to them. If he did not go away, his Holy Spirit would not come to them. If he departed, he would send them the Holy Spirit to abide in their hearts forever. The Holy Ghost would also be their teacher and would be their memory bank as it relates to everything that Jesus taught them. The Holy Ghost also has responsibility for executing search warrants on all things, including the deep things of God. In his writings to the Romans, Paul reminded us that the Spirit helps us with our infirmities. We do not know what we should pray for as we ought, but the Holy Spirit makes intercession for us with groanings that cannot be uttered.

When Jesus passed through Samaria, he went to the property that Jacob willed to his son, Joseph, in the city called Sychar. He was weary, hungry and thirsty, from his long journey from Judaea, and sat on the well, while his disciples went away to buy refreshments. A woman from Samaria came to draw water from the well and Jesus requested her to give him a drink of water from the well. Jesus promised the woman living water. He told her that if anyone drank from the well at Sychar, they would become thirsty again, but anyone who drink the water that he gives them would never thirst, but would have a well of living water (Holy Spirit) "springing up into everlasting life" (John 4:14).

Jesus promised the disciples that they will receive power after the Holy Ghost came on them and they will be his witnesses throughout the uttermost parts of the world. On the day of Pentecost, about 9 a.m., the apostles and others were all in one place and in one accord, in prayer and supplication before God. Suddenly, there was a sound from heaven as of a mighty rushing wind that filled all the house where they were having fellowship with God and one another. Cloven tongues like fire sat on each of them, filling them with the power of the Holy Ghost. The 120 persons in the upper room began to speak in other tongues as the Holy Spirit allowed them to speak, so that witnesses of the event believed that they were all drunk.

Peter preached that whoever shall call on the name of the Lord will be saved, and of the importance of the death, burial and resurrection of our blessed Lord and Savior Jesus Christ to their salvation. Peter's message was so convincing that the congregation inquired of the apostle what they needed to do (to be saved). Peter told them to "repent and be baptized every one of you in the name of Jesus Christ for the remission of sins, and ye shall receive the gift of the Holy Ghost" (Acts 2:38).

Cornelius was a professional officer of the Roman army, a Gentile, a devout and generous man who along with his entire household served the true and living God. He was, as always, praying to God and fasting, and about 9 a.m., while he was in an attitude of prayer and was fasting, he was visited by an angel of the Lord who informed him that his generosity and prayers were acknowledged and were recognized as a memorial by God. Cornelius then adhered to God's instructions to send to Joppa for Simon Peter, who was among the Jews that received the gift of the Holy Spirit on the day of Pentecost. The following day, about 6 a.m. when Peter was on the housetop praying, he too heard from God, who instructed him to go to Cornelius's house at Caesarea with Cornelius's servants without doubting anything. Peter obeyed God's instructions and went to Cornelius's house.

Cornelius expected Peter and had invited many of his friends and relatives to joint him to listen to what instructions God gave to Peter for him. Peter told the gathering that God was no respecter of persons, that in every nation everyone that fears God and does righteous works is accepted by him. He testified that God anointed Jesus with the Holy Ghost and power and he performed many miracles while he lived on this earth. He further testified that Jesus was murdered by the Jews, but God raised him from the dead, and that "everyone who believes in him receives forgiveness of sins through his name" (Acts 10:43 NIV).

While Peter was preaching, the Holy Ghost fell on all persons who heard the word and they magnified God and spoke with other tongues, leaving the Jews who accompanied Peter to Cornelius's house astonished that the Gentiles had also received the gift of the Holy Ghost.

Let us examine Cornelius's relationship with God. He prayed and fasted often and ensured that his family, friends and employees did the same. What is our status with God? Do we read the Bible, fast and pray often? Or are we just Sunday going-to-meeting Christians? Cornelius was wealthy and financially sound. His right relationship with God brought him eternal prosperity for the soul. God is willing and able to do the same for us but we must have the right attitude toward him.

REPENT THAT YOUR SINS MAYBE BLOTTED OUT

We must repent so that our sins may be erased from our record and thrown in the sea of God's forgetfulness. The Apostle Peter, in the name of Jesus, healed the man who was lame from birth and begged for his living at the gate of the temple, named Beautiful. The healed man was overjoyed and followed Peter and John into the temple. He had never walked before, but now he was walking and talking and leaping and praising God. The people were filled with great wonder and amazement at this great miracle that had taken place. Peter then preached about the death, burial and resurrection of our Lord and Savior Jesus Christ, and advised his listeners to "repent ye therefore, and be converted that your sins maybe blotted out" (Acts 3:19). When we repent of our sins and forsake them, God removes them from our record and remembers them no more.

REPENTANCE LEADS TO LIFE

Repentance leads to life. "When they heard this, they had no further objections, and praised God, saying, 'So then, God has granted even the Gentiles repentance unto life'" (Acts 11:18 NIV). Jesus did not die for the Jews alone. He gave his life for the whole world. Jesus came to offer abundant life. He came to offer eternal life. We receive eternal life simply by repenting of our sins and forsaking them. Jesus died on the cross that whosoever believes in him will not die but will have everlasting life and Christ will raise him up at the last day. The master put it this way: "He that heareth my word, and believeth on him that sent me, hath everlasting life, and shall not come into condemnation; but is passed from death unto life" (John 5:24).

Repent or Perish

We must repent or we will die.

> There were present at that season some that told him [Jesus] of the Galileans, whose blood Pilate had mingled with their sacrifices. And Jesus answering said to them, Suppose ye that these Galileans were sinners above all the Galileans, because they suffered such things? I tell you, Nay: but except ye repent ye shall all likewise perish. Or those eighteen on whom the tower of Siloam fell and slew them, think ye that they were sinners above all men that dwelt at Jerusalem? I tell you, nay; but except ye repent, ye shall all likewise perish. (Luke 13:1–5)

Jesus took the opportunity to use these two tragedies in order to highlight the importance of repentance. There are so many different tragedies that we experience in this world today. We hear of famines where several people die. There are earthquakes and several people die. There are air, sea, and road accidents and people violently die. There are outbreaks of diseases and many people die. There are acts of terrorism and many people die, etc. Jesus is teaching us that whatever our status in society, whatever our position in the church, whatever income we earn, we need to repent from our sins or face the consequences of eternal death. Good things will happen to wicked people, and conversely Christians will have terrifying experiences, but unless we repent, we will all perish. When such tragedies occur, such as were mentioned in Luke 13:1–5, we must not think the victims are greater sinners than anyone else. They may very well be saved and sanctified and called home to be with the Lord. The Bible teaches that there is one step only between life and death. We can be called home this very hour so we need to treat repentance as the first and most urgent item on our list to do.

REPENT FOR THE KINGDOM OF HEAVEN IS AT HAND

How do we define this foundational message of the church concerning the kingdom of God? What does Jesus mean when he told Pilate: "My kingdom is not of this world" (John 18:36). Jesus left the glory of heaven and counted it but loss. He came down to earth as King of kings but not to set up an earthly kingdom. The kingdom of heaven is not of this world but will be part of the world when he returns to reign with his believers.

The kingdom of God can be defined as that miraculous process by which Christ redeems us from our sins. It is not meat nor drink nor rules and regulations but: "righteousness and peace and joy in the Holy Ghost" (Rom 14:17). We were all guilty sinners but when we accept Christ by faith, the way we live is guided and directed by the Holy Spirit producing the positive outcome of righteousness, joy and peace with God and with others. The Holy Spirit then convicts and motivates us to perform tasks in advancing the kingdom of God.

There is one way only to obtain that righteousness, peace and joy in the Holy Ghost. We must be born again. Being born of water and of the Spirit is the required passport to enter the kingdom of God:

> There was a man of the Pharisees, named Nicodemus, a ruler of the Jews: The same came to Jesus by night, and said unto him, Rabbi, we know that thou art a teacher come from God, for no man can do these miracles that thou doest, except God be with

him. Jesus answered and said unto him, Verily, verily, I say unto thee, Except a man be born again, he cannot see the kingdom of God. Nicodemus saith unto him, how can a man be born when he is old? Can he enter the second time into his mother's womb, and be born? Jesus answered, Verily, verily, I say unto thee, Except a man be born of water and of the Spirit, he cannot enter the Kingdom of God. (John 3:1–5)

The kingdom of God is available to us by grace, through genuine faith and trust in our Lord. It focuses on its value. How much is the kingdom of God worth? How much is God worth? God is worth everything we own, above all else, because God is good for our joy and for our security. Stated differently, the kingdom of God is a priceless treasure that is worth everything. There is nothing more valuable than it and it is accompanied by joy and happiness. The kingdom of God is a priceless treasure that a person will give up, and if he loses all he has in his effort to secure it, he will be full of unspeakable joy. Paul counted everything that was profitable to him as loss for the sake of knowing Christ, for the sake of the treasures of the kingdom of God. Paul stated:

> What is more, I consider everything a loss compared to the surpassing greatness of knowing Christ Jesus my Lord, for whose sake I have lost all things . . . that I may gain Christ [that I may gain the kingdom of God]. and be found in him, not having a righteousness of my own that comes from the law, but that which is through faith in Christ—the righteousness that comes from God on the basis of faith. I want to know Christ—yes, to know the power of his resurrection and participating in his sufferings, becoming like him in his death. (Phil 3:8–10 NIV)

Paul is teaching that existence without Christ is worthless in contrast to everything gained from serving Christ.

We learn in Matt 19:27–30 that Jesus' disciples gave up all to follow him. Jesus reminded his disciples of the wonderful rewards that they will obtain in the kingdom of God because they gave up all for the shame and sufferings of the cross. God will reward us based on his righteous justice. We that believe in him, are rewarded with his ever-abiding presence in our hearts. Jesus reassured the disciples that when they give up something valuable for his kingdom, they will be repaid several times over. The sacrifices that we make now are for eternal benefits and not for the temporary benefits that last for a time or season and result in eternal death.

In the kingdom of God, which is eternal, secure and without restriction, Christ is the King and his dominion endures through all generations (Ps

145:13). His kingdom rules over all other kingdoms everywhere (Ps 103:19–20). He is sovereign and he is supreme. He manages his kingdom in an orderly manner because he is a God of order. If we are unwilling to give up everything for the sake of the gospel of the kingdom, we cannot be part of the family of God. The kingdom of God is an everlasting dominion that will not pass away and will never be destroyed. In this kingdom, God is the authority. Glory and sovereign power, and every person, regardless of language, shall worship him (Dan 7:13–17). It is at the feet of Jesus that every knee shall bow and every tongue shall confess, both in heaven and on earth, that Jesus is Lord.

You guessed it right. The kingdom of God is for the saints of the Most High God who will inhabit it forever and forever and forever (Dan 7:17–18).

THE MESSAGE OF JOHN THE BAPTIST WAS THE KINGDOM OF GOD

John the Baptist was called to prepare the way for Jesus' ministry here on earth. His key message was the kingdom of God. "In those days came John the Baptist, preaching in the wilderness of Judaea, and saying, Repent ye: for the kingdom of heaven is at hand" (Matt 3:1–2). He taught that we, as Christians, should produce fruits worthy of repentance. Jesus taught that the law and the prophets were proclaimed until John started preaching this message concerning the kingdom of God. The Old Testament era ended at that time and the New Testament period was ushered in. It is from this time that the good news concerning the kingdom of God and his Christ was preached (Luke 16:16). In other words, the arrival of Jesus Christ from heaven, upon this earth, in human form, fulfilled the Old Testament promises while at the same time establishing the new covenant.

JESUS' MESSAGE CONCERNED THE KINGDOM OF GOD

The principal theme of Jesus' teaching and preaching is the kingdom of God:

> And Jesus went about all Galilee, teaching in their synagogues, and preaching the gospel of the kingdom, and healing all manner of sickness, and all manner of disease among the people. (Matt 4:23)

And it came to pass afterward, that he [Jesus] went throughout every city and village, preaching and shewing the glad tidings of the kingdom of God: and the twelve were with him. (Luke 8:1)

Now after John was put in prison, Jesus came into Galilee, preaching the gospel of the kingdom of God, And saying, the time is fulfilled, and the kingdom of God is at hand: repent ye and believe the gospel. (Mark 1:14)

And his disciples went forth, and came into the city, and found as he had said unto them: and they made ready the passover. And in the evening he cometh with the twelve. And as they sat and did eat, Jesus said, Verily I say unto you, One of you which eateth with me shall betray me. And they began to be sorrowful, and to say unto him one by one, is it I? and another said is it I? And he answered and said unto them, It is one of the twelve, that dippeth with me in the dish. The Son of man indeed goeth, as it is written of him: but woe to that man by whom the Son of man is betrayed! good were it for that man if he had never been born. And as they did eat, Jesus took bread, and blessed, and brake it, and gave to them, and said, Take eat: this is my body. And he took the cup, and when he had given thanks, he gave it to them: and they all drank of it. And he said unto them, This is my blood of the new testament, which is shed for many. Verily I say unto you, I will drink no more of the fruit of the vine, until that day I drink it new in the kingdom of God. (Mark 14:16–25)

THE DISCIPLES' MESSAGE WAS THE KINGDOM OF GOD

Having benefitted intellectually and spiritually from the education, experience and wisdom that resulted from being taught by Jesus, the responsibility was given to the disciples to preach the message concerning the kingdom of God: "Then he called his twelve disciples together, and gave them power and authority over all devils, and to cure diseases. And he sent them to preach the kingdom of God, and to heal the sick" (Luke 9:1–2).

ST. PAUL'S MESSAGE WAS THE KINGDOM OF GOD

The premier message of the Apostle Paul was the kingdom of God:

> And when Paul had laid his hands on them, the Holy Ghost came on them; and they spake with tongues, and prophesied. And all the men were about twelve. And he went into the synagogue, and spake boldly for the space of three months, disputing and persuading the things concerning the kingdom of God. (Acts 19:6–8)

Paul also referred to his fellow ministers as his: "Fellow workers unto the kingdom of God" (Col 4:11). The Apostle Paul taught that Christians have already entered the kingdom of God. He wrote:

> Giving thanks unto the Father, which has made us meet to be partakers of the inheritance of the saints in light: Who hath delivered us from the power of darkness, and hath translated us into the kingdom of his dear Son: In whom we have redemption through his blood, even the forgiveness of sins. (Col 1:12–14)

Paul recognized the importance of thanking God for everything. We become partakers of the inheritance of the saints by accepting Christ as Lord and Savior and in the process, we were delivered from the dark power of Satan, and the penalty of sin, which is eternal death. We obtained new Spiritual light by faith, through the redeeming blood of Christ and by this, we are translated into the new environment of the kingdom of Christ. The inheritance will be given to us when we physically die and Christ returns to be with his saints.

Jesus taught: "But if I cast out devils by the Spirit of God, then the kingdom of God is come unto you" (Matt 12:28). Jesus, the King of the kingdom was right there on the spot to destroy the powers of evil. Jesus forcefully causes Satan to exit control of our lives so that the kingdom of God can take up permanent residence in our hearts.

The kingdom of God can also be described as a special, eternal province, that Christians will inherit when the King of Glory returns to earth, and which was prepared for us from the foundation of the world. The kingdom will include every person who has truly repented of their sins and lives a complete life in Christ Jesus. The Apostle Peter wrote:

> Wherefore the rather, brethren, give diligence to make your calling and election sure: for if you do these things, ye shall never fall: For so an entrance shall be ministered unto you abundantly into the everlasting -kingdom of our Lord and Savior Jesus Christ. (2 Pet 1:10–11)

Christians should not be led to commit sin by accommodating false doctrines and the glamour of sin that last but for a season. We should ensure that God's invitation to godly living and being God's choice for his kingdom is fully secured. We should be diligent, faithful and virtuous, do good deeds, exercise self-control, perseverance, show generosity, exercise godliness and ensure that we never ever fall back into the vomit of sin, and loose our inheritance in the kingdom of God. Our receipt of the inheritance depends on our relationship with Christ. We must become the children of God.

Jesus also taught that many persons will join with Abraham, Isaac and Jacob, and sit in the kingdom of heaven. The time is coming soon when the believers and unbelievers will be separated; the good seed will be separated from the tares; the sheep will be separated from the goats. The angels of the Most High will gather out of the kingdom all things that offend and them which do iniquity and shall cast them into the furnace of fire where there will be wailing and gnashing of teeth. Believers will shine forth as the sun in the kingdom of their Father. These believers are represented by those who have fed the hungry, given drink to the thirsty, clothed the naked and visited the sick and those who were incarcerated for the sake of the kingdom of God. It is these believers that will join the patriarchs in the kingdom of heaven.

THE KINGDOM OF GOD IS IN OUR HEARTS

The kingdom of God is in the mist of us today and has existed since the foundation of the world. Jesus' mission on this earth was never to set up an earthly political kingdom. His mission was to rule in our hearts. God's power and his truth is within our midst to guard, guide and protect us. He lives and reigns in our hearts and lives. The Pharisees demanded of Jesus when the kingdom of God should come. He told them that the kingdom of God does not come by observation, for no one can say it is here or it is there: "the kingdom of God is within you" (Luke 17:21). The Jews always looked forward to a messiah. They anticipated a powerful political leader who would liberate them to world prominence, but Jesus' message was the gospel of the kingdom of God, that they should repent of their sins and obey the gospel.

What Shall We Do regarding the Kingdom of God?

First, the Bible teaches that we must first seek the kingdom of God and his righteousness and all the blessings we need will be given to us:

> But seek ye first the kingdom of God, and his righteousness; and all these things shall be added unto you. (Matt 6:33)

The true and living God only will provide all that we need. The wealthy are commanded to recognize that God is the true source of their wealth and be generous with their riches. The material blessings of God are to be enjoyed and used for the advancement of his kingdom, and not for self-centered living. When material wealth is not available to us, we can be rich in good deeds. No matter how poor we are, we have something to share with someone.

Second, we must accept the kingdom of God with humility. Jesus taught that those who do not accept the kingdom of God as little children will not enter his Father's kingdom.

Third, we should pray that his kingdom should come. When Jesus taught his disciples to pray, he told them that they should pray for his kingdom to come and that his will be done.

Fourth, we must keep and teach his commandments. Jesus taught:

> Whosoever therefore shall break one of these least commandments, and shall teach men so, he shall be called the least in the kingdom of heaven: but whosoever shall do and teach them, the same shall be called great in the kingdom of heaven. For I say unto you, That except your righteousness shall exceed the righteousness of the scribes and Pharisees, ye shall in no case enter the kingdom Of heaven. (Matt 5:19-20)

Fifth, we must preach the gospel of the kingdom to the entire world:

> But the one who stands firm to the end, he will be saved. And this his gospel of the kingdom will be preached in the whole world as a testimony to all nations, and then the end will come. (Matt 24:13-14 NIV)

We are being reminded that no matter what our difficulties in this present life, whatever our challenges, whatever our afflictions, we must endure them, until Christ returns, because those persons that endure to the end will be saved. We must preach the gospel of the kingdom to the entire world and then the end of the age will come.

Jesus told the story of a farmer who went out to sow his seed. The farmer is the teacher and preacher and the seeds sown is the Word of God; the message of the kingdom of God. The parable of the soils, as it is sometimes called, warns of circumstances and attitudes that can keep anyone who has received the seed of the good news of the gospel of Jesus from producing a godly harvest. The suitability of the soil depends on the heart of each individual who is exposed to the message of the kingdom of God. The different soils on which the seeds fell represent the different methods in which we receive and follow the message. Some hearts are hardened and unprepared for the message. Some hearts are stony from disuse and some hearts lusts after the things of the world. The word is propagated in various parts of the world and the yield depends on where the Word is preached and how it is received.

As the farmer sowed, some seeds fell by the wayside, only for the birds to devour them. This is a case where someone hears the word of the kingdom, does not understand it, and give it no attention. The evil one snatches away that which was sown in their hearts. There is nothing wrong with the seed. The seed is the good seed of the kingdom of God and this does not change. Jesus came to set us free so that we can have eternal life in him in his coming kingdom. The question that arises is the quality of the soil and its preparation to receive seed of the message. They are unwilling to change their selfish behavior and they continue on their sinful journey to the path of doom. Their hearts become hardened to the word of God and the devil comes and snatches away the message of the kingdom that was sown in their hearts.

Some of the seeds fell on stony ground where they did not have much earth, and immediately they grew up, but when the sun came up, they were scorched and withered away. This is the category of persons who hear and joyfully receive the Word of God, but because God's Word does not take deep root in their hearts, their Christian experience endures for a short time, but soon stumbles off the Christian journey when challenged by tribulation or persecution. This can happen if the Word is not preached correctly, or if conversion is primarily about the characteristics of the church. The Christian pathway is not a bed of roses, without thorns. Jesus said that believers would be persecuted and reviled for the sake of the kingdom of God, and that all who would be his followers must deny themselves, take up their crosses and follow him. The life of a Christian is hard because many persons hate the gospel and will hate Christians because they believe on him and trust him. The stones of this world are the temporal things that will perish compared to the eternal kingdom of God which God will establish forever. There is a great day coming when Jesus will judge the world in righteousness, and when we are judged, we need to know that our sins are covered by the blood of our Lord and Savior Jesus Christ. This gospel of the kingdom is good news to those who are perishing. If you allow this good seed to fall by the wayside, your Christian life, not being rooted in the Word, will be scorched, then wither away and die and you will be lost for all eternity. Long-standing members in the church should also be careful, because they can retreat to a condition where they have no root in themselves and have no firm and lasting conversion to the kingdom of God. Any church member can have a stony heart if they are not rooted and grounded in the teachings of the gospel of the kingdom of God and daily practice its principles.

Some seeds were sown among thorns and the thorns sprang up and choked them. This category of Christian hears the Word and commences their Christian journey with enthusiasm but along the way, they are deceived by the glamour of this world and are deceived by riches and become unproductive. The worries of this life are temporal materials, property, wealth, riches, and the lust for other things that choke the Word, making it unfruitful and unprofitable, and causes us to lose our souls in hell, for all eternity. The possession of great wealth or significant income is not recognition of God's favor and neither is their lack recognition of God's disfavor. Jesus advised the rich young man that he would inherit eternal life if he gave all his wealth to the poor. Jesus was not telling us that there is anything evil about wealth but reminding us about our evil attitudes toward them. The root of evil is not the money but the love of it. Jesus chastised Simon Peter, telling him: "Get thee behind me, Satan: thou art an offence unto me: for thou savourest not the things that be of God, but those that be of men" (Matt 16:23). Peter had put the cares of the world before the things of God in his actions, his priorities and his thinking. As Christians our focus must be entirely on God and the importance of eternal life by trusting God and believing in his promises.

Some seeds were sown on fertile soil and yielded crops of varying quantities. This category hears the word, understands it, and wins other persons into the kingdom of God. They make a positive response to the gospel message and endure to the end.

The field where the seeds are sown is the world and the seeds are sown by teachers and preachers of the Word as well as other leaders that are called by God. The good seeds are the children of God, while the tares are the children of the devil. The harvesting of the fruits take place at the end of the age and those appointed to reap the crops are the angels of God. At that time the angels will gather and separate the tares from the wheat. The tares, who have offended God and practiced lawlessness, will be burned in the furnace of everlasting fire, where there will be wailing and gnashing of teeth. On the other side, the good seed, will shine forth as the sun in the kingdom of God.

Jesus lived the kingdom, preached the kingdom and exhibited the kingdom in Word and in deed. He released his kingdom on earth in our hearts on good soil that germinates and produces a harvest of souls into his kingdom. The kingdom message, the Word of God is sowed as seed in our hearts. The seed germinates and brings forth good fruits, which produce other seeds that produce more fruits. The seeds are multiplied, and the fruits of repentance are also multiplied. It is our responsibility to ensure that our priorities are right and that we do the things to make our soil fertile and our harvest bountiful.

GOD'S STANDARD FOR ENTRANCE IN THE KINGDOM OF GOD

God has set the standard that we must attain in order to gain entrance into the kingdom of God. Jesus taught his disciples that, "except your righteousness shall exceed the righteousness of the scribes and Pharisees, ye shall in no case enter the kingdom of heaven" (Matt 5:20).

Scribes were well-educated men who studied, transcribed, interpreted and taught the law of Moses, and were often associated with the sect of the Pharisees. Their advice and instructions went way beyond what was written in the Scriptures because they introduced many man-made regulations and traditions which became more important than the Scriptures themselves.

In Mark 2:16, the scribes and Pharisees complained that Jesus ate with publicans and sinners. Jesus reminded them that they that were well did not need a doctor, only those that were sick and that he did not come to call the righteous to repentance, but sinners.

In Mark 3.22, when Jesus cast out devils, the scribes said: "He hath Beelzebub, and by the prince of the devils casteth he out devils." Jesus told them that Satan could not cast out Satan. Nor could a kingdom or a house divided against itself stand. The pride of the scribes did not allow them to admit that Jesus had supernatural power from above to perform miracles and they accused him of getting his power from Satan, but Jesus showed up the nonsense of their argument.

In Mark 2:1–12, when Jesus was in Capernaum teaching in a house, he healed a paralytic man. He told the sick man: "Son, thy sins be forgiven thee" (Mark 2:6), but the scribes accused him of blasphemy. Jesus informed them that the "Son of Man" had power on earth to forgive sins.

We learn that the scribes and Pharisees were filled with indignation (Luke 6:11) and watched Jesus to determine whether or not he would heal on the Sabbath day (Luke 6:7) that they might accuse him of breaking Moses' law. Jesus taught that it was fitting and proper to do good deeds and to save lives no matter which day of the week it was.

The story is told in John 8:1–11 of how the scribes and Pharisees brought a woman to Jesus that had committed the sin of adultery. A person cannot commit the sin of adultery alone but only one offender was brought to Jesus. The male partner was allowed to escape. Jesus knew that the scribes and the Pharisees were trying to trap him, seeking something for which they could accuse him. Jesus simply reminded them that we are all sinners but if we cease from sinning, we will stand before God without condemnation.

In Mark 11:18, we learn that the chief priests joined with the scribes to seek methods by which Jesus could be murdered because they were afraid of his teaching and saw him as a dangerous threat to their way of life.

And in Luke 23:10, we learn that the chief priests again joined with the scribes and vehemently accused Jesus when he was brought before Herod.

The Pharisees were a group of religious leaders who opposed Jesus. They considered themselves to be the mortal enemies of Christ and often met to plan how they would entangle him and test him on his mastery of the Scriptures. This sect was started by one who had a great zeal for the law. The word Pharisee literally means "one who is separated." They separated themselves to holiness. Through this devotion to holiness, they received respect for piety and righteousness that was unparalleled and received the lofty praise of men. They were considered experts in religion and made many elaborate Jewish regulations. They sat in seats of honor and power and could not tolerate Jesus. They were considered his mortal enemies but thought of themselves as separated to holiness. They considered themselves superior to everyone else on earth and at banquets, they would sit in the most privileged seats. They prayed and fasted in public places, and gave alms to beggars in order to be noticed by onlookers so that people would regard them as pious and righteous. Jesus with good reason called them snakes, a brood of vipers, blind guides, blind fools and children of hell.

In Matthew 23, Jesus pronounced seven woes (warnings, grief, denunciation, distress) on the scribes and Pharisees. It was during this sermon on the mountainside that Jesus taught his disciples that the righteousness of the scribes and the Pharisees was not enough to gain entrance into the kingdom of God. Jesus commended the scribes and Pharisees for paying tithes and suggested that they should continue to worship God with their tithes but in the right way so that their gifts would be accepted by him. With regard to their public prayers, Jesus said that they have received their reward in full. He, however condemned them because they neglected the more important matters of the law: justice, mercy, and faithfulness. The scribes and Pharisees were to be respected because of their authoritative position but what they did should not be emulated because they did not practice what they preached.

What are some of the Pharisee-like characteristics that Christians need to overcome before they can be considered fit and proper to enter heaven? First, the Pharisees were proud. Jesus told the story of the Pharisee and the sinner who went to the temple to pray (Luke 18:9–14). The "I-Man" Pharisee prayed with himself: "God, I thank thee, that I am not as other men are, extortioners, unjust, adulterers or even as this publican. I fast twice a week, I give tithes of all that I possess."

Can we see ourselves in the mirror? "I go to church each time the doors are opened. I do not know why that sinner John Browne does not stay away from this church." Do we in our pride, like the Pharisee, look down on others. God's most beautiful angel, Lucifer, was cast out of heaven because of his pride. Jesus taught that all that is in the world is the lust of the eyes, the lust of the flesh and the pride of life. On the other side, the tax collector humbled himself before God. He recognized that he was a sinner, and he prayed that God would save him from his sins. All of us who exalt ourselves will be brought low. God will uplift the humble.

Second, the Pharisee fasted at least twice a week. We are not to underscore the power of fasting as a magnificent weapon to fight our spiritual battles against principalities, against powers, against the rulers of darkness of this world and against spiritual wickedness in heavenly places (Matt 17:14–21; Mark 9:14–29). Jesus taught us that when we fast, we are not to be like the hypocritical Pharisees and fast to be seen and praised by others. We must fast to be seen by God only, who is in the secret place, observing and noting our actions, so that he can openly reward us (Matt 6:16–18). Fasting looses the bonds of wickedness, undoes heavy burdens, sets free the oppressed, and breaks every yoke (Isa 58:6).

Third, the Pharisees prayed three times a day as was the custom of the Jews. In the story that Jesus told about the Pharisee and the publican who went to the temple to pray, the Pharisee prayed, not about his sins and his wrongdoing, but about the sins that other had committed, because he thought that he was more righteous than others. He was not like robbers, adulterers or evildoers. After all, he was the holy one, who did not need to repent of his sins. They stood in the streets, synagogues and other public places and prayed, so that others can see them and praise them. Jesus' message to us is clear: "Men ought always to prayer and not to faint." He further taught that we must pray that God forgive our trespasses and sins. How often do we pray and what is our attitude when we approach God's throne of grace and mercy? Do we desire to have and have not or do we covet what rightly belong to others but still do not get what we want to have? Have you been praying in accordance with God's will so that he will hear and answer our prayers and give you grace and mercy in your time of need? You will not hear from God if you ask with the wrong motives or ask so that you may spend God's resources on riotous living. God will not hear your babbling and long meaningless prayers. Your prayer must be righteous, powerful and effective in the eyes of God.

Fourth, the Pharisee tithed but omitted the weightier matters of the law: justice, mercy, and faith. Jesus encouraged them to continue to pay their tithes but condemned them because they would strain out a gnat and swallow a camel. In different words, Jesus is teaching us that paying tithes is important, but our focus must be on greater matters of ensuring that God's people are treated with love, justice, and mercy, and that they were faithful to God. Jesus never issued harsh words to publicans and prostitutes. We spend so much time arguing about minor matters and forget such matters as feeding the hungry, comforting the sick and afflicted, and ensuring that all are treated fairly. Most importantly, we must put God first in our lives because God will not trade first place with anyone.

Fifth, the scribes and Pharisees were missionaries. Jesus taught that they traveled land and sea to make one convert, just to make then twice the child of hell. The problem is that there was numerical increase, and outward appearance of conversion, but no conversion took place in the hearts of the converts. Let us again look at ourselves in the mirror. Examine if our living is in harmony with that of Christ or if we are a stumbling block in the way of others who want to be followers of Christ. What about when persons are converted to Christ? Is it for the glory of God or is it for our credit and advantage? The church, through Christians, has the important role to preach and teach the good news of salvation to the entire world. We must travel land, sea and air to compel those that are lost in their sins to find hope and joy in Jesus Christ, the God of our salvation. There is more joy in heaven over one sinner that repents and turns from his sins than over those who have already repented.

The point is that our relationship with God must be superior to that of the scribes and Pharisees in order to gain the entry ticket to the kingdom of God.

GOD'S FORGIVENESS

> And Jesus said unto him, This day is salvation come to this house, forasmuch as he also is a son of Abraham. For the Son of man is come to seek and to save that which was lost. (Luke 19:9–10)

Jesus of Nazareth, the third person of the Godhead, God in human flesh, was passing through the city of Jericho. He was on his way to Jerusalem to die on the cross at Mount Calvary for the sins of the whole world. On his way there, he explained to his disciples that he would be rejected of men and murdered but would be resurrected from the dead. Jericho's chief tax collector, Zacchaeus, wanted to see who Jesus was. He was a very short man and could not see him because of the large crowd that had gathered, also to see and hear Jesus. Zacchaeus ran ahead of the crowd and climbed a sycamore tree. A sycamore tree was a very tall tree, with large leaves and low branches that was very easy to climb.

Zacchaeus, who was very rich, was a thief, an extortionist, and fraudster, who overcharged the taxpayers of Jericho and pocketed the excesses. He wanted to get a glimpse of Jesus to see who Jesus was. He climbed the tree and probably hid among the large leaves with a sufficiently clear view that he could see the Master when he passed by. When Jesus came to the sycamore tree where Zacchaeus was, he stopped and looked up in the tree at Zacchaeus. He told Zacchaeus to come down immediately because he had invited himself to be a guest at his house for the day. Jesus knows all things and he knew Zacchaeus's name and he called him by name. Jesus knows all of us by name and when our Father draws us, he calls us by our name. He knows the number of hairs on our heads.

Zacchaeus was excited because Jesus would be a guest at his house. This news caused those following Jesus to complain. The complaint laid was that Jesus would be the guest of a sinner. They simply did not believe that Jesus should have fellowship with such a person. The crowd saw Zacchaeus as a notorious sinner with whom Jesus should not associate. Jesus' mission, however, is to call sinners to repentance. They thought of themselves as righteous and we are all like that. We can see the mote in our brother's eye without first addressing the beam that is in our own eyes.

When Zacchaeus arrived at his house with Jesus, he confessed to Jesus that he was a sinner and that he was sorry for the sins he had committed. The Bible teaches that

> if we say we have no sin, we are deceiving ourselves, and the truth is not in us. If we confess our sins, he is faithful and righteous to forgive us our sins, and cleanse us from all unrighteousness. If we say that we have not sinned, we make him a liar, and his word is not in us. (1 John 1:8–10)

The psalmist David confessed his sin to God when he said: "Then I acknowledge my sin to you and did not cover up my iniquity. I said, 'I will confess my transgressions to the Lord.' And you forgave the guilt of my sin" (Ps 32:5).

The people who were following Jesus were disturbed because Jesus was going to Zacchaeus's house. They wanted to know why Jesus was associating with sinners. Jesus saw past the sins that Zacchaeus had committed just as he saw past the sins that Moses had committed, that (Saul of Tarsus) Saint Paul had committed and just as he saw past all our sins. It does not matter the gravity of the sin. God will crush them to oblivion and bring us to the state just as if we had not sinned.

Zacchaeus recognized the need for a Savior and the Savior of all mankind was on the spot seeking to save him. He knew that he could not hold on to mammon and Jesus at the same time. He had to give up that which separated him from God. He was not overwhelmed by the weight of his possessions. Zacchaeus told Jesus that he would give half of what he owned to the poor and would repay all he had cheated, four times the amount he cheated them of. Jesus recognized Zacchaeus's broken and penitent heart. He told him: "Today salvation is come to this house."

Zacchaeus's repentance brought salvation not only to himself, but to his entire household as well.

REDEMPTION

Redemption may be properly defined as the repurchasing of lost mankind from the burden of sin by Jesus' death on the cross. God made us. He owns us, but we became slaves to sin and that separated us from him. Yet, he needed us to love, obey, trust and worship him, and he was willing to put up a ransom for us. He gave his own life on the cross to deliver, ransom or redeem us from the slavery of sin.

REDEMPTION THROUGH HIS BLOOD

> In whom we have redemption through his blood, the forgiveness of sins, according to the riches of his grace; Wherein he hath abounded toward us in all wisdom and prudence. (Eph 1:7–8)

The Bible teaches that all mankind sinned and fell short of God's glory. We became separated from God and became slaves to sin: "Whoever commits sin is a slave to sin" (John 8:34), and as such, we felt no obligation to righteousness. However, every slave looks forward with great expectation that one day, someone would rescue him from those chains and set him free. God sent his only begotten son, Jesus Christ, to be the ultimate sacrificial ransom for our release from the chains and the curse of sin, the curse of the law, and eternal death.

REDEMPTION SAVES US FROM THE WRATH TO COME

We are redeemed from sin so that we may be protected from the wrath of God that will be revealed from heaven against the godlessness and wickedness of men. We were by nature the children of wrath:

> But God commendeth his love toward us, in that while we were yet sinners, Christ died for us. Much more then, being now justified by his blood, we shall be saved from wrath through him. (Rom 5:8–9)

God has not appointed us to suffer his wrath but to obtain salvation through our Lord Jesus Christ. It is a fearful thing to fall into the hands of the living God.

The Bible teaches that after death there is the great white throne judgment for the unrighteous dead:

> And I saw the dead, small and great, stand before God; and the books were opened: and another book was opened, which is the book of life: and the dead were judged out of those things which were written in the books, according to their works. And the sea gave up the dead which were in it, and death and hell delivered up the dead which were in them: and they were judged, every man according to their works. And death and hell were cast into the lake of fire. This is the second death. And whosoever was not found written in the book of life was cast into the lake of fire. (Rev 20:12–15)

When we believe in Jesus and obey his Word, we will be granted everlasting life. However, the time will come when the dead will hear Jesus' voice and live because he has Life in himself and has the authority to execute judgment:

> Marvel not at this, for the hour is coming, in the which all that are in the graves shall hear his voice, And shall come forth; they that have done good, unto the resurrection of life; and they that have done evil unto the resurrection of damnation. (John 5:28–29)

REDEMPTION THAT WE MIGHT BE GUARANTEED EVERLASTING LIFE

We are redeemed that we should not perish but have everlasting life. Our primary task is to believe in Jesus and we will have eternal life. The Bible teaches: "For God so loved the world, that he gave his only begotten Son, that whosoever believeth in him should not perish, but have everlasting life" (John 3:16). However, if we reject him, we will not see life because his wrath remains on those who reject him.

When Jesus volunteered his life on the cross, he abolished the law of sin and eternal death for all who will accept him as Christ and Lord. He conquered death and its sting by triumphantly exiting the grave with the keys of death and hell. He is the first that rose from the dead to a life of immortality and incorruption, and because he rose from the dead, all God's people will be resurrected to eternal life. This is our hope. This is why we endure the affliction and the shame of the cross. Our perishable bodies will become imperishable and the mortal will put on immortality, death being swallowed up in victory: "But is now made manifest by the appearing of our Saviour Jesus Christ, who hath abolished death, and hath brought life and immorality to light through the gospel" (2 Tim 1:10).

REDEMPTION THAT WE MAY BE ADOPTED AS GOD'S OWN CHILDREN

> Even so we, when we were the children, were in bondage under the elements of the world: But when the fulness of the time was come, God sent forth his Son, made of a woman, made under the law, To redeem them that were under the law, that we might receive the adoption as sons. And because ye are sons, God hath sent forth the Spirit of his Son into your hearts, crying Abba, Father. Wherefore thou are no longer a servant but a son; and if a son, then an heir of God through Christ. (Gal 4:3–7)

Before Christ's death, burial and resurrection, we were all slaves to the law and we followed the law to death thinking that we would be saved by it. In addition to the law given by Moses, the scribes and the Pharisees saddled God's people with many burdensome rules, ordinances and regulations which were very difficult if not impossible to observe. This practice received the condemnation of Christ because the scribes and Pharisees did not keep the observances themselves, although they forced others to do so. This yoke was as unbearable for our foreparents as it is for us. Jesus' death resulted in our redemption from the bondage of the law that we might receive the adoption as children and heirs of God. We are no longer slaves of the law but free in Christ Jesus to go boldly before the throne of God, our Father, having received the righteousness of Christ in our hearts.

REDEMPTION THAT WE MIGHT BE PURIFIED

> For the grace of God that bringeth salvation hath appeared to all men, Teaching us that, denying ungodliness and worldly lusts, we should live soberly, righteously, and godly in this present world; Looking for that blessed hope and the glorious appearing of the great God and Savior Jesus Christ; Who gave himself for us, that he might redeem us from all iniquity, and purify unto himself a peculiar people, zealous of good works. (Titus 2:11–14)

God's grace, yes, God's free and unmerited mercy on the human race has saved us from sin, through Christ's obedience to his violent and merciless death on the cross. We are transformed from a sinful life to a Christian life through faith in Jesus Christ and are justified freely by his grace through the redemption that came by him and through him. God makes this grace available to all of us and it is through this grace that we have the power to forsake sin and live a new purified life in Christ Jesus. It is through Christ that we have redemption through his blood, the forgiveness and cleansing of sins, in accordance with the riches of his grace. God's grace is God's gift to us which we accept by faith in him.

This same grace has appeared to all humankind and teaches us that since we have accepted Christ as Lord and Savior of our lives, we must deny all impiety no matter how it raises its ugly head and we must deny or not act on the vicious temptation of worldly passions no matter how severe the temptation. It is this same grace of God that teaches us how to live self-controlled, upright and godly lives in our current lifetime, because there is no repentance beyond the grave. If we die with unrepentant sin in our hearts, we will have to face the consequences of sin, which is eternal death. Christians are to be sober, reverent, temperate, honest, generous, obedient and faithful to God, and although we will not be saved by our work, God expects us to give service to our church, our communities, our work environment and the organizations to which we are attached.

God took our sins in his body by his death on the cross so that through his grace, by faith, we might be redeemed from the bondage of sin and the curse of eternal death and be purified for himself as his special people, zealous of good works. We are a chosen generation, a royal priesthood, a holy nation, God's own special people, that we may proclaim his praises because he mercifully called us from the darkness of sin into his marvelous light of righteousness.

REDEMPTION THAT WE MIGHT RECEIVE THE HOLY SPIRIT

> Do you not know that your bodies are temples of the Holy Spirit, who is in you, whom you have received from God? You are not your own; you were bought at a price. Therefore, honor God with your bodies. (1 Cor 6:19–20 NIV)

> Keep watch over yourselves and all the flock of which the Holy Spirit has made you overseers. Be shepherds of the church of God, which he bought with his own blood. (Acts 20:28 NIV)

Paul has two important questions for us. Can you define the Christian body, and can you tell who is its owner? Paul then answers the questions for us. Our bodies are the temple of the living God and the home of the Holy Spirit. We are not allowed to treat this temple as we like. We are not allowed to have drunken bodies nor are we allowed to abuse our bodies with illegal substances. We must not be gluttons. We are not allowed to have sexual intercourse outside the bond of holy matrimony, and we must keep the temple clean. We are to honor God with our bodies. Jesus bought us with his blood, which he spilled on the cross, and is the owner and controller over us. He has given us permission to use our bodies with the understanding that our bodies are his home and must be treated well. It must not be allowed to run to ruin with the dust and ravishes of sin. We cannot abuse it; period. We have no equity in it and at anytime the owner can call for the keys. I therefore urge you in the name of Jesus Christ our Lord, that you keep a diligent watch over God's holy temple because God has bought all of us with the price of his life and sent his Holy Spirit to reside in us. There is no room for garbage or filth.

REDEEMED TO BE KINGS AND PRIESTS

Christ redeemed us to God by his blood and someday coming soon, he will unite us with fellow believers on the earth to be kings and priests to our God:

> And they sung a new song, saying, Thou art worthy to take the book, and to open the seals thereof: for thou wast slain, and hast redeemed us to God by thy blood out of every kindred, and tongue, and people, and nation; And hast made us unto our God kings and priests: and we shall reign on the earth. (Rev 5:9–10)

Thanks be to God.

Chapter 5

Conversion

The final step in the process of salvation is called conversion. A person is converted by turning from his sins, embracing God's plan of salvation for eternal life, and confessing Jesus Christ as Lord and Savior of his life. The process occurs in our hearts by faith. It is a complete change of attitude with respect to the wrong actions of our past sinful life while accepting our new resolve to do the right things all the time, by focusing on Jesus Christ as our present help to abstain from committing sins of any kind. The prophet Isaiah put it this way: "Let the wicked forsake his way, and the unrighteous man his thoughts: and let him return unto the Lord, and he will have mercy upon him; and to our God, for he will abundantly pardon" (Isa 55:7).

We must turn our backs on sin and take our places once again in God's garden of Eden, the same spiritual and moral position that Adam was in before he sinned against God. We have to make adjustments to our thoughts, our attitudes, our habits and our actions, and do what is right and well pleasing to him. The Apostle Paul had this to say: "And be not conformed to this world: but be ye transformed by the renewing of your mind, that you may prove what is that good, and acceptable, and perfect will of God" (Rom 12:2).

We were once entangled with the yoke of sin of its varying kinds, and Paul is advising us to turn away from that way of life and live a new and transformed life guided by the Holy Spirit of Jesus our Lord. Our thoughts, motives and actions must be renewed and different. The cornerstone of everything that we do, think and say must be God centered and we must learn what God's will is because it is his will that is good, acceptable and perfect.

The psalmist explained conversion this way: "Depart from evil, and do good; seek peace, and pursue it" (Ps 34:14).

Peter replicated this same message: "They must turn from evil and do good; they must seek peace and pursue it" (1 Pet 3:11 NIV).

The converted Paul's message to the Hebrews is significant:

> Therefore, since we are surrounded by such a great cloud of witnesses, let us throw off everything that hinders and the sin that so easily entangles, and let us run with perseverance the race marked out for us, fixing our eyes on Jesus, the pioneer and perfecter of our faith. For the joy set before him he endured the cross, scorning its shame, and sat down at the right hand of the throne of God. (Heb 12:1–2 NIV)

He went on to say: "Stand fast therefore in the liberty wherewith Christ hath made us free, and be not entangled again with the yoke of bondage" (Gal 5:1).

Paul's Letter to the Philippians provides further insights:

> But whatever were gains to me I now consider loss for the sake of Christ. What is more, I consider everything a loss because of the surpassing greatness of knowing Jesus Christ my Lord, for whose sake I have lost all things. I consider them garbage that I may gain Christ. And be found in him, not having a righteousness of my own that comes from the law, but that which is through faith in Christ—the righteousness that comes from God and is by faith. I want to know Christ—yes, to know the power of his resurrection and participation in his sufferings, becoming like him in his death, and so, somehow, to attain to the resurrection from the dead. (Phil 3:7–11 NIV)

CONVERSION OF MANASSEH

Manasseh was a Hebrew king who commenced his reign at the tender age of twelve years old. He was a remarkably evil king and engaged himself in the terrible worship of the old forms of idols, and sacrificed his own children as burnt offerings in the valley of Hinnom. His advisors were spirit mediums, fortune-tellers and sorcerers. He persecuted and murdered large numbers of innocent true worshippers of God and corrupted the worship of the true and living God at the temple. He made the temple a place of idolatry, cult astrological worship, and turned the temple into an idolatrous brothel.

Manasseh and his people ignored God's warning and generous promises, and God sent in the Assyrian army to capture him and put him in prison. While he was in captivity and afflicted, he prayed to the Lord God of heaven and humbled himself greatly before him. He recognized that the Lord was really God and repented of his sins. God heard his prayer and restored his kingdom.

Manasseh's life changed dramatically. He removed the idols from the hills and from the temple and destroyed the pagan altars. He then rebuilt the altar of the Lord and offered sacrifices to God. He also instructed the people of Judah to serve the true and living God. This is a true example of conversion. Manasseh was a notorious sinner who repented and turned from his sins, to serve the true and living God Almighty: "The Lord your God is gracious and compassionate. He will not turn his face from you if you return to him" (2 Chr 30:9 NIV).

CONVERSION OF PAUL

We are all familiar with the rich ministry of Paul. Paul preached and taught Jesus Christ, his crucifixion and resurrection from the dead, and the kingdom of God. But Paul was not always Paul. Before his new name was written down in glory, Paul was the notorious sinner called Saul. Yes, the Apostle Paul was the notorious Saul who was born in Tarsus, a Roman city. His parents were native Jews, which made him a natural Jew. He was educated at Tarsus, where he studied philosophy and Greek poetry. He went on to study divinity and Jewish law at Jerusalem where he was able to study under the tutorship of the eminent, brilliant Pharisee professor Gamaliel. Additionally, Saul was an excellent tent maker. He was technically and academically brilliant.

Saul, the intellectual that he was, was certainly motivated to practice the knowledge he had attained. He was young and ambitious and would have wanted to distinguish himself as an eminent scholar. He found a project to challenge his intellectual capacity. There were at Jerusalem some perceived unlearned and ignorant men who were preaching and teaching the gospel and spreading the good news of Christ and salvation to all who were willing to listen. Saul took on a mission to exterminate this gospel of Jesus Christ and anyone who made its continuity possible. He led a vigorous and vicious campaign of threats and murder against the church at Jerusalem with the support and goodwill of the chief priests.

First, it was Stephen, a man full of faith; a man of grace and power, who did great wonders and signs among the people. Stephen was such a powerful man of God that he was able to dispute and argue with members of the Synagogue of the Freemen, Jews of Cyrene and Alexandria, as well as the provinces of Cilicia and Asia. They could not stand up against his wisdom or the Spirit with which he spoke. Stephen was a man of honest report, full of the Holy Ghost and wisdom. He was among the seven chosen and appointed to lead the food distribution program of the early church at Jerusalem and was indeed a powerful minister of the gospel of Christ. Saul masterminded his murder.

Saul continued his threats and murder against the church and obtained arrest warrants from the high priest to the synagogue at Damascus, for anyone, man or woman, caught teaching or preaching the gospel, to be handcuffed and brought to Jerusalem. Paul was near the end of his journey and was about to enter the city of Damascus when a light from heaven, which was brighter than the sun, encompassed him causing him to fall to the ground. So great was the glory of that light that it caused Paul to become blind. Saul then heard and responded to the powerful voice of Jesus. Paul had no defense against Jesus' charge of being persecuted by him. He immediately accepted him as Lord and Master of his life and inquired what Jesus wanted him to do. Jesus informed him that he had ordained him to be a minister of his gospel and as a witness of his Damascus Road conversion, and of the further instructions that would be given to him. Paul's mission was to evangelize the Gentiles specifically and also to evangelize the entire world, ensuring that spiritual eyes were opened and that God's people were changed from the pathway of Satan and darkness, so that they may receive forgiveness of sin and an inheritance among those that are sanctified by the faith that is in Christ Jesus.

This is the true definition of conversion. Paul was a sinner of the worst kind. He met Jesus, made a right-about turn in his life and lived a life of obedience to Christ and self-denial to the point of willingness to die for Christ's sake. God forgave his sins and he was baptized in the name of the Lord Jesus.

Paul gave believers an important example for us to follow at the time of conversion. Immediately after conversion, he fasted for three days and nights as he prepared for his new mission. This is a great example for the church and individuals on how to approach missions and God's work. Paul accepted his mission from Christ with the knowledge that as a missionary of Christ, he would have to endure various degrees of suffering. Our Christian lives are not different from that of Paul's. We will have to endure and conquer much affliction until we complete this race so that we can receive our inheritance in the kingdom of God.

Chapter 6

We Must Be Holy

> For this is the will of God, even your sanctification, that you should abstain from fornication: That every one of you should know how to possess his vessel in sanctification and honour, Not in the lust of concupiscence, even as the Gentiles which know not God: That no man go beyond and defraud his brother in any matter: because that the Lord is an avenger of all such, as we also have forewarned you and testified. For God has not called us unto uncleanness, but unto holiness. He therefore that despiseth, despiseth not man, but God, who hath given unto us his Holy Spirit. (1 Thess 4:3–8)

When we accept Christ as Lord and Savior of our lives, we are forgiven for our sinful actions and omissions of actions, but the root from which our sins originated in the first place continues to have a deleterious impact on our Christian living, and must be put to death through the blood of Christ, so as to prevent new or repeat manifestations of sin. The process of eradicating this root of sin is called sanctification. It is the cleansing of the heart and the old sinful nature from inbred sin through the application of the blood of Jesus Christ, by faith. It is the process of making a person holy and setting them apart for God's service. It is God's second distinct work of grace. The Holy Spirit purifies us, eradicates our sinful nature, and gives us his divine nature with the characteristics of the image and likeness of God, the true image and likeness with which we were created. The work of the

Holy Spirit takes place in our hearts whereby we become the workmanship of God, created in Christ.

The life of righteousness that we embark on must be a life without sin, and of service to our Lord and his people. Our sinful and selfish nature is crucified with Christ and this results in the complete destruction of our body of sin, which is rendered powerless and we are no longer the servants of sin. The old nature dies and a new creation comes into existence. Paul testified that he (the flesh with all of its affections and lusts) was crucified (nailed to the cross) with Christ so that Christ could live in him. His life was no longer controlled by the flesh but by his faith in the Son of God. Paul became dead to the reigning power of sin but alive to God, through Jesus. His selfish heart was replaced by a new spiritual heart. He was different on the inside because he was resurrected to a new life, and our Lord and Savior Jesus Christ was in complete control, living and reigning inside of his heart. The old Paul, with his selfish rebellion against God's will, was totally and completely annulled. However, Paul did not cease to exist. He stated that the life that he lived in the flesh, he lived by faith in God. His orientation had changed because he died to sin and selfishness and his goals and ambitions were transformed by the indwelling Christ. Paul died to sin and was renewed in knowledge after the image of God, who created him.

Christ dwells in our hearts through faith, and this is the message that Paul presents in his Epistle to the Galatians. He reminded the churches at Galatia that their Christian experience was based on their faith in God, and not on keeping the Mosaic law. He inquired of them if they received the Holy Spirit by observing the law or by believing the gospel of Christ; he also asked: "Are ye so foolish? Having begun in the Spirit, are ye now made perfect by the flesh?" (Gal 3:3). Abraham, the great-grandfather of humankind and world hero, was saved by faith and not by keeping the law. He was justified by faith and this was counted as righteousness. Good works never bring about the life of righteousness. The blood of our Lord Jesus, who was murdered on the cross, changed our lives from lives of sin to lives of righteousness and we have to completely surrender the remainder of our lives to him by faith.

A life surrendered to Christ means that we are completely in subjection to our Lord for as long as we should live. We are no longer in control but have surrendered our members to the obedience of Christ, who is our Lord and Master. The Apostle James gave this exhortation: "Submit yourselves therefore to God. Resist the devil and he will flee from you" (Jas 4:7).

The Apostle Peter put it this way:

> As obedient children, not fashioning yourselves according to the former lust in your ignorance. But as he which has called you is Holy, so be ye holy in all manner of conversation; Because it is written, be ye holy, for I Am holy. (1 Pet 1:14–16)

We surrender our lives with all of life's problems, decisions, issues, situations, and circumstances; both known and unknown; past, present and future. We daily surrender our entire life, and personality and being, for as long as we have breath, to Jesus' control.

Our new relationship with Christ destroys the power of the Adamic nature with which we were born and gives us the ability to live in accordance with our new divine nature, without violating God's laws of salvation. We are transformed into the image of Christ as exemplified by love, peace, patience, kindness, goodness, faithfulness and self-control.

Sanctification returns us to oneness with Christ: "For both he that sanctifieth and they who are sanctified are all of one: for which cause, he is not ashamed to call them brethren" (Heb 2:11). Sanctification is important because God suffered on the cross that we might be cleansed from sin; and without holiness, "no man shall see the Lord" (Heb 12:14). Our unity with Christ destroys the power of the old nature and associates us with the likeness of Christ, who gives us the authority to exist in accordance with our new divine nature. It also means a resurrection to new living and separation from the dominion of the sinful nature, because our sinful nature was crucified with Christ on the cross. The goal of sanctification is to conform the Christian to the image and likeness of Christ, and it is his Spirit who changes us into that same image from glory to glory. The power of the Spirit put to death the deeds of the body.

Sanctification is the work of God but it is also the work of every Christian. We must give up our own wills, desires, and ambitions and let God have his own way in our lives. Paul advises the Christian: "Having these promises, dearly beloved, let us cleanse ourselves from all filthiness of the flesh and spirit, perfecting holiness in the fear of God" (2 Cor 7:1). He besought us:

> I beseech you therefore, brethren, by the mercies of God, that ye present your bodies a living sacrifice, holy, acceptable unto God, which is your reasonable service. And be not conformed to this world: but be ye transformed by the renewing of your mind, that ye may prove what is that good, and acceptable, and perfect, will of God. (Rom 12:1–2)

As part of the sanctification process, the Christian is required to:

- flee from idolatry (1 Cor 10:14);
- purify ourselves from everything which contaminates the body and spirit; perfect holiness out of reverence to God (2 Cor 7:1);
- flee youthful lust; pursue righteousness, faith, love, and peace (2 Tim 2:22);
- extricate ourselves from worldly fables (1 Tim 4:7);
- by the Spirit, put to death the misdeeds of the body (Rom 8:13);
- live by the Spirit (Gal 5:16);
- be an example for believers in conversation, in life, in faith and in purity; read the Bible; do not neglect your gift; watch your life and doctrine (1 Tim 4:12–15);
- bear each other's burdens (Gal 6:2).

So then, there is a correlation and conjunction of both human and divine agencies in the work of sanctification.

OLD NATURE

Let us return for a moment to the story of creation. God created us in his own image after his own likeness. He created us without sin and in a holy state. We chose to disobey him and our disobedience separated us from him. Our sinfulness was inherited from Adam and the result is that all humankind is born with a sinful nature (spiritually dead). We serve sin and self and thus exclude God from of our lives. This sinful nature is sometimes referred to as the old man, the sinful flesh, or carnal nature. As Paul put it:

> For we know that the law is spiritual: but I am carnal, sold under sin. For that which I do I allow not: for what I would, that do I not; but what I hate, that do I. If then I do what I would not, I consent unto the law that it is good. Now then it is no more I that do it, but sin that dwelleth in me. For I know that in me (that is, in my flesh), dwelleth no good thing: for to will is present with me; but how to perform that which is good I find not. For the good that I would I do not: but the evil I would not, that I do. Now if I do what I would not, it is no more I that do it, but sin that dwelleth in me. I find then a law, that, when I would do good, evil is present with me. For I delight in the law of God after the inward man. But I see another law in my members, warring against the law of my mind, and bringing me into captivity to the law of sin which is in my members. O wretched man

> that I am! Who shall deliver me from the body of this death? I thank God through Jesus Christ our Lord. So then with the mind I myself serve the law of God, but with the flesh the law of sin. (Rom 7:14–25)

Paul went further and explained that to be carnally minded is death (Rom 8:6), because the carnal mind is hostile toward God and cannot submit to God's law, neither can it please him (Rom 8:7–8). The carnal person is dominated by self-life and is obedient to that which is fallen and sinful in the old Adamic nature, and in which nothing good is produced. Self-seeking is wrong and is inconsistent with the true service of God or imitation of Christ.

The flesh is the name by which the Bible refers to our fallen nature. Our spirit, soul and body, were under the power of sin. It is the sinner we were before we became Christians. Our powers, that is, intellect, emotions and will were under the power of the flesh. Nothing good comes from the flesh and it is the mind of the flesh that is at enmity with God. The sinful flesh must be put to death so that we might be free from the chains of sin. St. Paul put it this way:

> Knowing this, that our old man is crucified with him, that the body of sin might be destroyed, that henceforth we should not serve sin. For he that is dead is free from sin. (Rom 6:6–7)

Paul further noted:

> And they that are Christ's have crucified the flesh with the affections and lusts. (Gal 5:24)

The new life with Christ begins with the destruction of selfishness. All our conflicts, affections and lusts have been nailed to the cross and brought under Christ's control.

The unsaved person is a slave to the things of the flesh and simply leaves God out of his life. The believer has two choices. He can either serve God or succumb to the old nature by leaving God out of his life. The Bible teaches us that we should "walk in the Spirit, and ye shall not fulfil the lust of the flesh. For the flesh lusteth against the Spirit, and the Spirit against the flesh; and these are contrary the one to the other: so that ye cannot do the things ye would" (Gal 5:16–17). We cannot walk in the Spirit and fulfill the lust of the flesh at the same time, because it is impossible to perform these two opposites at once: "Ye cannot drink of the cup of the Lord, and the cup of devils: ye cannot be partakers of the Lord's table, and the table of devils" (1 Cor 10:21).

The Holy Spirit never leads to immorality, strife, jealousy, factions, and other sins. The Spirit always led and continues to lead us to treat other persons the way that Jesus would treat them, with compassion, gentleness, kindness, humility, and forgiveness. The Christian is given a new heart, a new conscience. His new life in Christ starts with the death of selfishness. The conscience rejects selfishness as its commander-in-chief and determines that he should walk in the Spirit; soberly, righteously, and godly in this present world. Paul wrote to the Ephesians

> that ye put off concerning the former conversation the old man, which is corrupt according to the deceitful lusts; And be renewed in the spirit of your mind; And that ye put on the new man, which after God is created in righteousness and true holiness. (Eph 4:22–24)

Walking in the Spirit does not mean a trouble-free life. Christians have to endure all the conflicts and sufferings of life, but we must decide not to allow them to lead us in the wrong pathway. There will be conflicts between the will and Satan; conflicts between the heart and the world; conflict with habits; conflicts with polluted imaginations; conflicts with temptations resulting from our association with others. Jesus taught: "If any man will come after me, let him deny himself, and take up his cross daily, and follow me" (Luke 9:23). We have to take up our crosses of affliction and suffering every day; whether it is in our bodies, in our finances, in our businesses, in our families, in our churches, in our communities, in our schools, or in our countries. Paul said that he kept his body under his complete discipline by treating it like his slave, so that his preaching would not be in vain but that he would be on the winner's podium to accept his reward from Jesus.

NEW NATURE

The old self was corrupted in accordance with our deceitful desires, but we are now sanctified because Christ offered his body on the cross once for all. What was begun in the spirit, we cannot perfect in the flesh. We must allow God's Holy Spirit to have dominion over every thought and imagination of our hearts, every word that we speak, and every action performed, so that we do not gratify the desires of our sinful nature. God himself has covenanted with us to put his laws in our hearts, write them on our minds, and remember our sins and lawless acts no more:

> I will sprinkle clean water on you, and you will be clean; I will cleanse you from all impurities and from all your idols. I will

give you a new heart and put a new spirit in you; I will remove your heart of stone and give you a heart of flesh. And I will put my Spirit in you and move you to follow my decrees and be careful to keep my laws. (Ezek 36:25–27 NIV)

He will be our God and we will be his people.

We were corrupt and rotten on the inside before we accepted Christ as our Lord. We must therefore ensure that dirty old man of filthy thoughts, filthy conversation and filthy actions are totally and completely destroyed, and we must follow Christ with a renewed mind, a renewed way of speaking, and renewed actions. The old sinful self must be discarded like the disposition of garbage never to raise its ugly head again. We must change our behaviors to match that of our calling in Christ Jesus. We must put to death the components of our earthly nature: sexual immorality, impurity, lust, evil desires, and greed, which is idolatry, and put on the likeness of Christ: compassion, kindness, humility, gentleness, and patience. We must not make provision for the flesh to fulfill its lusts and we must walk in the image and likeness of our Lord Jesus. In other words, we are to exhibit the characteristics and attitudes of our new divine nature by imitating Christ in all aspects of our lives. We must continue our journey in the Spirit, ensuring that we do not perfect in the flesh what the new life began in the Spirit.

We are the circumcision which worship God in the Spirit and in truth, rejoice in Christ Jesus and have no confidence in the flesh. Here is what Paul said:

> In whom ye are circumcised with the circumcision made without hands, in putting off the body of the sins of the flesh by the circumcision of Christ. Buried with him in baptism, wherein also ye are risen with him through the faith of the operation of God, who hath raised him from the dead. (Col 2:11–12)

GOD SANCTIFIED HIS CHOSEN PEOPLE ISRAEL

God demands holiness from all his people. He has not called us to impurity, but to holiness. With regards to his chosen people, Israel, God chose them to be holy and to be his special treasure above all others, and this was in exchange for their obedience to him. He told them:

> For thou art a holy people unto the LORD thy God, and the LORD hath chosen thee to be a peculiar people unto himself, above all nations that are on the face of the earth. (Deut 14:2)

WE MUST BE HOLY

> Now if you obey me fully and keep my covenant, then out of all nations you will be my treasured possession. Although the whole earth is mine, you will be for me a kingdom of priests and a holy nation. (Exod 19:5-6 NIV)

As Christians, as descendants of Abraham, we are also sanctified for God's service just as the Israelites were sanctified. We too will have to be obedient to him in order to benefit from his special treatment. The Apostle Peter wrote:

> As obedient children, not fashioning yourselves according to the former lusts in your ignorance: But as he which has called you is holy, so be ye holy in all your conversation; Because it is written, be holy for I am holy. (1 Pet 1:14-16)

Peter continued:

> But ye are a chosen generation, a royal priesthood, an holy nation, a peculiar people, that you may shew forth the praises of him who called you out of darkness into his marvelous light. (1 Pet 2:9)

And this is the universal Christian message, that all his people, Israelites and Gentiles alike, must be holy because God is holy. God has chosen all of us without exception and made us his special treasure for his special purpose.

NEW HIGHWAY

Having accepted Christ as Lord and Savior, we have made that important spiritual directional change in our way of living that has determined our Christian travel plan to destination eternal life. We were traveling on the broad and dusty road of sin and destruction that leads to the destination of eternal death. One day we made contact with Jesus and his Holy Spirit, who convicted us of sin and convinced us to change lanes from that broad and dusty road to the narrow road, the highway of holiness, which leads to heaven. This is the highway for the blood-washed pilgrim, the sinner saved by the grace of God, through faith in his Son, Jesus Christ. The Bible teaches:

> And a highway will be there; it will be called the Way of Holiness. . . . The unclean will not journey on it; wicked fools will not go about on it. No lion will be there, nor will any ravenous beast; they will not be found there. But only the redeemed will walk there. (Isa 35:8-9 NIV)

This highway is for those with clean hands and pure hearts. It is a highway for those who believe in God and trust him as their Savior. This is a road for those redeemed by the blood of the Lamb, and no impostors nor wicked persons will have a passport for this journey of God's elite.

God's Glory Will Provide Lighting for This City

The Apostle John reported from the Isle of Patmos:

> I did not see a temple in the city, because the Lord God Almighty and the Lamb are its temple. The city does not need the sun or the moon to shine on it, for the glory of God gives it light, and the Lamb is its lamp. The nations will walk by its light, and the kings of the earth will bring their splendor into it. On no day will its gates ever be shut, for there will be no night there. The glory and honor of the nations will be brought into it. Nothing impure will ever enter it, nor will anyone who does what is shameful or deceitful, but only those whose names are written in the Lamb's book of life. (Rev 21:22–27 NIV)

We can look forward with great anticipation and excitement to the wonders and splendor and glory and honor of the city where God's presence will outshine the sun. All darkness is eliminated from that city. It will be a city of holy people abiding with their holy, holy, holy God. God himself and the sacrificed Lamb that took away our sins are the temple. God and the human race will be reunited in that city, never to be separated again, and of course, there will be no sin there. God will be praised and worshipped and given thanks.

New Heaven and New Earth

> And I saw a new heaven and a new earth: for the first heaven and the first earth were passed away; and there was no more sea. And I John saw the holy city, new Jerusalem, coming down from God out of heaven, prepared as a bride adorned for her husband. And I heard a great voice out of heaven saying, behold, the tabernacle of God is with men, and he will dwell with them, and they shall be his people, and God himself shall be with them, and be their God. And God shall wipe away all tears from their eyes; and there shall be no more death, neither sorrow, nor crying, neither shall there be any more pain: for the former things were passed away. (Rev 21:1–4)

WE MUST BE HOLY TO SERVE IN GOD'S ARMY

The filthy condition of our former lives does not prevent God from calling us into active service for his purposes. God calls us and forgives our sin. He sanctifies us by his word, for his special purposes. Moses committed murder, the most hideous of crimes, and yet God called him into active service to lead his people Israel from the slavery of Egypt. After Moses committed his crime and became an outlaw, he came face to face with the presence of God. He had visited God's mountain, Mount Horeb, and there he met God, who talked to him from a flame of fire, out of the middle of a nonconsuming burning bush. God commanded Moses to take off his shoes of sinfulness and fear and stand on the principle of holiness because he called him to the important duty of freeing the oppressed Israel from the bondage of Egypt. Yes, Moses was a hideous criminal, but he had the right attitude toward God's own people. God called him despite the spiritual dead condition that he was in at the time and sanctified him for his special purpose.

After the death of Moses, God called Joshua into action to ensure that the Israelites took the safe passage into the promised land, but Joshua had to be sanctified for God's work. Joshua was commanded to take of the sandals of impurity and to stand on God's principles of holiness before he took on his successful leadership role in the service of the Lord.

In the year that King Uzziah died, Isaiah saw the Lord sitting on his throne, high and lifted up. He learned of God's holiness and concluded that he did not measure up to his righteous requirements because he had a dirty mouth and those people he lived with and among also had filthy mouths. God sent his angel to him and God forgave his transgressions and purged him from all his sins. Isaiah was then ready to proclaim God's word to the people of Israel and let the world know that God would inhabit the world in human flesh and volunteer his life for the sins of the all humanity.

Before Jeremiah was conceived, God knew him, and before he was born, God sanctified him and ordained him to be a prophet to the nations. God appointed him to serve over nations and kingdoms to root out, pull down, destroy, and throw down, to build and to plant.

God's Spirit entered Ezekiel's heart before he sent him to the rebellious nation of Israel to be their watchman and to proclaim God's word.

The apostles were required to wait at Jerusalem for the promise of the Father, the baptism of the Holy Ghost, so that they could have the power to be witnesses to the world of Jesus' death, burial and resurrection. On the day of Pentecost, cloven tongues like fire cleansed them and the Holy Ghost entered their hearts.

Paul, before he began his ministerial work in the service of the King of kings, was overshadowed by a light from heaven that left him blind. It was in that state of blindness that Paul recognized it was Jesus whom he persecuted. The Light of the world had cleansed him from his sin and he immediately acknowledged that Jesus was his Lord. God chose Paul to bear his banner before the Gentiles, kings, and the people of Israel. Ananias, one of Jesus' disciples, laid his hands on him and the scales that had blinded him physically and spiritually were removed from his eyes. He received his physical and spiritual sight and the gift of the Holy Ghost and became a premier minister of the gospel of Christ.

We too must be holy if God is to use us in his service to bear fruits worthy of repentance. No matter what position or situation God has called us from or to serve in, we must be holy. Everyone who is called by the name of Christ must be holy. God demands it, and we must accept it without wavering.

God's Standard Is Holiness

As recorded in 1 Thessalonians 4, we must live in accordance with God's will, and it is God's will that we be sanctified and avoid sexual immorality. We must exhibit control over our bodies in a way that is holy and respectable. It is God's command that we be holy. If we are to be holy, it is important then, that our body of sins be crucified with Christ on the cross and our living become the life as characterized by the image and likeness of Christ.

First Thessalonians also suggests that both body and soul should be cleansed and made holy. God has not called us to uncleanness but to live holy and honorable lives. Paul wrote: "Having therefore these promises, dearly beloved, let us cleanse ourselves from all filthiness of the flesh and spirit, perfecting holiness in the fear of God" (2 Cor 7:1). Paul is teaching us how to live righteous lives. He tells us that our lives will be perfected if we completely cleanse ourselves from all the filthiness of the flesh and mind by plunging into God's rich cleansing blood stream that flows from the cross of Calvary. He further states:

> Husbands love your wives, even as Christ also loved the Church and gave himself for it; That he might sanctify and cleanse it with the washing of water by the word, That he might present it to himself a glorious Church, not having spot, or wrinkle, or any such thing, but that it should be holy and without blemish. (Eph 5:25–27)

Paul teaches that we must present our bodies as a living, holy sacrifice, that will be acceptable to God. We should glorify God in our bodies and in our Spirits because they belong to him.

BODY, SOUL, AND SPIRIT MUST BE SANCTIFIED

The Apostle Paul wrote:

> And the very God of peace sanctify you wholly; and I pray that your whole spirit and soul and body be preserved blameless unto the coming of our Lord Jesus Christ. Faithful is he who calleth you, who also will do it. (1 Thess 5:23–24)

Sanctification of the body, soul and spirit is the total surrender of all our appetites and propensities to the entire control of God. Some of these appetites and propensities originate in the body, and some have their origin in the mind, but all must be brought under God's control.

When a person is saved and sanctified, he exhibits faith, hope and love. At the early stage in our Christian walk with the Lord, we are but babes in him and needs must breast feed on the sincere milk of the word before going on to the weightier matters of the word. In other words, Christianity is like a seed which is planted in the ground, which germinates and brings out the vine, then the blossoms, and then the full fruit. That is to say, a Christian is expected to grow spiritually just as a baby is expected to grow physically.

We are saved from our sins but because of our sinful nature, may have sinful desires. God requires holiness and Paul prays that the Author of our peace, our God of the universe, would sanctify us to the fullest extent of the perfection of our nature, and that our entire spirit, soul and body, be preserved without sin, until our Lord returns. To put it differently; God needs to completely purify us from all filthiness of the flesh and spirit perfecting holiness in the fear of the Lord, so that we can become his peculiar people, zealous of good works. God will reconstruct us in his own image, so that we can be presented as a glorious church without spots or wrinkles, or any such things, but washed in the blood of the Lamb of God.

Complete sanctification brings peace from the God of peace, presenting our whole spirit, soul and body as blameless and to be preserved by his faithfulness, who also will bring it to past. Entire sanctification cast out the fear of yielding to temptation and the fear of affliction and persecution. Paul is teaching that our entire life and personality and being must be completely sanctified.

OUR SPIRIT MUST BE SANCTIFIED

The Apostle Peter writes:

> Elect according to the foreknowledge of God the Father, through sanctification of the Spirit, unto obedience and sprinkling of the blood of Jesus Christ: Grace unto you, and peace, be multiplied. Blessed be the God and Father of our Lord Jesus Christ, which according to his abundant mercy hath begotten us again unto a lively hope by the resurrection of Jesus Christ from the dead, To an inheritance incorruptible, and undefiled, and that fadeth not away, reserved in heaven for you, Who are kept by the power of God through faith unto salvation ready to be revealed in the last time. (1 Pet 1:2–5)

The Lord Jesus Christ has saved us, not by the righteous deeds we had done, but according to his abundant mercy, through the washing of new birth and renewal by the Holy Spirit. He chose us from the beginning to be saved by sanctifying our spirits through his death on the cross, by faith in the truth. He has called us to a living hope of forever being with him in glory, and because of our obedience to him, we will be rewarded with an incorruptible and undefiled inheritance in heaven.

The Deeds of the Flesh Must Be Destroyed

We were once slaves to the flesh and if we continue in bondage to the flesh, we will die, but if we want to live, we must ensure the death of the deeds of the flesh. The spirit and the flesh are diametrically opposed to each other. The flesh craves what is contrary to the Spirit and the Spirit desires what is contrary to the flesh. The Christian's pathway must be in accordance with the Spirit of God, and not in accordance with the desires of the flesh, such as sexual immorality, impurity, sensuality, idolatry, sorcery, enmity, strife, jealousy, anger, rivalries, dissensions, divisions, envy, drunkenness, and orgies. If we sow to the flesh, we will from the flesh reap corruption, but if we sow to the Spirit, we will from the Spirit inherit eternal life; and an inheritance that is incorruptible, undefiled, does not fade away and that is reserved in heaven for us. As God declared in Ezekiel: "I will give you a new heart and put a new spirit in you" (Ezek 36:26 NIV).

The Bible teaches that those who live according to the flesh have their minds set on what the flesh desires; but those who live in accordance with the Spirit have their minds set on what the Spirit desires, which is life and peace. The mind governed by the flesh is hostile to God; it does not submit to God's law, nor can it do so. The sinful mind is hostile to God. It does not submit to God's law, nor can it do so. Those controlled by the sinful nature cannot please God. You, however, are controlled not by the sinful nature but by the Spirit, if the Spirit of God lives in you. And if anyone does not have the Spirit of Christ; he does not belong to Christ (Rom 8:5–9 NIV). The mind of the unsaved person is evil, degenerate and desperately wicked and will incur the wrath of God. Christians should have minds similar to the mind of Christ; minds that are in total submission to God. Our thoughts, plans, professions, and programs must conform to God's will. We must renew our minds daily in exhibition of the mind of Christ. We must not conform to the evil that is in the world but must be transformed by the renewing of our minds so that we can accomplish the perfect will of God; by doing what is right in his sight; separating ourselves for his service with pure minds; and doing the good deeds which God appreciates. Our concentration should be on what is excellent and praiseworthy.

We Must Be in Control of Our Spirit

The Bible also teaches that we must control our spirit because: "He that hath no rule over his own spirit is like a city that is broken down, and without walls" (Prov 25:28). We must control our anger, our emotions, our attitudes, and our desire to eat and to drink. Self-control strengthens our inner being. It builds a wall of defense and secures us against the wiles of the devil. When we rage out of control, we can cause immeasurable damage to relationships, marriages, homes, and reputations. We can lose employment, business, and friends, and we can commit murder when we lack control in our lives. The person who exhibits self-control is a person of sound character and wisdom. He controls his appetites and passions and does not permit rebellion against reason, conscience, thoughts, desires, inclinations, and resentments.

OUR BODIES MUST BE SANCTIFIED

The Apostle Paul wrote to the Romans:

> Therefore do not let sin reign in your mortal body so that you obey its evil desires. Do not offer any pars of yourself to sin, as an instrument of wickedness, but rather offer yourselves to God, as those who have been brought from death to life; and offer every part of yourself to him as an instrument of righteousness. For sin shall not be your master, because you are not under law, but under grace. (Rom 6:12–14 NIV)

There is no excuse for misuse or abuse of our bodies. Christ died on the cross that our bodies may be kept holy and kept preserved until he returns. Our bodies are not our own and we have no right to give them over to sin or dishonor them with fleshy activities. The body belongs to the Lord and is to be used as instruments of his righteousness. We must not allow sin to control our mortal body. Our bodies must be controlled by the Holy Spirit.

God requires that we present our bodies as a living sacrifice, holy, pleasing to him, because this is a true and proper way to worship him. This is God's will for our lives. Paul admonishes us to abstain from evil and prays that our God of peace will sanctify us completely, and that our entire spirit, soul and body be preserved in a holy state until our Lord returns.

We should strive to be free from all those illnesses of whatever kind that are a direct result of abuse or misuse of our bodies We should abstain from illegal drugs, alcohol addiction or gluttony, because these destroy the body. We should ensure that we get the right amount of exercise, eat the right food, and drink clean water in the right amounts, because this will assist in keeping our bodies healthy and prolonging our lives. Physical and medical checkups at appropriate times will bring to light any unusual or deleterious activities occurring in our bodies so that, if necessary, treatment may be prescribed at an early stage. We should use our bodies for holy purposes that bring honor and glory to the God of our salvation.

God owns our bodies and we have sometimes used his property as it suited us, but instead of destroying us, he repurchased our bodies through his death on the cross and we ought to honor and glorify him by taking good care of his temple. God himself, completely sanctifies our whole spirit, soul and body and he will preserve us without blame until he returns, but we must remain faithful to him.

Our Bodies Are Members of Christ

The church is the body of Christ and we are not only members of the church, we are also members of Christ. When we commit sins against our own bodies, we disgrace ourselves, we disgrace the church and we disgrace Christ. St. Paul in his epistle to the Corinthians put it in this manner:

> Know ye not that your bodies are the members of Christ? Shall I then take the members of Christ, and make them members of a harlot? God forbid. What? Know ye not that he which is joined to a harlot is one body? For two, saith he, shall be one flesh. But he that is joined unto the Lord is one spirit. Flee fornication. Every sin that a man doeth is without the body; but he that

> committeth fornication sinneth against his own body. What? Know ye not that your body is the temple of the Holy Ghost which is in you, which ye have in God, and ye are not your own? For ye are bought with a price: therefore, glorify God in your body, and in your spirit, which are God's. (1 Cor 6:15-20)

Some of us, yes, Christians, do not consider promiscuous sexual relationships with the seriousness it deserves, but we must bear in mind that when we come together as sexual partners, we become one flesh (Gen 2:24). Our relationship with Christ is spiritual, but it involves the physical body and can be destroyed by physical sins. Of course, fornication is very common and is tolerated and accepted in our society and unfortunately, in some congregations.

Illicit sexual activity sells newspapers, products, movies, and so on. Paul says that we are to flee from it. We are not to talk about it. We can be trapped by it. We can become addicted to it. We can contract all types of sexual diseases from it. We can die (physically, spiritually, eternally) because of it. Sexual immorality contributes to the decay in our society. Homes are broken because of it. There are many unwanted pregnancies because of it. Marital separation and divorce result from it. Hatred, envy and murder result from it and of course it weakens the church. We are to flee from it. It is simply vanity and vexation of the spirit. Paul says that there must not even be a hint of it or any kind of impurity simply because these are improper for God's holy people (Eph 5:3).

OUR SOULS MUST BE SANCTIFIED

The soul is a combination of the mind, will and emotions. Our feelings and our power to make decisions are in our souls. Our mind, our ability to think, is in our soul. The soul is the most important part of our life because the battle in life is for our souls. There is warfare for the souls of our children, our families and the nation as a whole. The devil battles with God for our souls. "I speak after the manner of men because of the infirmity of your flesh: for as you have yielded your members servants to uncleanness and to iniquity unto iniquity, even so now yield your members servants to righteousness unto holiness" (Rom 6:19).

Let us again return for a moment to the story of creation. Remember Satan craftily deceived Adam to disobey God and eat from the tree of knowledge of good and evil (Gen 3:1-7), and that sinful act of disobedience ruined our nature as exemplified in our spirit, soul and body, and alienated us from God, making us his enemies. Remember that "the Lord God formed man of the dust of the ground, and breathed into his nostrils the breath of life; and man became a living soul" (Gen 2:7). God breathed into us our mind, emotions and will, giving us the authority to manage our lives as we determine right. Sin corrupted our souls and God needed to bring us back into line with the nature of his holiness. God wants to transform us by renewing our minds, so that we may prove what is good and acceptable, and perfect will of God (Rom 12:2). God wants our souls purified and consecrated to him alone.

There is nothing in the universe more powerful than the human will. It is man's most precious gift from God, and it controls our destiny. The will decides how man will perform God's work on earth, but it can act against God. The will lives in our subconscious mind, which is the heart. The more something is repeated, the more permanent what is heard take residence in our hearts, and when ungodly information takes up residence, it leaves us in trouble because the heart is the center of thought and it holds the key to life, so that whatever or whoever controls what is in our heart will also control our life. A person is as he thinks in his heart. We are whatever is in our heart, and that is why we have to keep our distance from what is ungodly and sinful. The Bible teaches that the heart is deceitful above all things and desperately wicked. We speak from the heart and it is from within, out of our hearts that there are evil thoughts, sexual immorality, theft, murder, adultery, greed, malice, deceit, lewdness, envy, slander, arrogance and folly. Once information takes up residence in our hearts, even when we are not conscious of it, it continues to work, and if the wrong message is sent, what is in our heart is activated and can either make us great or can totally and completely destroy us.

It is the heart that determines our future and our destiny. We become what we see and hear and sometimes we become plagued with habits we are desperately trying to annihilate. We should read, mark and inwardly digest the word of God found in the Bible and we should allow our hearts to be guided and directed by God's word so as to cultivate the right habits that will bring us personal benefits and blessings for others. The heart has emotions and passions. It decides what is morally right or wrong. It is from our hearts that we love or hate; we are sorrowful or happy; we are sane or insane; we do evil or good. It is from the heart that a decision is made to serve God or worship the devil. The intent of man's heart was evil from his youth.

Our Souls Are Purified through Obedience

The Apostle Peter wrote: "Seeing you have purified your souls in obeying the truth through the Spirit unto unfeigned love of the brethren, see that ye love one another with a pure heart fervently" (1 Pet 1:22).

God demands our obedience to the gospel of truth through the Spirit unto unfeigned love of the brethren. Jesus is the way, the truth and the life. He is that Word that became flesh and lived among us and was full of truth and glory. He is the Spirit of truth that will guide us into all truth and show us things to come. He is the comforter, who has come from the Father and testify of his Son, Jesus. It is with the purified soul that we have the capability to love sincerely and unequivocally.

We Must Love Fellow Christians Fervently

Peter reminds us that an important ingredient of sanctification of the soul is sincere love for each other. He further teaches that we should love as brothers, be tender-hearted, humble and must love the brotherhood of believers, fear God and honor the king, because love covers a multitude of sins. Christ gave us a new commandment that we love each other as much as he loves us, and this love is our Christian identity. How much does Jesus love us? With his life. Paul teaches us that our love must be without dissimulation; we must be devoted to each other in continued brotherly love, and we should outdo ourselves in honoring each other.

We Must Love Our Enemies

Christ taught us:

> But I say unto you which hear, Love your enemies, do good to them which hate you, Bless them that curse you, and pray for them which despitefully use you. And unto him that smiteth thee on the one cheek, offer also the other; and him that taketh away thy cloak forbid not to take thy coat also. Give to every man that asketh of thee; and of him that taketh away thy goods, ask them not again. And as ye would that men should do unto you, do ye also to them likewise. For if ye love them which love you, what thank have ye? For sinners also love those that love them. And if ye do good to them which do good to you, what thank have ye? For sinners also do even the same. And if you lend to them of whom ye hope to receive, what thank have ye?

> For sinners also lend to sinners, to receive as much again. But love your enemies, and do good, and lend, hoping for nothing again, and your reward shall be great, and ye shall be the children of the Highest: for he is kind unto the unthankful and the evil. Be ye therefore merciful, as your Father also is merciful. (Luke 6:27–35)

Paul's message is just as clear:

> If thine enemy hunger, feed him: if he thirst, give him drink: for in so doing thou shall heap coals of fire on his head. Be not overcome of evil, but overcome evil with good. (Rom 12:20–21)

God Predestinated Us to Be Holy

Paul wrote in his Letter to the Ephesians:

> According as he has chosen us in him before the foundation of the world, that we should be holy and without blame before him in love: Having predestinated us unto the adoption of children by Jesus Christ to himself, according to the good pleasure of his will. (Eph 1:4–5)

There is no escape. We must be holy. Holiness is God's predestination plan for us. To be holy means that our past sins are covered by the blood of Christ and permanently removed from our records. We are just as if we had never sinned and we are separated for God's specific purpose and use. God chose those people who would accept his plan of redemption through Jesus Christ, even before the world existed. He predestined us to be holy, without blame, set apart and committed to his righteousness. He predestined us to be his adopted children in accordance with his good pleasure and his will. He restores us, redeeming our sins with the price of his spilled blood, ordained us, and gave us the will to do good deeds and not evil deeds. Let us follow God's command. Let us comply with his will. Let us be holy, even as he is holy.

Chapter 7

Christian Perfection

Christian perfection maybe defined as the process of living a life of purity and completeness in Christ our Lord. It means accepting and living a spotless and unblemished life in accordance the attributes, characteristics and likeness of Christ. Simply put, it is the restoration of the Christian to the same state of holiness and uprightness as Adam was before he disobeyed God's command not to eat of the fruit from the tree of knowledge of good and evil. This is achieved through the process of entire sanctification of body, spirit and soul by the blood of our Lord and Savior, Jesus Christ. The Bible teaches us that we must become more and more perfect every day, by refusing to return to our own evil vomit of sin, for which we will need to return to God in repentance for his forgiveness and mercy: "Therefore leaving the principles of the doctrine of Christ, let us go on to perfection; not laying again the foundation of repentance from dead works and faith toward God" (Heb 6:1). Paul exhorts us to move on to perfection and not to sin again and return to the same position of separation from God that we were in before experiencing the saving grace and keeping power of Jesus. This same Apostle Paul instructs us, that despite various afflictions and sufferings, we must not be ashamed, because we know in whom we believe, and in whom we have confidence and conviction, that Christ has the power to keep us from sin for himself, until he returns to rapture his church and for all eternity.

Christian perfection also refers to God's keeping grace; God's power to keep us from the evil one and from falling prey to his temptations and tricks. St. Paul put it this way:

> Whereunto I am appointed a preacher, and an apostle, and a teacher of the Gentiles. For the which cause I also suffer these things: nevertheless, I am not ashamed: for I know whom I have believed and am persuaded that he is able to keep that which I have committed unto him against that day. (2 Tim 1:11–12)

The Apostle Jude wrote this liturgical formula of praise and glorification to God (doxology):

> Now unto him that is able to keep you from falling, and to present you faultless before the presence of his glory with exceeding joy, To the only wise God our Savior, be glory and majesty, dominion and power, both now and forever. Amen. (Jude 24–25)

In Jude's day, they were immoral citizens and false teachers; godless teachers operating among the people, who perverted God's grace. They were teaching believers that being saved by grace gave them a license to sin, without fear of God's punishment. Jude unequivocally proclaims that God has the power to keep Christians from sinning; from returning to the depravity of feeding on the husks that pigs refused to eat. In other words, Christians, by the power of the Holy Ghost, can live free from sin and can be triumphant over the craftiness of Satan. Glory be to God.

The Master teaches that we must be perfect. One day a very rich young man went to Jesus and inquired of him what he needed to do to inherit eternal life. He had kept all the commandments from his youth, but recognized that something was missing from his spiritual life. He was not a murderer; he was not an adulterer; he was not a thief and he was not a false witness. He honored his parents and loved his neighbors as much as he loved himself, but he perceived that he was not in the right spiritual position to enter God's kingdom. His life failed the test of Christian perfection that would allow him to be identified as an adopted child of God and joint heir with Christ in his coming kingdom:

> Jesus said unto him, if thou wilt be perfect, go and sell that thou hast, and give to the poor, and thou shalt have treasure in heaven: and come and follow me. (Matt 19:21)

Let us look at ourselves in the mirror. Is there anything that we have to give up in order to benefit from the treasures of heaven? What is it that we are holding on to that we must give up in order to be perfect Christians?

This rich young man had to give up the sin of selfishness. Jesus required that he give special attention to the poor and needy. Let us lay it all on the altar; every weight and the sin that so easily beset us, in complete surrender to our Lord and Savior, Jesus Christ, and let us run with patience the race that is set before us.

The passionate prayer of Jesus is recorded in the Gospel of St. John chapter 17:

> And for their sakes I sanctify myself, that they also might be sanctified through the truth. Neither pray I for these alone, but for them also which believe on me through their word; That they all may be one: as thou, Father, art in me, and I in thee, that they may also be one in us, that the world may believe that thou hast sent me. And the glory which thou gavest me I have given them; that they may be one, even as we are one: I in them, and thou in me, that they may be made perfect in one; and that the world may know that thou hast sent me, and hast loved them as thou hast loved me. (John 17:19–23)

Christ is teaching that if we are to live perfect Christian lives, we must be sanctified by the truth. We must become one in the truth, one in the Holy Spirit, and one in the Father. If we abide in him, and he in us, we lose our ability to commit sin because we have become part of his divine nature. We must not allow sin to creep into our hearts after receiving the knowledge of truth. The burden is on us to ensure we are in oneness with Christ and the Father. He sanctified himself that he may sanctify us; make us pure and holy, and set us apart for service and worship in his kingdom.

This teaching is corroborated:

> Whosoever abideth in him sinneth not: whosoever sinneth hath not seen him, neither known him. Little children, let no man deceive you: he that doeth righteousness is righteous, even as he is righteous. He that committeth sin is of the devil; for the devil sinneth from the beginning. For this purpose the Son of man was manifested, that he might destroy the works of the devil. Whosoever is born of God doth not commit sin; for his seed remaineth in him and he cannot sin because he is born of God. In this the children of God are manifest, and the children of the devil: whosoever doeth not righteousness is not of God, neither he that loveth not his brother. (John 3:6–10)

Paul gave this exhortation: "Awake to righteousness and sin not; for some have not the knowledge of God: I speak this to your shame" (1 Cor 15:34).

If we are to be righteous, we must be properly aligned with God's authority. This includes but is not limited to an active response to the poor by sharing with them. Ezekiel declares that part of the responsibility of the righteous is to take good care of the poor and needy: "[He] gives his food to the hungry and provides clothing for the naked" (Ezek 18:7). In the gospel of St. Matthew chapter 25 we hear from the Master detailing the significance of sharing with the needy:

> When the Son of Man comes in his glory, and all the angels with him, he will sit on his glorious throne. All the nations will be gathered before him, and he will separate the people one from another as a shepherd separates the sheep from the goats. He will put the sheep on his right and the goats on his left. Then the King will say to those on his right, "Come, you who are blessed by my Father; take your inheritance, the kingdom prepared for you since the creation of the world. For I was hungry and you gave me something to eat, I was thirsty and you gave me something to drink, I was a stranger and you invited me in, I needed clothes and you clothed me, I was sick and you looked after me, I was in prison and you came to visit me." Then the righteous will answer him, "Lord, when did we see you hungry and feed you, or thirsty and give you something to drink? When did we see you a stranger and invite you in, or needing clothes and clothe you? When did we see you sick or in prison and go to visit you." The King will reply, "Truly I tell you, whatever you did for one of the least of these brothers and sisters of mine, you did for me." Then he will say to those on his left, "Depart from me, you who are cursed, into the eternal fire prepared for the devil and his angels. For I was hungry and you gave me nothing to eat, I was thirsty and you gave me nothing to drink, I was a stranger and you did not invite me in, I needed clothes and you did not clothe me, I was sick and in prison and you did not look after me." They also will answer, "Lord, when did we see you hungry or thirsty or a stranger or needing clothes or sick or in prison, and did not help you?" He will reply, "Truly I tell you, whatever you did not do for one of the least of these, you did not do for me." Then they will go away to eternal punishment, but the righteous to eternal life. (Matt 25:31–46 NIV)

Let us reexamine our lives. Are we doing anything positive to help the poor, the downtrodden, the outcast, the sick, the incarcerated and all those who generally need help? What type of assistance are we giving them? Is it the best that we can do? The early church was successful because believers were united as one and "had everything in common." They sold their properties and goods and made distributions based on individual needs.

Zacchaeus, the chief tax collector, whom the people detested, came into a right relationship with Christ and made the decision to give half of his property to the poor, and return four times the amount of property he had stolen from any person. Jesus saved him and his entire household.

Cornelius was a centurion in the Italian Regiment, and his prayers and generosity to the poor was recognized by God as a memorial offering. As a result, Cornelius, his entire house, and his friends were saved and received the gift of promise, the Holy Ghost.

Lady Tabitha Dorcas was a saint who did good deeds and was generous toward the poor. She became ill and died. The disciples sent for Peter and by the power of the resurrected Jesus, Dorcas was raised from the dead, and the result was that many people believed the gospel.

GOD FORGETS OUR SINS

I have already explained that all the human race is guilty before God of committing the rebellious act of sin against him. If we say that we have not sinned, we make God a liar, and his word is not in us. His truth is not in us. God will blot out our transgressions for his own sake and will not remember them (Isa 43:25; Heb 8:12; Heb 10:14-18; Ps 103:12). The Christian becomes a new creation. The new birth (being born again) is a birth without sin, a birth through the Holy Spirit, by the blood of Christ. That is to say, the new birth brings justification by our faith in the saving grace and keeping power of our Lord and Savior. Christ forgives us completely for all our past sins and demolishes them in his wilderness of forgetfulness. We are sanctified to sin no more and must keep it that way:

> For by one offering he hath perfected forever them that are sanctified. Whereof the Holy Ghost also is a witness to us: for after that he had said before, This is the covenant that I will make with them after those days, saith the Lord, I will put my laws into their hearts, and in their minds will I write them; And their sins and iniquities will I remember no more. Now where remission of sin is there is, no more offering for sin. (Heb 10:14-18)

Paul went a little further:

> Now the God of peace, that brought again from the dead our Lord Jesus, that great shepherd of the sheep, through the blood of the everlasting covenant, Make you perfect in every good

work to do his will, working in you that which is well pleasing in his sight, through Jesus Christ; to whom be glory for ever and ever. Amen. (Heb 13:20–21)

Peter tells us that God has called us by his own glory and goodness and by his divine power gave us all that we need for godly living through a personal relationship with him, so that we may be part of his divine nature that ensures we escape the corruption of sinful desires.

We Are Sealed by the Holy Spirit

When we surrender to Christ as Lord and Savior of our lives, the Holy Spirit of promise seals us until the day of redemption to preserve our faith in in him, confirm that we are his adopted children and joint heirs with Christ, and offers us protection from the evil one (from sin). The Holy Spirit seals us to separate and distinguish us from the children of the world. The Holy Spirit produces fruits in our lives such as love, joy, peace, long suffering, gentleness, goodness, faith, meekness and temperance. These fruits are evidence of the Spirit's supreme control in our hearts and lives. It is the Holy Spirit that seals us until the day of redemption, complete and free from the corruption of sin and hell.

There are three specific Scripture references that I will use which justify this unequivocal Christian fact. The first is:

> And you also were included in Christ when you heard the word of truth, the gospel of your salvation. When you believed, you were marked in him with a seal, the promised Holy Spirit, who is a deposit guaranteeing our inheritance until the redemption of those who are God's possession—to the praise of his glory. (Eph 1:13–14 NIV)

Note that we (God's possessions) are marked in him through adoption by the Holy Spirit (sealed by the Holy Spirit) as our protection from sin and a down payment guaranteeing our eternal inheritance in heaven until he returns. We become the children of God through adoption and are preserved in him until our Lord returns.

Paul writes:

> For it is impossible for those who were once enlightened, and have tasted of the heavenly gift, and were made partakers of the Holy Ghost, And have tasted the good word of God, and the powers of the world to come, if they shall fall away, to renew

them again unto repentance; seeing they crucify to themselves the Son of God afresh, and put him to an open shame. (Heb 6:4)

When Christians sin, they are crucifying God afresh. They drive fresh nails in his hands and feet and put him to open shame, the shame of his crucifixion. To avoid this repeated crucifixion of Christ, Christians must not sin.

The second Scripture that will be used is Eph 4:30: "And do not grieve the Holy Spirit of God, with whom you were sealed for the day of redemption" (NIV). Paul is here recognizing that Christians have the propensity to commit sin and sin will grieve the Holy Spirit out of our lives. Sin will break the seal of redemption. The Holy Spirit is perfectly holy, and sin is an offense to him. The result of sin is that we will again lay the foundation for repentance from dead works and faith toward God. The Lord Jesus Christ is the true vine, while God our Father is the gardener:

> He cuts off every branch in me that bears no fruit, while every branch that bears fruit, he prunes so that it will be more fruitful. You are already clean because of the word that I have spoken to you. Remain in me, and I will remain in you. No branch can bear fruit of itself; it must remain in the vine. Neither can you bear fruit unless you remain in me. I am the vine; you are the branches. If you remain in me and I in you, you will bear much fruit; apart from me you can do nothing. If you do not remain in me, you are like a branch that is thrown away and withers; such branches are picked up, thrown into the fire and burned. (John 15:2–6 NIV)

If Christians remain faithful to their calling in Christ, if they remain attached to the true vine, with our heavenly Father as the husbandman, they will endure to the day of redemption. However, Jesus is pointing out that if Christians become detached from him (because of sinful acts); they become like a literal branch from a tree that becomes dry and is perfect wood for the fire. The key to remaining sealed is to remain in him (do not sin) by allowing his Holy Spirit to have complete authority in our hearts.

Paul warned the foolish Galatians against perfecting in the flesh, what was begun in the Spirit. He supported Jesus' teaching from St. John's Gospel. He wrote to the Romans:

> Granted. But they were broken off because of unbelief, and you stand by faith. Do not be arrogant, but tremble. For if God did not spare the natural branches, he will not spare you either. Consider therefore the kindness and sternness of God: sternness to those who fell, but kindness to you, provided that you

continue in his kindness. Otherwise, you also will be cut off.
And if they do not persist in unbelief, they will be granted in, for
God is able to graft them in again. (Rom 11:20–23 NIV)

Paul gives the reasons why branches are cut off (unsealed). They are cut off because of unbelief. Unbelief is a lack of faith in God's authority. It is the wrong and evil attitudes lodged in the deep recesses of our hearts that cause all kinds of wicked outcomes (sin), and that will destroy our relationship with him. Jesus taught:

> For from within, out of a person's heart, that evil thoughts come—sexual immorality, theft, murder, adultery, greed, malice, deceit, lewdness, envy, slander, arrogance and folly. All these evils come from inside and make a man unclean. (Mark 7:21–23 NIV)

When Moses led God's chosen people, the Israelites, through the wilderness, their principle failure to enter the promised land was the wrong attitudes in their hearts toward God:

> Harden not your hearts, as in the provocation, in the days of temptations in the wilderness: When your fathers tempted me, proved me, and saw my works forty years. Wherefore I was grieved with that generation, and said, They do always err in their heart; and they have not known my ways. So I sware in my wrath, they shall not enter into my rest.) Take heed, brethren, lest there be in any of you an evil heart of unbelief, in departing from the living God. (Heb 3:8–12)

The Israelites did not trust God and disobeyed him. They committed other sins because of wrong attitudes and unbelief. They wanted to please themselves and rejected God's authority over their lives. Their sin of unbelief kept them in the wilderness for forty years.

In the story of the parable of the sower, Jesus reminds us that sometimes his word falls on rocky ground, and although we believe and accept the word with joy, they have no firm root and commit sin in times of temptation. It is our lack of faith (our refusal to trust in God's word), that make it impossible to please God; whatsoever is not of faith is sin; sin separates us from God and unless we repent, we will reap the wages of sin, which is eternal death. Whosoever believes in him is not condemned to eternal death but whoever does not believe stands condemned already because he has not believed in the only begotten Son of God. The Bible teaches that the unbelieving shall have their part in the lake which burns with brimstone and fire, which is the second death (Rev 21:8). However, he that believes in the only begotten Son of God shall be saved (Mark 16:16).

Paul again warns us to be careful that we do not give up our faith in the true and living God because of an evil heart of unbelief (refusal to trust and obey God). Unbelief will destroy our relationship with Christ. Our lack of faith causes us to think things that are not true, and it is very easy to think things that are not true. We exhibit wrong attitudes and refuse to change; we harden our hearts against God. We should be comforted by the words of the Apostle Paul: "For God is able to graft them in again." In other words, if sin causes us to become detached from Christ, God will graft us back into the True Vine to a right relationship with him.

My third reference to being sealed by God is:

> Now it is God who makes both us and you stand firm in Christ. He anointed us, set his seal of ownership on us, and put his Spirit in our hearts as a deposit, guaranteeing what is to come. (2 Cor 1:21–22 NIV)

Who created us? The person who created us owns us. The Holy Spirit owns us and protects us against the craftiness of the devil, providing an escape route from sin and eternal death. The seal is a deposit which guarantees eternal life and the hope of being forever with the Lord. The Holy Spirit is given to Christians as confirmation that we belong to God and he belongs to us. The Holy Spirit adopts us as heirs and joint heirs with Christ and presents us with our title deposit guaranteeing eternal life. Sometimes ownership changes hands. We need to hold on to our new birthright. Anytime a Christian sins against God, he breaks the title covenant of ownership, the Holy Spirit leaves him, and he dies spiritually. Sin separates him from God. The light of God goes out in his heart and is replaced by the devil's darkness. Light and darkness are perfect opposites that cannot coexist. One gives way to the other. If we are to remain sealed, we must be careful not to disobey God. Remember that we can resist the Holy Spirit. Stephen accused the Jews of being stiff-necked and uncircumcised in heart and ears and of always resisting the Holy Ghost, as their fathers did (Acts 7:51). We must keep God in the driver's seat. He is the one who will steer our faithfulness in him and cause us to stand on his principles of holiness and steadfastness.

We are sealed (preserved) without sin when we become a new creation in Christ. We are born sinners. However, the new birth is a new life of righteousness, without sin. The Holy Spirit cannot seal sin within himself or us, and if sin remain in us, that means we were not sealed. We cannot be sealed in our old sinful nature. We cannot be preserved in our sins. God will keep all that we have committed to him until he calls us home or raptures us. The Bible teaches us that

> those who are in the realm of the flesh cannot please God. You, however, are not in the realm of the flesh but are in the realm of the Spirit, if indeed the Spirit of God lives in you. And if anyone does not have the Spirit of Christ, they do not belong to Christ. (Rom 8:8–9 NIV)

When we are sealed, we are free from the corruption of sin and hell. Sin corrupts our relationship with Christ. Sin displeases God and separates us from him. We thus give up the title deeds of his righteousness and lose our down payment to our eternal inheritance with him. When we abide in him, we do not sin, and we sin because we do not know him. He is faithful, just and merciful, and will forgive our sins, cleanse us from all unrighteousness and remember our sins no more.

The Holy Spirit seals us without sin and makes us his divine possessions so that we are owned by him forever. Paul's advice to Timothy is this: "Nevertheless the foundation of God standeth sure, having this seal, the Lord knoweth them that are his. And, let everyone that nameth the name of Christ, depart from iniquity" (2 Tim 2:19). A life without sin is a life of honor, sanctified, meet for the Master's use and completely prepared for every good work. Amen.

We Are Secured in the Arms of Jesus

The Bible teaches us:

> My sheep hear my voice, and I know them, and they follow me: And I give unto them eternal life; and they shall never perish, neither shall any man pluck them out of my hand. My Father, which gave them me, is greater than all; and no man is able to pluck them out of my Father's hand. (John 10:27–29)

In John 17, Jesus' prayer of intercession to our Father in heaven was that God should keep through his own name all that he had given to him. While Christ was on earth with those whom the Father had given to him, he kept them in his Father's name, and none of them were lost, except for the son of perdition, that the Scripture might be fulfilled. And there will be many sons of perdition in this present world. That is to say, there will be many who will participate in the work of the church and do good deeds, but unfortunately, the hearts of these unbelievers will not be cleansed from sin and they would not be protected by God's banner of love and security.

God has given us eternal life, which is an imperishable and incorruptible sinless life. We cannot sin if God is holding us in his hands. If we sin, we are not in his hands, because sin separates us from God and God will not hold sin in his hands. He has nailed them to the cross and remembers them no more. He holds us in the hull of his hand so that no one can take away our salvation. Our salvation is safe and secured when we are in his arms. Jesus reminds us that he is the shepherd of the sheep and has control over them. He has such a firm grip on them that no one can pluck them from his hands nor his Father's hands. The Apostle Paul was persuaded that neither death nor life, nor angels, nor principalities, nor powers, nor things present, nor things to come, nor height, nor depth, nor any other creature shall be able to separate Christians from God's love.

God chose us in himself. He has predestined us in accordance with his plan and has worked out all things in conformity with the purpose of his will. The good news for Christians is that God the Father has given us to God the Son, and Christ will never drive us away. It is God's will that all of us remain in the safe protection and ownership of Christ until he raises us up on the last day. Our basic task is to look to him in faith and believe in him and we will never perish but will have eternal life. We can also be comforted because no one can snatch us from the Father's hand. We are saved to the uttermost; to sin no more. We must not allow sin to reign in our mortal bodies nor should we allow our members to be used as instruments of unrighteousness, nor should we permit sin to dominate us. We cannot be sinners and saints at the same time. We have been exonerated from the pangs of sin and eternal death. We serve in the service of the King and must bear fruits of holiness that will lead others to repentance and be a source of encouragement for those who already know Christ. God saves us completely, but we must come to God through Christ who lives to intercede for us.

THE FATHER'S WILL

> All that the Father giveth me shall come to me; and him that cometh to me I will in no wise cast out. For I came down from heaven, not to do mine own will, but the will of him that send me. And this is the Father's will which hath sent me, that of all which he hath given me I should lose nothing, but should raise it up again at the last day. (John 6:37-39)

No person can go to Jesus unless he is drawn to him by the Father. When we go to Jesus and accept him as our Lord and Savior, he will not turn us away.

Our Lord has returned to heaven to prepare a place for us so that he will come again and receive us to himself and we can be forever with him. When God calls us, he cleans us up and makes us worthy of his calling:

> Then I will sprinkle clean water upon you, and ye shall be clean: from all your filthiness, and from all your idols, will I cleanse you. A new heart also will I give you, and a new spirit will I put within you: and I will take away the stony heart out of your flesh, and I will give you an heart of flesh. And I will put my Spirit within you, and cause you to walk in my statutes, and ye shall keep my judgements, and do them. (Ezek 36:25–27)

The Holy Spirit teaches us and we learn from him. All whom God gives to Christ will be preserved from sin and eternal death. It is the Father's will that all of us whom he gave to Christ will remain with him and he will raise them up in glory and power at the last day. It is the Father's will that everyone who looks to the Son and believes in him will have eternal life. However, if we sin, unless we repent, and restore our broken relationship with him, we will face the consequences of eternal death.

Our Lord made an earnest prayer for all whom the Father gave him. All that the Father give him belong to him and he is glorified in them. God does not glory when sin is in our hearts. He prayed that our Holy Father would keep all Christians from evil, through his own name, and that they be sanctified through the truth; his Word is truth. While Jesus was with them in the world, he kept all that the Father gave him in the Father's name and none of them were lost except "the son of perdition; that the scripture might be fulfilled" (John 17:12). Judas Iscariot, the son of perdition, a thief with direct access to Jesus, and one of the twelve disciples whom the Father gave to Jesus betrayed him and rather than repent of his sins, committed suicide and made up his bed in hell for everlasting destruction. Christians are not them who draw back to perdition (destruction); but of them that believe to the saving of the soul (Heb 10:39).

Jesus taught that a corrupt tree will bear evil fruits while every good tree will bear good fruits. Trees that bear evil fruits are cut down and thrown into the fire of hell. Many that are called will not be chosen to enter the kingdom of God. The Bible teaches that

> not everyone that says unto me, Lord, Lord, shall enter the Kingdom of heaven; but he that doeth the will of my Father which is in heaven. Many will say in that day, Lord, Lord, have we not prophesied in thy name? and in thy name have cast out devils? And in thy name have done many wonderful works? And then

will I profess unto them, I never knew you: depart from me ye that work iniquity. (Matt 7:21–23)

Christians must set aside all evil and accept the word of God with humility. We must be doers of the word of God, and not hearers only, because the doers of the word of God are justified, and God will bless them in accordance with his glorious riches.

CHRIST COMMANDS CHRISTIAN PERFECTION

God has called us to Christian perfection because God is perfect. Christ himself taught: "Be ye therefore perfect, even as your Father in heaven is perfect" (Matt 5:48). The Christian is called with a holy calling and God will sustain our spiritual lives without fault until the day of our Lord Jesus Christ. We must be sincere and without sin, being filled with the fruits of righteousness of our Lord and Savior, Jesus Christ. God created Adam a perfect being, but he gave Adam the power of choice. Adam's sinful choice had a contagious, deleterious effect, on the entire human race for all generations. When we accept Christ as our Lord and Savior, we are born again, and brought to that state of Christian perfection by the cleansing, sanctifying blood of Christ, through faith in him. We have the power of choice that God gave to all mankind. For sure the enemy of our souls will tempt us sore in an all-out effort to bring our relationship with Christ to naught. We can say yes or no to the temptations of the devil. John the Apostle wrote:

> My little children, these things write I unto you, that ye sin not. And if any man sin, we have an advocate with the Father, Jesus Christ the righteous: And he is the propitiation for our sins: and not for ours only, but also for the sins of the whole world. And hereby we do know that we know him, if we keep his commandments. (1 John 2:1–3)

> If we confess our sins, he is faithful and just to forgive us our sins, and to cleanse us of all unrighteousness. (1 John 1:9)

John advises us not to sin. However, if perchance, in our folly, we commit sin, our relationship with God has ended and we have returned to our wicked ways and our evil thoughts, and have to be returned to our position of blamelessness and faultlessness through the forgiving and cleansing grace of Jesus. When a Christian finds himself at such a crossroad, he is not faced with making a decision as to whether or not he will do the will of God. At the beginning of his holiness journey, he had surrendered forever all situations and problems that his life will encounter, including his past, those he was currently experiencing, and those that will present themselves in the future. His current response to that crossroad situation is to find what is the will of God and do it. But of course, we can choose not to act in accordance with the will of God, and allow sin to take root in our hearts, thus violating our life of surrender to Christ. We sometimes refuse to accept and follow the will of God by substituting our own will and desires to the particular situation with which we are faced and break our surrender covenant with God. We must keep his commandments because this is our certificate which exemplifies our personal relationship with him. The Bible teaches: "Blessed are they which do his commandments, that they might have right to the tree of life and may enter in through the gates of the city" (Rev 22:14). Sin separates us from God. The blood of Christ restores the broken relationship.

Paul advises us in Heb 6:1 that the Christian must go on to perfect Christian living and must not lay again the foundation of repentance from dead works and of faith toward God. In his second letter to the church at Corinth, Paul commanded the church to "be perfect" and to live in peace and love so that the God of peace would be with them (2 Cor 13:11). We cannot enjoy the pleasures of sin and hopelessness and simultaneously have a relationship with Christ. The Bible teaches: "You cannot drink the cup of the Lord and the cup of demons too; you cannot have a part in both the Lord's table and the table of demons" (1 Cor 10:21 NIV). Sin destroys our relationship with him. He that commits sin belongs to the devil (1 John 3:3–9). The Apostle John is teaching us that we must purify ourselves and keep ourselves pure. Purity is God's passport for every believer's entry in the kingdom of God. When we abide in him (are sealed in him by the Holy Spirit), we will not sin, because sin is of the devil and not of God. We belong to God and he to us. When we are born into a relationship with him, we will not sin, because Christ's seed of holiness and perfection are given to us and remain in us. Christ teaches us that we must be born again. To be born again means to be born of God. To be born of God means to be born of the Holy Spirit of God. The new birth is not of natural descent, nor of human decision nor of a husband's will, but as the Master taught, Christians are born of water and of the Spirit: "No one can enter the kingdom unless he is born of water and the Spirit. Flesh gives birth to flesh, but the Spirit gives birth to Spirit" (John 3:5–6 NIV). Christians look upward with confidence to the future for the promised new heavens and new earth wherein dwells righteousness, and we are diligent to be found of him in peace, spotless and blameless, and without the stains of sin.

> Whosoever believeth that Jesus is the Christ is born of God: and everyone that loveth him that begat loveth him also that is begotten of him. (1 John 5:1)

> Being born again, not of corruptible seed, but of incorruptible, by the word of God which liveth and abideth forever. (1 Pet 1:23)

There is a correlation between the birth of Jesus Christ and the new birth of the Christian. With regards to the birth of our Lord, the angel of the Lord visited Mary and told her that she had found favor with God and that she will give birth to the Son of God, who will be called Jesus; be given the throne of David; will reign over the house of Jacob forever, and his kingdom will be an everlasting kingdom:

> Then said Mary unto the angel, How shall this be, seeing I know not a man? And the angel answered and said unto her, The Holy Ghost shall come upon thee, and the power of the highest shall overshadow thee: therefore, that holy thing which shall be born of thee shall be called the Son of God. (Luke 1:34–35)

Jesus never sinned because he was conceived by the Holy Ghost. He was not born of corruptible seed that perishes. He was born of imperishable seed. He was born to Mary by the power of the Holy Ghost and God took on the nature of man. He became God/man.

Jesus taught that a man must be born again; must be born of water and of the Holy Spirit. A Christian is born of the imperishable and incorruptible seed (of God), through the enduring word of God which lives and abides forever. The Christian birth (new creation from above) is an adoption through the Holy Spirit into the family of God as heirs of God, and heirs and joint heirs with Christ, into the coming kingdom of God. The Holy Spirit of God is active in our new birth. We are born again of water and of the Holy Spirit, and humans become recipients of the divine nature of God, as adopted children of God. The Holy Spirit returns to us that state of righteousness that Adam lost through his act of disobedience and gives us that divine character or quality in our new life. To put it differently, when we are born again, that old corrupt sinful nature, also known as the flesh, is destroyed, and we put on the new man, which after God is created in righteousness and true holiness and without sin. We are like the prodigal son, returning home from a sojourn of lawlessness and pig food. We receive God in our hearts as the Lord of our lives, and covenant with him to go and sin no more.

We cannot and must not view Christian perfection from the point of view of our physical birth. We are physically born in sin and separated from God. We are born sinners. Our new spiritual birth is a birth of righteousness in Jesus Christ by faith in him. Jesus was perfect. Yet he was tempted just as we are tempted, but he did not sin. If he had sinned, he would have become imperfect. We will be tempted despite our spiritual birth from above. The key is that, like Jesus, we must not yield to the temptation because yielding is sin, sin makes us imperfect and separates us from him.

The active participation of the Holy Spirit into the sinless birth of Jesus and the new birth of the Christian into the family of God, are compatible, mysterious, and without condemnation. The Bible teaches: "If ye know that he is righteous, ye know that everyone that doeth righteousness is born of him" (1 John 2:29). Sin causes the Holy Spirit to lose control of our being and permits the enemy of our souls to take his seat behind our lives' steering wheels. The light of God gives way to the darkness of Satan because light and darkness cannot coexist. We cannot serve God and the devil at the same time. If we sin, we are deemed as sinners in need of repentance. "We know that whosoever is born of God sinneth not; but he that is begotten of God keepeth himself, and the wicked one toucheth him not" (1 John 5:18).

This is a true saying that not one of us will see the Lord except we exhibit holiness in our daily living (Heb 12:14). The psalmist in Psalm 24 asked the questions: Who may ascend the hill of the Lord? Who may stand in his Holy Place? He answers the two questions in v. 4: "He who has clean hands and a pure heart" (NIV). We must therefore press to attain that true state of God's holy perfection that will allow us to enter with him in the portals of his glory whenever he should come or call. Christ taught:

> Enter ye in at the straight gate: for wide is the gate, and broad is the way that leadeth to destruction, and many go in thereat: Because straight strait is the gate, and narrow is the way, which leadeth unto life, and few there be that find it. (Matt 7:13-14)

Paul puts it this way:

> Nevertheless, the foundation of God standeth sure, having this seal, the Lord knoweth them that are his. And, let everyone that nameth the name of Christ, depart from iniquity. (2 Tim 2:19)

When we repent of our sins, we are agreeing with God that it is wrong to commit sin, and so we turn from sin to righteous living. God put his seal within of our hearts as a stamp of recognition that we are his and he is ours. We abide in him and he dwells in us. It is through faith, by the blood of Christ, that we are saved and kept from the evil one by his divine power. If we have his seal, if we belong to him; if we are the children of God, if we are named by the name of Christ, we must stop sinning, period. Let us listen to the Apostle Paul again as he addressed the church at Rome:

> What shall we say then? Shall we continue in sin, that grace may abound? God forbid. How shall we, that are dead to sin, live any longer therein? Know ye not, that so many of us as were baptized into Jesus Christ were baptized into his death? Therefore we are buried with him by baptism into death: that like as Christ was raised up from the dead by the glory of the Father, even so we also should walk in newness of life. For if we have been planted together in the likeness of his death, we shall be also in the likeness of his resurrection: Knowing this, that our old man is crucified with him, that the body of sin might be destroyed, that henceforth we should not serve sin. For he that is dead is freed from sin. (Rom 6:1–7)

Paul is teaching that our old man, our sinful nature, the very root of sin, was crucified with Christ on the cross, that the body of sin might be destroyed, so that we should no longer be slaves to sin and the devil, but be servants of God and his righteousness.

God is able to keep us from sinning and to present us faultless in his glorious presence with exceeding joy. Christ loves the church and gifted his life on the cross:

> That he might sanctify and cleanse it with the washing of water by the word, That he might present it to himself a glorious church, not having spot, or wrinkle, or any such thing; but that it should be holy and without blemish. (Eph 5:26–27)

In other words, the blood of Christ, the suffering of Christ, cleanses and sanctifies the church from her old ways of sinning and sets her apart for his special service. We are saved by the washing of regeneration and renewing of the Holy Ghost: "That being justified by his grace, we should be made heirs according to the hope of eternal life" (Titus 3:7).

BELIEVERS GOD RECOGNIZED AS PERFECT

We need must know and believe that when we accept Jesus as Lord and Savior of our lives, we can afterward live perfect Christian lives. All of us will not get it right the first time we accept him as Lord and Savior, there might be pitfalls along the way, and for all of us, there is a learning curve. If we stumble or fall, that is, if we sin, we must not remain in that sinful position, but ask God to forgive us and continue on our journey rejoicing in the hope of our salvation. God is our present help in times of trouble and whatever challenge we encounter, we can call on him because he is wide awake and available at all times to take care of us.

Throughout the Bible, God has identified and recognized individuals as perfect, and in Revelation, God identified perfect churches for our edification, example, and encouragement along this pilgrim journey. Let us go on to perfection. Let us be perfect because God commands and demands it. Let our loyalty and faithfulness to him be that unblemished service of servanthood and humility to him that he expects and demands of us. The Almighty God called Abraham when he was ninety-nine years old and commanded him: "Walk before me and be thou perfect" (Gen 17:1). The Bible tell us to "mark the perfect man and behold the upright: for the end of that man is peace" (Ps 37:37).

JOB

The Bible teaches us that Job was blameless and upright, and one who feared God, shunned evil and held fast to his integrity. It was this Job who was so faithful to God that the devil unsuccessfully sought to completely destroy him, and without cause. Here is how the Lord interrogated Satan about Job's perfection: "Hast thou considered my servant Job, that there is none like him in the earth, a perfect and an upright man, one that feareth God, and escheweth evil? and still he holdeth fast his integrity, although thou movedst me against him, to destroy him without cause" (Job 2:3). God allowed Job's faithfulness to be tested and Satan's attack on him was so severe that Job's wife told him to curse God and die, but Job remained faithful to God despite all of his challenges. Job passed the test of perfection with flying colors, and as a result he received double God's blessings for all his loyalty and commitment to him. The psalmist sings:

> Blessed is the man whose transgression is forgiven, whose sin is covered. Blessed is the man unto whom the Lord imputeth not iniquity, and in whose spirit there is no guile. (Ps 32:1–2)

NOAH

We learn that

> Noah was a just man and perfect in his generations, and Noah walked with God. (Gen 6:9)

Paul wrote:

Without faith it is impossible to please him: for he that cometh to God must believe that he is, and that he is a rewarder of them that diligently seek him. By faith Noah, being warned of God of things not seen as yet, moved with fear, prepared an ark to the saving of his house; by the which he condemned the world, and became heir of the righteousness which is by faith. (Heb 11:6–7)

DAVID WAS PERFECT

The psalmist testified:

> The Lord rewarded me according to my righteousness; according to the cleanness of my hands hath he recompensed me. For I have kept the ways of the Lord and have not wickedly departed from my God. For all his judgements were before me; and as for statutes, I did not depart from them. I was also upright before him and have kept myself from mine iniquity. (2 Sam 22:21–24)

Listen to what God said about his servant David:

> Who kept my commandments; and who followed me with all his heart, to do that only which was right in mine eyes. (1 Kgs 14:8)

> David did that which was right in the eyes of the Lord and turned not aside from anything that he commanded him all the days of his life, save only in the matter of Uriah, the Hittite. (1 Kgs 15:5)

David had confronted his sins head on. He repented of his lust, covetousness, idolatry, adultery and murder and never returned to a life of sinfulness. He was perfect before God and God identified him as a man after his own heart.

THE APOSTLE PAUL WAS PERFECT

Paul was an apostle who was loyal and faithful to the cause of Christ even to the risk of his own life and truly merits the crown of righteousness which God has set aside for him and all who look forward to his second coming. The Apostle Paul, who spoke from a pure conscience, recognizing that he was about to die, wrote this passionate dying declaration:

> For I am now ready to be offered, and the time for my departure is at hand. I have fought a good fight, I have finished my course, I have kept the faith. Henceforth, there is laid up for me a crown

of righteousness, which the Lord, the Righteous Judge, shall give me at that day: and not to me only, but unto all them also that love his appearing. (2 Tim 4:6–8)

A great testimony indeed from a great servant of Christ.

Paul admonishes us: "Let us therefore, as many as be perfect, be thus minded: and if in anything ye be otherwise minded, God shall reveal even this unto you" (Phil 3:15). Christian maturity is not a stagnant experience. We need to move forward from where we are and press harder and harder, toward that prize for the high calling of God, in Christ.

AND THERE ARE OTHERS WHO WERE PERFECT

Before Enoch was translated, his testimony was that he pleased the Lord (Heb 11:5). Joseph, Jesus' earthly father, was a just man (Matt 1:19). Zacharias and his wife, Elizabeth, were both righteous (Luke 1:5–6). Simeon was a just and devout man (Luke 2:25). John the Baptist was a just and holy man (Mark: 6:20). Cornelius was a devout man; a just man, that feared God with his whole house (Acts 10:1).

GOD'S PATHWAY FOR CHRISTIAN GROWTH

> And he gave some Apostles; and some prophets; and some evangelists; and some pastors and teachers. For the perfecting of the Saints, for the work of the Ministry, for the edifying of the body of Christ. Till we come in the unity of the faith, and of the knowledge of the Son of God, unto a perfect man, unto the measure of the stature of the fullness of Christ. (Eph 4:11–13)

The Bible teaches that every one of us is given grace (special abilities and individual tasks) according to the measure of the gift of Christ. Apostles, prophets, evangelists, pastors and teachers are gifts that Jesus gave to the church to help her grow bigger and better. These gifts to the church are for the purpose of perfecting the saints, doing God's ministry and edifying the body of Christ. All Christians are to participate in the in the work of the ministry and in the edification of the body of Christ. Apostles, pastors and evangelists ensure that the church experiences bigger and better growth in terms of its spiritual maturity and congregation expansion. Christians must exhibit faith in the Son of God through their profound knowledge in him. We need to fully grow into Christ's own image, so that we can perfectly attain entire completeness in him. Paul informs us that we are to have specific Christian experiences: unity of the faith and of the knowledge of the Son of God; we are to come to a perfect man; we are to come to a measure of the stature of the fullness of Christ. We have the ability and capability to attain this perfection, not by our own efforts, but by "the righteousness of God which is by the faith of Jesus Christ unto all and upon all of them who believe" (Rom 3:22).

THE PERFECT CHURCHES OF REVELATION

The question of whether we can have Christian perfection has to be answered in the positive. Yes, we can. In the book of the Revelation of our Lord, the Apostle John reminds us that God knows our works, where we live, and where Satan resides. Jesus Christ as the head of the church, commanded the exiled Apostle John to write to the seven churches of Turkey, each one with its distinguishing features and carrying the same message, which has application for all ages, including today's churches.

God needs his church to be perfect so that she can be presented to him as a glorious church, not having spot or wrinkle or any such thing, but that she should be holy and without blemish. Unfortunately, some of our churches are imperfect, while there are others that have a combination of perfect and imperfect members. There is the loveless church at Ephesus, the compromising church at Pergamos, the worldly church at Thyatira, and the lukewarm church of the Laodiceans. These churches are required to fall on their knees in repentance before God or suffer the consequences of eternal death for their sinfulness.

THE DEAD CHURCH AT SARDIS (REV 3:1-6)

The church at Sardis was reputed to be alive and kicking and for those looking on, it appeared to be very vibrant indeed. This church was far from being alive; it was in fact spiritually deceased. It looked good and sounded good on the outside, but within, it was full of dead bones and nastiness. It appears that the anointing of God was lacking in this church and this spiritual lifelessness received Jesus' condemnation. This church was filled with unsaved members who acted and behaved like Christians. God determined that their works were not perfect before him and they were in need of repentance.

There were a few saved persons in this church that did not participate in sinfulness. They walked faithfully with God and received God's protection. Jesus promised these overcomers, these "born again" Christians, and faithful soldiers of the cross, that he would not erase their names from the Lamb's Book of Life, but would confess their names before his Father and his angels, and they would walk with him clothed in garments of white (white representing their purity). God required these faithful soldiers of the cross to hold fast to their profession of serving him in spirit and in truth. This small section of the congregation was perfect before God.

THE PERSECUTED AND SUFFERING CHURCH AT SMYRNA (REV 2:8–11)

The church of Smyrna was a perfect church. God recognized the experiences of this church; their tribulations and their perceived poverty. He called out the blasphemy of those from the synagogue of Satan. This is the first of two completely perfect churches mentioned in the book of Revelation. The Christians of Smyrna were pure and strong in the Lord with a depth of spiritual wealth which would not be taken from them. The message from Christ was sent to prepare them for coming persecution and encourage their perseverance and endurance: "Do not be afraid of what you are about to suffer. I tell you the devil will put some of you in prison to test you and you will suffer persecution for ten days. Be faithful even to the point of death, and I will give you the crown of life" (Rev 2:10 NIV). Christians must not be afraid of the challenges of sufferings and persecution. We must hold firmly to our faith in God because he will reward us with the crown of life eternal for our patience and endurance.

This church at Smyrna will not be hurt by the second death. In other words, the gates of hell will not prevail against this church, which will be part of the first resurrection and which will be caught up with the other perfect churches to meet our Lord in the air to be forever with him.

THE FAITHFUL CHURCH AT PHILADELPHIA (REV 3:7–13)

This is a church that God did not have to discipline, he did not have to warn them, and he did not have to threaten to bring judgment on them, because this church is true, faithful, loyal and godly. Jesus praised and rewarded this church:

> I know your deeds. See, I have placed before you an open door that no one can shut: I know that you have a little strength, yet you have kept my word, and have not denied my name. Since

you have kept my command to endure patiently, I will keep you from the hour of trial that is going to come upon the whole world, to test those who live on the earth. (Rev 3:8, 10 NIV)

This church is required to hold fast to what they have, so that their crown will not be taken away. Jesus promised these overcomers: "Him who overcomes, I will make a pillar in the temple of my God. Never again will he leave it. I will write on him the name of my God and the name of the city of my God, the New Jerusalem, which is coming down out of heaven from my God. And I will also write on him my new name" (Rev 3:12 NIV).

THE BIG QUESTION

If you are a faithful Christian for many years and you commit a sinful act before you die, and you did not confess that one sin to God and repent before you physically die, will you go to heaven with the other saints? The prophet Ezekiel, who was directed by God to involve himself personally in the Divine Word, answers with an emphatic *no*! Ezekiel was a prophet who saw visions of God when the heavens opened and the word of the LORD came to him. He was directed by God to faithfully preach God's word of divine judgment to the Jews. Ezekiel was required to preach about God's eminent judgment on the rebellious nation of Israel and of their future redemption: a new exodus, a new covenant, a restored Jerusalem and the coming of Christ to the world. Here is what God instructed Ezekiel to tell his chosen people:

> But if a righteous man turns from his righteousness and commits sin and does the same detestable things the wicked man does, will he live? None of the righteous things which he does will be remembered. Because of the unfaithfulness he is guilty of and because of the sins he has committed, he will die. (Ezek 18:24 NIV)

The psalmist David put it this way:

> The face of the LORD is against those who do evil, to cut off the memory of them from the earth. (Ps 34:16)

Ezekiel repeats the answer in v. 26:

> If a righteous man turns from his righteousness and commits sin, he will die for it; because of the sin he has committed he will die.

In Ezek 33:12–13, the prophet who was given instructions from God continued his firebrand preaching:

> Therefore, thou son of man, say unto the children of thy people, The righteousness of the righteous shall not deliver him in the day of his transgression: as for the wickedness of the wicked, he shall not fall thereby in the day that he turneth from his wickedness; neither shall the righteous be able to live for his righteousness in the day that he sinneth. When I shall say to the righteous, that he shall surely live; if he trust to his own righteousness, and commit iniquity, all his righteousness shall not be remembered; but for his iniquity that he hath committed, he shall die for it. (Ezek 33:12–13)

Ezekiel then gives a pathway out of the sinful situation:

> Therefore, I will judge you, O house of Israel, every one according to his ways, saith the Lord God. Repent, and turn yourselves from all your transgressions; so iniquity shall not be your ruin. Cast away from you all your transgressions, whereby ye have transgressed; and make you a new heart and a new spirit: for why will ye die, O house of Israel? For I have no pleasure in the death of him that dieth, saith the Lord God: wherefore turn yourselves, and live ye. (Ezek 18:30–32)

A Christian must not sin, period. Christ died for our sins. His death on the cross was total and complete victory over our sin and the wrath as a result of unforgiven sin. For our sakes, Christ was made sin although he did not sin, so that we might become the righteousness of God in him. God forgave all our trespasses and sins and brought us from the pathway that leads to eternal death to a pathway wherein we can boast with great confidence that we are alive unto God, forevermore.

If a Christian sins, he has a responsibility to himself and to God through our Advocate and Intercessor, Jesus the Righteous, to repent and turn from his sins so that he can live spiritually and have an eternal home in heaven. It is also true that if he does not repent, he will die in his sins and suffer the consequences of spiritual death and an eternal home in the pits of hell with the devil, the false prophets and the antichrist, and with all those other goats who do not know Christ as Lord and whose names are not written in the Lamb's Book of Life.

Simply put, God does not tolerate sin. He knows how to deliver Christians out of temptations:

For if God spared not the angels that sinned, but cast them down to hell, and delivered them into chains of darkness, to be reserved unto judgment; And spared not the old world, but saved Noah the eighth person, a preacher of righteousness, bringing in the flood upon the world of the ungodly; And turning the cities of Sodom and Gomorrha into ashes condemned them with an overthrow, making them an ensample unto those that after should live ungodly; And delivered just Lot, vexed with the filthy conversation of the wicked: (For that righteous man dwelling among them, in seeing and hearing, vexed his righteous soul from day to day with their unlawful deeds;) The Lord knoweth how to deliver the godly out of temptations, and to reserve the unjust unto the day of judgment to be punished. (2 Pet 2:4–9)

Let us look at the prophesy of Isaiah: "Awake, awake, O Zion, clothe yourself with strength. Put on your garments of splendor, O Jerusalem, the Holy City. The uncircumcised and defiled will not enter you again" (Isa 52:1 NIV).

In the book of the Revelation of Jesus Christ, which he gave to John to show his servants what must soon take place, we learn: "Blessed are those who washed their robes, that they may have rights to the tree of life and may go through the gate of the city" (Rev 22:14 NIV).

God's eyes are too pure to look on evil (Hab 1:13).

PART TWO

God's Pathway to Prosperity

Chapter 8

Prosperity through Wisdom

"Wisdom is the principal thing; therefore get wisdom: and with all thy getting get understanding" (Prov 4:7). King Solomon, the wisest human being, ever, advised us to choose instruction rather than silver and knowledge rather than choice gold. Wisdom is better than rubies, and all the things that we desire cannot be compared to her. It is the principal thing and we must strive with every sinew in our veins to obtain her, above all else. The wise Solomon states:

> Wisdom like an inheritance, is a good thing and benefits those who see the sun. Wisdom is a shelter as money is a shelter, but the advantage of knowledge is this: Wisdom preserves those who have it. (Eccl 7:11–12 NIV)

The Bible teaches us that it is more important to have wisdom than to have money, because you can have money today and be broke tomorrow. It is far more beneficial to teach a person to fish than give him a fish because you would be relieved of the problem of providing fish for him again. Wisdom preserves those persons who possess her because they know how to earn income. When we have wealth, God does not want us to forget him. He had to remind the Israelites that he loved them and delivered them from the chains of Egypt because they were his holy people; his treasured possession. He led them through the vast and dreadful desert, provided water and food for them, and protected them from the venoms of the wilderness. He told them:

> You may say to yourself, my power and the strength of my hands have produced this wealth for me. But remember the Lord your God, for it is he who gives you the ability to produce wealth. (Deut 8:17–18 NIV)

God is faithful to give us new, workable ideas, the ability to generate abundant wealth. Money will disappear in a flash, but God will give you knowledge, understanding and wisdom that no one can take from you.

WISDOM DEFINED

Wisdom is the ability to determine what is right and then following the right course of action to achieve a predetermined accurate result. It is that predetermined plan to achieve a predetermined result and its perfect execution that achieve the most efficient and effective predestined goal. It exhibits the ability to develop sound judgments. Do not forsake her and she will guard you; love her and she will watch over you; prize her and she will exalt you; she will honor you if you embrace her (Prov 4:6–8). In its simplest form, wisdom is knowledge of what is true or right and includes just and merciful adjudications, as to actions. Wisdom teaches us the right way to do things. It gives us control over the best methods and the best means of doing things for our own good and the good of others.

The Apostle James defined the wise person as one who shows that by good conduct, and good conversation, that his works are done in the meekness of wisdom. The wise person is not an achiever by craftiness, bitterness, envying, strife, and such like which is earthly, sensual, and devilish. True wisdom comes from our Father which art in heaven and exhibits the following characteristics: it is first pure, then peaceable, gentle, and easy to be entreated, full of good fruits, without partiality and without hypocrisy. Stated differently, wisdom is the ability and capability to recognize God's perspective and act in accordance with his word.

We measure wisdom by the depth of a person's character, by his actions. True wisdom produces peace and goodness while foolishness leads to disorder:

> Who is a wise man and endued with knowledge among you? let him show out of a good conversation his works with meekness of wisdom. But if ye have bitter envying and strife in your hearts, glory not, and lie not against the truth. This wisdom descendeth

not from above but is earthly, sensual, devilish. For where envying and strife is, there is confusion and every evil work. But the wisdom that is from above is first pure, then peaceable, gentle, and easy to be intreated, full of mercy and good fruits, without partiality, and without hypocrisy. (Jas 3:13–17)

WISDOM IS OF GOD

Wisdom in its fullness is manifested in the true and living Jehovah God, because he is naturally and completely and invariably wise. It is God who uses his attributes in a way to accomplish his predetermined purposes by the best means possible. God is wise in heart and mighty in strength and all wisdom and power belong to him. Counsel and understanding are his (Job 12:13). Perfect wisdom comes from God and all the wisdom used in the world is distributed by him. His perfect wisdom is unchangeable. It transcends anything attainable by mankind. God owns these qualities. Wisdom is not acquired or imparted to him. It belongs to him, necessarily and always:

> God is mighty in strength and wisdom. (Job 35:5)

> Lift up your eyes and look to the heavens: who created all these? He who brings out the starry host one by one and call forth each of them by name. Because of his great power and mighty strength, not one of them is missing. Do you not know? Have you not heard? The Lord is the Everlasting God, the creator of the ends of the earth. He will not grow tired or weary and his understanding no one can fathom. (Isa 40:26, 28 NIV)

In Exodus 31, Moses was required to build a tabernacle for the service of the Lord, for God's own honor and glory. God told him to select the qualified builder Bezaleel to build this tabernacle which architectural plan God had described in detail. God filled Bezaleel with his Spirit in wisdom and understanding, and in knowledge, and in all manner of workmanship necessary to complete and decorate the tabernacle, according to God's specifications so that he might receive honor and glory. This is exactly what God does for us when he calls us into service. He gives us the ability and capability to complete the tasks according to his specifications, so that he will receive honor and glory.

In 1 Chronicles, God endowed the young Solomon with wisdom to manage the kingdom of Israel, with the added responsibility to build his house of worship. Solomon's father, King David, was a man of war from very young and God determined that he was unfit to build his house of worship, because he had shed too much blood during wars against all the enemies of Israel. God's house is for the saving of souls and not for the destruction of precious human lives: "for the Son of man is not come to destroy men's lives, but to save them" (Luke 9:56). God ordained Solomon to build his house before he was born. God told King David that he would give him a son to be called Solomon, and he shall build a house in my name (1 Chr 22:9-10).

God warned Solomon to take heed to fulfill the statutes which he had charged Moses with:

> Only the Lord give thee wisdom and understanding, and give thee charge concerning Israel, that thou mayest keep the law of the Lord thy God. Then shall thou prosper, if thou takest heed to fulfill the statutes and judgements which the Lord charged Moses with concerning Israel. Be strong, and of good courage, dread not, nor be dismayed. (1 Chr 22:12-13)

God promised Solomon wisdom and prosperity. However, these promises were conditional on him studying and adhering to the word of the Lord.

Our God Almighty will, at some time in the future, further demonstrate the mystery of his wisdom when he unifies all things in Christ, in heaven and on earth.

GOD CREATED THE WORLD BY WISDOM

God's creation of the world is an amazing, magnificent, and glorious example of his rich, creative genius, demonstrated in pure unadulterated wisdom. Give special attention to the creation of the human being. Each of us is unique. We have varying skills, abilities, talents, and gifts. Some of us are doctors, lawyers, engineers, architects, farmers, maids, bus drivers, and such, and each of us can be specifically identified:

> O Lord, how manifold are thy works! In wisdom hast thou made them all: the earth is full of thy riches. So is this great and wide sea, wherein are things creeping innumerable, both small and great beasts. There go the ships: there is that leviathan, whom thou hast made to play therein. These wait all upon thee; that thou mayest give them their meat in due season. (Ps 104:24-27)

Psalm 104 wholly exhibits the power of God's wisdom when he created the world. God, by pure, unimaginable wisdom, created the heaven and earth and everyone and everything in them with immeasurable variation and outstanding creativity. He created the sun to rule the day and the moon and stars to rule the night. He filled the earth and sea with water, food and fresh air. In fact, there is nothing that God left out in his magnificent and glorious creation of the world. He created day and night and a light to rule each of them. He created times and seasons. The earth spins on its axis at the same speed and without variation. A person can travel to any part of the world and return to their house and it has not moved an inch from where it was left. Washington has not been relocated and London has remained unmoved. Barbados is still the most easterly of all the islands in the Caribbean and has remained, perhaps, the most beautiful, peaceful and delightful tourist and investment attraction in the world.

SALVATION IS ACHIEVED IN THE WISDOM OF GOD

The first epistle of Paul to the Corinthians is heavily concentrated on wisdom. The people of Corinth were puffed up in their imaginary wisdom but separated from God. The gospel message was foolishness in the eyes of these worldly beings who believed that they were wise. These pretenders to wisdom and education could not fathom lowly fishermen preaching that Christ died on the cross for the sins of the whole world, that Christ is no longer in the grave but rose from the dead and ascended to heaven and is now seated on the right hand of God, our Father, pleading and interceding our cause, and that Christ will redeem us from the world of sin and bring us to the position just as if we had not sinned. They perceived that these uneducated and ignorant messengers of God were preaching foolishness and the message of the gospel was not accepted. That is why in the very first chapter of 1 Corinthians, Paul addressed the subject of wisdom: "For after that in the wisdom of God the world by wisdom, knew not God, it pleased God that by the foolishness of preaching to save them that believe" (1 Cor 1:21). In other words, the wisdom of God is exhibited in the preaching of the gospel by humble messengers sent by God.

This highly educated apostle had rejected the gospel news of salvation until he was humbled by God, while on the road to Damascus to persecute those who propagated this "foolish" gospel. In v. 26, Paul states: "For ye see your calling, brethren, how not many wise men after the flesh, not many mighty, not many noble, are called."

Paul's message is strong and powerful. Christianity does not discriminate. It is completely impartial. It does not confirm the mighty in their Christian seats. The status of Christianity is not for the educated. It is not for the rich and famous. It is not for the powerful nor is it for any of us who are wise in our own conceit. Christianity is for everyone who will believe the gospel of the kingdom of God. The rich and poor have the same access to it. The famous, underrated and berated have the same access to it. The wise and the foolish have the same access to it. The one road to Christianity is by way of the cross of Jesus Christ and it is available everyone. In v. 27, Paul reminds us: "But God has chosen the foolish things of the world to confound the wise; and God has chosen the weak things of the world to confound the things that are mighty." God is so wise that he chose the things of the world that appear to us as foolish to put to shame those of us who are wise in our own estimation. If it was any other way someone would step forward and claim that it was him who introduced, followed through and saw it to completion. God does not share his glory with anyone. The power of the gospel is not in the bearer of the news but rather in the message of the cross. The power of the gospel is that Christ died for our sins on the cross, that he was buried, and that he came forward triumphantly from the grave to become the firstfruits of them that sleep.

It is important to acknowledge that sometimes God chooses from the most outcast and rejected by our societies. He chose Moses after he had murdered an Egyptian. Isaiah confessed that he was undone and a man of unclean lips spending time with like people of unclean lips. And yes, God chose Paul, who bore responsibility for the murder of so many Christians. What about heroine Rahab? After all, she was a prostitute, liar, deceiver and traitor, but God chose her as the lineage through which our Lord and Savior would come into the world.

God examines us to determine whether we can be used as vessels of honor, and despite our perceived condition in the eyes of the world and sometimes our own eyes, he chooses us. My message to you is this: be in the right position at the right time and with the right attitude toward God's message of salvation and you will be God's important choice to proclaim his message. Moses stood on holy ground. Isaiah experienced a vision of the exalted God, high and lifted up. Paul was on the right road and had the right attitude. He talked directly to our Lord and did not reject him nor his counsel. Rahab's faith led her into action and this act of faith pleased God.

CHRIST IS THE WISDOM OF GOD

"But unto them which are called, both Jews and Greeks, Christ the power of God, and the wisdom of God" (1 Cor 1:24). Christ is the power of God and the wisdom of God. It is through this wisdom, by his blood outpoured on the cross, that the entire world can be saved from sin and eternal damnation.

The wisdom of Christ is that he suffered to death to bear our sins in his own body and transferred our eternal death sentence to himself.

No one knows or can even comprehend the riches of the wisdom and knowledge of Christ. His judgments are unsearchable and no one has the ability or capability to trace his paths. No one knows the mind of Christ and no one has ever advised or counseled him. When we accept Christ as Lord and Savior, he changes our lives. He takes away our Adamic, sinful nature and unites us as one with him and with one another. Christ then gives us his Spirit of wisdom so that we may know him better, that we may know the hope to which he has called us, the riches of his glorious inheritance in his holy people and his incomparable power for all believers. All of the treasures of wisdom and knowledge are hidden in him.

BENEFITS OF WISDOM

There are many benefits of wisdom, including happiness, health, and success. It is hoped that we will benefit together from them, as we accentuate and actualize what we learn from what God is teaching us from his holy Scriptures. In addition to the three benefits mentioned, we also note that wisdom builds strong homes and promotes happy family relationships. Wisdom exalts us before others and brings us favor in the workplace. Wisdom diffuses angry people and angry situations. Wisdom enables us to overcome major obstacles and opposition.

Happiness

Wisdom offers happiness. The wisest man ever, Solomon, states in Proverbs 3, that when we find wisdom and understanding, we find happiness. He writes that wisdom is more profitable than silver and yields greater returns than gold. Wisdom is more precious than rubies and there is nothing that we desire that can be compared with her. Wisdom is the principal thing and whatever we try to accomplish, we should seek it with our whole heart to ensure that she occupy the principal location in our armory. This is the pure wisdom found in Christ Jesus our Lord.

Health

Wisdom provides health to our navels and marrow to our bones (Prov 3:8). In the book of Proverbs chapter 2, the author invites us to listen to wisdom and energetically seek and apply the benefit of understanding to our lives, because God will guide and reward our sincere and persistent search for this principal and important treasure. The author also invites us to seek and find the knowledge of God and in return God will give us victory in all aspects of our lives. He will be our shield. He will guard our course and protect our way. To put it another way, God will give us that pure wisdom that will guard and protect us from our violent enemies, and all other enemies, known and unknown, who will seek to physically harm us. He will guard and protect our physical bodies from injuries and all manner of illnesses and diseases. Wisdom will lead us to live healthy lives.

Wisdom Saves Us from Immorality

> It [wisdom] will save you from the adulteress, from the wayward wife with her seductive words, Who has left the partner of her youth and ignored the covenant she made before God, For her words leads down to death and her path to the spirits of the dead. None who go in to her return or attain the paths of life. (Prov 2:16–19 NIV)

God is so serious about adultery that as far back as Lev 10:20, God imposed capital punishment on both adulterer and adulteress who committed the crime of adultery. Adultery is still a serious issue today. We must not commit adultery, period. When we commit adultery, we also commit several other sins. We are coveting and taking another person's spouse. We break our marriage covenant to be faithful to our partner until death, and we break our covenant relationship with our God. Wisdom will save us from the evil woman and from the flattering tongue of strange women. If we take fire in our bosom, our clothes will be burned. If we walk on hot coals, our feet will be burned. And if we have sexual intercourse with our neighbor's spouse, we will be guilty of adultery, from which the penalty for adultery can be imposed.

When we righteously apply wisdom, she will save us from the forbidden woman, from the enticing, smooth-talking adulteress, who leads us to commit sins against our God, that results in the wrath of God, and physical, spiritual and eternal death. Wisdom is the principal thing, and Christ is our wisdom who saves us from sin and death.

We also define adultery in terms of our ability to separate ourselves from our covenant relationship with God. We wander away from God by sinning against him. When we break off our relationship with God, we are committing spiritual adultery against him. The Bible teaches us that the whore of Babylon seduces us to commit adultery with her. In Psalm 51, David acknowledges that his sin is not only against Uriah's wife, Bathsheba, but also against God. He prayed for forgiveness:

> Wash me thoroughly from mine iniquity, and cleanse me from sin. For I acknowledge my transgressions: and my sin is ever before me. Against thee only, have I sinned, and done this evil in thy sight: that thou mightiest be justified when thou speakest, and be clear when thou judgest. (Ps 51:2–4)

Wisdom Makes a Person Successful

"If the axe is dull and he does not sharpen the edge, then he must exert more strength. Wisdom has the advantage of giving success" (Eccl 10:10). We are taught by example that wisdom makes a person successful. The people of Solomon's day were very wealthy and prosperous. They were proud and often became angry when matters did not work out to their complete satisfaction. We are being taught in this verse that wisdom is profitable to direct the ruler, so that rather than being angry with each other, rather than being proud, we should act with prudence, mildness and good temper. This attitude will normally result in good success. We need to know the right way to do things and then follow that right path to complete the task. If the axe is dull, it will not be possible to cut the wood no matter how angry we are, how proud we are, how famous or prosperous we are. Sharpening the axe will give a successful result in cutting the wood.

We must use the best plans, the best methods and the best ways and means to complete a specific task. What is the task that we must bring to a successful completion? What road map is available to us to direct us to bring the task from ground zero to the successful end? Wisdom will instruct us how we should handle the task and it matters little if the task is small or great. We must not rush into the project. We must not let pride tell us we are so knowledgeable we can perform the task without thinking or planning the best methods and ways to complete it. We must not think of some form of vengeance in response to something that may or may not have affected us. We must allow wisdom to prevail and proceed with the right attitude and the right temperament, and we will reap the necessary success.

WISDOM MAKES A PERSON SUCCESSFUL: THE SUCCESS OF JOSHUA

> This book of the law shall not depart out of thy mouth, but thou shall meditate therein day and night, that thou mayest observe to do all that is written therein: for then thou shall make thy way prosperous, and then thou shall have good success. (Josh 1:8)

Israel wandered in the wilderness for forty years after their miraculous exit from the slavery and entanglement of Egypt. They were disobedient to God and had lost faith in him. Moses died and Joshua was chosen as the spiritual and military leader of Israel. God promised Joshua to be with him as he was with Moses, but he had to fearlessly demonstrate courage and strength. Joshua's prosperity and good success depended on his teaching and preaching God's word daily and nightly, meditating on God's word daily and nightly and obedience to the word of the Lord.

Prosperity and great success do not come from having an enormous amount of power, influential personal contacts, outstanding ambitions, or some outstanding listing of academic achievements or work experience. Joshua followed God's unique battle strategy, and conquered Jericho by marching around the city thirteen times, blowing trumpets and shouting. They subsequently lost the battle of Ai because one of the Israelites, Achan, disobeyed God and coveted the accursed thing (Josh 7). Once Israel was cleansed from Achan's sin, Israel conquered the small town of Ai.

Joshua knew how important it was to obey God, and as a result of this obedience, he was very successful in conquering all the enemies of Israel and ensuring that God's people were properly settled in the promised land. The standard for success and prosperity is not set by the affluent, wealthy, academics, or famous in our society. We must adjust our minds to God's way of thinking and be obedient to God's word because it is God who set the standards for lasting prosperity and success in this current physical life.

WISDOM MAKES A PERSON SUCCESSFUL: THE EARLY SUCCESS OF JACOB

Jacob's Pathway to Prosperity

I can say without fear of contradiction that God knows what plans he has for us. The LORD says, "I will guide you along the best pathway for your life. I will advise you and watch over you" (Ps 32:8 NLT). Our first task is to ascertain what God's plan and pathway is, and then execute it to the best of our abilities and capabilities in accordance with his plan and his will. God had a plan for Jacob and it was committed to Jacob to follow God's plan with perfect execution, if the plan was to be successful.

God planned Jacob's prosperity from the time Jacob was in his mother's womb. Isaac, Jacob's father, was forty years old when he married Rebekah, who was barren. Isaac prayed to God on her behalf and she became pregnant with twins. The babies jostled each other during her pregnancy, and she inquired of the Lord why this was happening. The Lord told her that she carried two nations in her womb and that the two peoples within her womb would be separated; that one will be stronger than the other, and that the younger son will have dominion over the older son. God had chosen Jacob to be stronger than his older brother, Esau, and to rule over him. Under ordinary circumstances, the younger of the two sons would be subservient to the older son. Jacob's elevation to the higher calling can be attributed to God's divine plan and not to natural or worldly development.

Esau Transfers His Inheritance Right to Jacob

One day, Esau came home from work starving. Jacob, his younger brother, had prepared stew and Esau must have thought that the stew was the right medicine that the doctor ordered and he requested that Jacob give him some of it because he thought that he was about to die. Jacob told Esau that he could have some of the lentil stew in exchange for his birthright. Esau then gave away his most valuable, although intangible, asset, his birthright, in exchange for immediate self-gratification. Here is what Jesus taught:

> For whosoever want to save his life shall lose it, but whosoever loses his life for me and for the gospel will save it. What good is it for a man to gain the whole world, yet forfeit his soul? Or what can a man give in exchange for his soul? (Mark 8:35–37 NIV)

In other words, what is the value of our souls? What are we willing to give up our souls for? There is nothing on this earth or any planet that can buy a single soul. Our souls are permanent while everything else on this earth is temporary and will pass away. Our souls will live forever. We can melt away our lives focusing on things that does not matter, and that may even bring hurt to us and others. Each and every single day we trade our souls for something. What are we trading our souls for? Esau despised his birthright. God will hold us accountable if we despise our spiritual heritage and leave him out in the cold. Paul teaches us that we should not be godless like Esau, who for a single meal sold his inheritance rights as the oldest son. We must give special attention to our eternal inheritance rather than that which has temporary value. And that is exactly what Jacob did.

Isaac Pronounces Blessings on Jacob

> So he [Isaac] went to him and kissed him. When Isaac caught the smell of his clothes, he blessed him [Jacob] and said, ah, the smell of my son is like the smell of the field that the Lord has blessed. May God give you of heaven's dew and of earth's richness—an abundance of grain and new wine. May nations serve you and peoples bow down to you. Be lord over your brothers and may the sons of your mother bow down to you. May those who curse you be cursed and those who bless you be blessed. (Gen 27:27–29 NIV)

God knows what our character will be even before we are born. He knows what our qualifications will be, whether we are going to be doctors, agriculturalist, or fisher folk. He knows what or attitudes, our mentality, and our relationship with him will be. And God knew that Esau would not have been careful about his spiritual and eternal heritage. He knew that Esau would have placed more value on a mess of pottage than on saving his soul. He knew that Esau would marry ungodly wives who did not believe in God nor would trust him. On the other side, God knew that Jacob would be worthy of the blessings of a first son and did in fact determine while he was in his mother's womb that he would rule over Esau, and gave his mother the news of his plan. When Isaac realized that he was deceived by Jacob, he could have reversed the blessings but chose not to do so. He, at last, recognized that God had elevated Jacob to be the heir to Abraham's heritage.

Jacob Receives the Blessings of Abraham

> May God Almighty bless you and make you fruitful and increase your numbers until you become a community of peoples. May he give you and your descendants the blessing given to Abraham, so that you may take possession of the land where you now live as an alien, the land that God gave to Abraham. (Gen 28:3–4 NIV)

The words of Isaac as he reaffirmed God's blessing on Jacob. Isaac's prayer is that Jacob become the heir to Abraham's blessing; that is, that he may receive the inheritance of the promised Canaan land and of course, that he become the line through which the promised seed, the incarnate Messiah, will present himself to the world. This was a prayer of faith, and at the same time, it was prophetic confirmation that Jacob would receive the same blessing that God promised Abraham and his seed after him. And through Jacob, the nation of Israel would multiply until the church from every kindred and nation and people and tongue multiply to a numberless quantity. Jacob inherited dominion over the land of Canaan, and this included the spiritual inheritance of heaven for which Abraham and all the other patriarchs had a glimpse and looked forward excitedly to being part of this better country.

Jacob Obeyed His Father

> So Isaac called for Jacob and blessed him and commanded him: Do not marry a Canaanite woman. Go at once to Paddan Aram, to the house of your mother's father Bethuel. Take a wife for yourself there, from among the daughters of Laban, your mother's brother. May God Almighty bless you and make you fruitful and increase your numbers until you become a community of peoples. May he give you and your descendants the blessings given to Abraham, so that you make take possession of the land where you now live as an alien, the land God gave to Abraham. Then Isaac sent Jacob on his way, and he went to Paddan Aram, to Laban, son of Bethuel the Aramean, the brother of Rebekah, who was the mother of Jacob and Esau. (Gen 28:1–5 NIV)

This passage of Scripture is a timely reminder of obeying our parents in the Lord. It is a reminder that when we honor and obey our parents God will reward us with long lives. It is a reminder that it is righteous to obey our godly parents. Jacob obeyed his parents and as a result, he started a new life with God and became very prosperous.

Jacob's First-Time Encounter with God

The scheming, deceiving Jacob had to flee from his father's house at Beersheba, to escape the fury and indignation of his brother's quest to permanently destroy him because Jacob had schemed him of his birthright and his father's blessing. When Jacob was fleeing from the wrath of Esau, he stopped to rest for the night at Bethel and it was on that spot that he had his first experience with God. While Jacob was resting, he had a dream. He saw a ladder reaching up to heaven and angels ascended and descended from heaven while the Lord stood above the ladder. That night, God revealed himself to Jacob for the very first time, forcing Jacob to acknowledge: "Surely, the Lord is in this place and I was not aware of it" (Gen 28:16 NIV). It was there at Bethel that God covenanted with Jacob to give him the land at Bethel, to multiply his descendants as the dust of the land, to bless the whole world through him, and to be with him until his promise to him was executed. Jacob believed God and trusted him with regard to the promises that he made to him. Jacob promised that the Lord will be his God if God in turn would provide him with protection, food, clothing and shelter. Jacob's encounter with God at Bethel that night brought a righteous change in his personal life. He was no longer the deceiver. He gave up his scheming and manipulative attitude. He understood that prosperity and protection depended on a righteous relationship with God and he committed to the principle of tithing. Like Jacob, we should give God honor and exaltation for his Holy Spirit in our lives and of course, we should reinvest our resources through tithing and serving.

Jacob was now exiled in Syria, at his uncle's house, where he became a shepherd in Laban's employ. Jacob was conned into faithfully laboring for Laban for fourteen years with only his two wives to show for it. The time came for Jacob to return to his homeland at Beersheba. He requested his uncle to release him so that he could return to his homeland along with his family and some material possessions for the purpose of taking care of his family. Laban had difficulty releasing such an outstanding employee who had an excellence in service report card, and whose productivity resulted in significant increased profitability and growth for Laban's estate. Laban was forced to recognize that it was through God's blessing for Jacob that he was blessed and had become extremely prosperous. If Jacob is to be released from his employment, he would have to work for another six years, because Laban had no intention of severing Jacob.

Jacob longed to return to his relatives in Canaan and requested that Laban give him permission to leave with his family. It seems to me that Jacob was also politely requesting severance payment because he did not have enough resources to sustain his large family. Laban was unwilling to release him because he significantly prospered under Jacob's stewardship and leadership. Laban recommended that Jacob work for him for another seven years but this time he would be paid for his service. He told Jacob to decide his remuneration and he would agree to it. Jacob came up with one big and bright idea. He did not accept a fixed salary from Laban but told him that he was willing to go on shepherding the livestock provided he was allowed to go through his flocks removing every speckled or spotted sheep, every dark-colored lamb and every speckled or spotted goat which will become his wages. Jacob determined that at the end of the working period, he would finally be ready to move on with his family. He was determined to trust God and allow his righteousness to testify for him as to the accuracy of his wages. Any goat in his possession that was not speckled or spotted, or any lamb that was not dark colored would be considered stolen.

Laban without hesitation agreed to the terms and conditions of Jacob's renewed work contract. Laban found this contract easy to sign because goats in that city were dark brown or black, but seldom white or spotted. The sheep were mainly white and occasionally black or spotted. In Jacob's plan, he would continue to shepherd all Laban's white livestock and would receive the rarer of the animals as his income. The contract began immediately when all the spotted and speckled flock were identified and set aside as Laban's property and taken three days journey to be managed by Laban's sons. Jacob was left only with the white sheep. All the speckled and spotted animals were owned by Laban, and by taking all the spotted or speckled animals from among the flock there appeared little opportunity for the reproduction of the spotted and speckled animals. It seemed impossible for white sheep to produce spotted or speckled sheep, however, with God nothing is impossible. To put it differently, all things are possible with God and if God be for us who can be against us. Jacob's task was to shepherd the unspotted, non-speckled and unstriped flock owned by Laban. All the newborn speckled or spotted flock only would become Jacob's property and the remainder would be Laban's property.

Jacob recognized how valuable he was to Laban's business and was totally committed and loyal in service to him. He was also committed to his family and took responsibility to provide for them. Laban attempted to deceive and cheat Jacob of his equity by changing his contract for income on ten occasions, but God continued to prosper Jacob.

Jacob's Family Meeting

The angel of the Lord spoke to Jacob and showed him the process to follow in order to get a successful outcome in terms of his prosperity. This was a supernatural miracle in which God caused the animals to have altered genetics although Jacob thought that it was due to his outstanding shepherding skill. Jacob's success caused his relationship with Laban's sons to deteriorate. Laban's attitude with Jacob also weakened. Jacob called a meeting with his two wives in the fields where his flocks were and planned his return to his father's home, with them as God had directed. Jacob then took his family and all his possessions back to Canaan. He returned home a very wealthy man; a man who learned to depend on God and his word.

WISDOM MAKES A PERSON SUCCESSFUL: THE SUCCESS OF JOSEPH

Joseph was the first of Jacob's sons, born to the beautiful Rachel, and he quickly became his father's favorite son. His father gave him a beautiful coat with many colors, which made his brothers jealous of him, harbored hatred in their hearts for him, and there was no peace between them. One night, Joseph dreamed that he would be their brother's leader and would have dominion over them and this made his brothers hate him more. Joseph dreamed a second dream. This time he dreamed that his father, mother, and brothers bowed down to him. This caused his brothers to envy him more, but Jacob took note of what Joseph said. One day, when Joseph went to visit his brothers and the flock in the fields, his brothers sold him as a slave to Ishmaelites who were traveling to Egypt from Gilead:

> And Joseph was brought down to Egypt; and Potiphar, an officer of Pharaoh, captain of the guard, an Egyptian, bought him of the hands of the Ishmaelites, which had brought him down thither. And the Lord was with Joseph, and he was a prosperous man; and he was in the house of his master the Egyptian. And his master saw that the Lord was with him, and that the Lord made all that he did to prosper in his hand. And Joseph found grace in his sight, and he served him: and he made him overseer over his house, and all that he had he put into his hand. And it came to pass from the time that he had made him overseer in his house, and over all that he had, that the Lord blessed the Egyptian's house for Joseph's sake; and the blessing of the Lord was upon all that he had in the house, and in the field. And he left all that he had in Joseph's hand; and he knew not ought he had, save the bread which he did eat. And Joseph was a goodly person, and well favoured. (Gen 39:1–6)

Potiphar was a rich man who promoted Joseph to manage his property with administrative responsibility for his entire estate. The Lord was with Joseph so that he prospered in everything that he did. He was wonderfully blessed, despite being sold to Potiphar as a slave. Potiphar knew that when Joseph was in charge of his business, he would be more prosperous than if he was himself in charge. Joseph had been treated unfairly by his brothers, but God was with him so that he was elevated to very high office in short order.

More trouble awaited Joseph. Potiphar's wife made daring sexual advances to test Joseph's chastity and when he resisted this temptation, telling Potiphar's wife: "There is none greater in this house than I; neither hath he [Potiphar] kept back anything from me, but thee, because thou art his wife; how then can I do this great wickedness, and sin against my God" (Gen 39:9). He was sentenced to prison for a crime he did not commit on the false testimony of Potiphar's wife. Christians, let us be reminded that false testimony is wicked and sinful. Remember the truth will always win, no matter how it appears that we are getting away with our lies. There is nothing hid that will not be revealed and Christ will judge our secrets.

Joseph response to Potiphar's wife's advances is a perfect example of how to use our God-given wisdom to resist the temptation of the devil and make him flee from us. Joseph resisted sin as though he was resisting an army that closed in on him and had him completely surrounded with no way of escape. God's grace was sufficient for Joseph, and it gave him the power to resist and overcome the fiery darts of the evil one. This escape from the temptation to commit sin was as daring as the escape of the three Hebrews that were thrown into the scorching, fiery furnace or Daniel's miraculous escape from the den of hungry lions. Joseph recognized that he would have committed a great sin against God, against his nature and his dominion, and that was not a part of God's plan for Joseph's life. God had a great plan for Joseph, which included carrying on the legacy of Abraham and Isaac and his father, Jacob.

Jesus himself suffered temptation but committed no sin. He was slandered, spat on, beaten, falsely accused, and tried from one judgment hall to the next, convicted and condemned to death on the basis of false testimony and eventually succumbed to death on the cross at the hands of wicked men. Our friends and enemies alike may take away our achievements, may demote us from our promotions at work, or even imprison us, but they cannot take away the wisdom and the grace that God has made sufficient for us. We may be separated from relatives and friends. We may sojourn in alien lands but wherever we are we can be assured of God's presence. We must maintain our faithfulness and loyalty to God because he will be faithful to us, as he was with faithful Joseph and with our forefathers.

> But while Joseph was there in the prison, the Lord was with him; he showed him kindness and granted him favor in the eyes of the prison warden. So the warden put Joseph in charge of all those held in the prison, and he was made responsible for all

that was done there. The warden paid no attention to anything under Joseph care, because the Lord was with Joseph and gave him success in whatever he did. (Gen 39:21–23)

You cannot keep a righteous man down. Joseph was disgraced by Mrs. Potiphar's accusation that resulted in his conviction and subsequent imprisonment. He was innocent of the charge, his good reputation had been tarnished, but he flourished in prison and once again, he was elevated to a management position. God had his eyes and his care on Joseph because God "Hears the needy and does not despise his captive people" (Ps 69:33). It does not matter where we are, what condition we are in, what our circumstances are, our Lord Jesus is in the mist to pronounce his favor on us. It behooves us then, to live pure and holy lives which God accepts and is our reasonable service. Joseph's success must therefore be attributed to his faithfulness and loyalty to God. He showed so much strength of character and demonstration of power to resist temptation that he earned the favor of God and man. First, his father showed him favor. Potiphar showed him favor. The prison warden showed him favor, and God's favor was on him, because he had outstanding success in every task assigned to him. Praise be to God.

While Joseph was imprisoned, Pharaoh, the king of Egypt, imprisoned his chief butler and his chief baker. One night, both the chief butler and chief baker had separate dreams that bothered them. Joseph interpreted their dreams and in accordance with Joseph's interpretation, the chief butler was reinstated to office while the chief baker received the death penalty. The imprisonment and dreams of the chief baker and butler were no coincidences. These were Joseph's pathway to greater success, prosperity and authority. Joseph was now imprisoned for a further two years and the chief butler forgot about his promise to him to make favorable mention of him to King Pharaoh so that he too could be exonerated from prison.

It was now King Pharaoh's time to dream. He had two separate dreams in one night and neither the magicians nor the wise men of the entire country of Egypt could interpret the dreams. Joseph rightly stated that "interpretation belongs to God" (Gen 40:8). The chief butler confessed that he failed to mention of Joseph's wisdom and that Joseph was the one who could possibly interpret his dreams. God works in his time. His timing is perfect. He is never late and never show up too early. Joseph's time had come to be exalted to the second highest office in the land, that of prime minister of Egypt. Joseph told Pharaoh: "It is not me. God shall give Pharaoh an answer of peace" (Gen 41:16). Joseph went on to interpret Pharaoh's dream and provided a strategic plan for perfect execution.

> And Pharaoh said unto his servants, Can we find such a one as this is, a man in whom the Spirit of God is? And Pharaoh said unto Joseph, Forasmuch as God hath shewed thee all this, there is none so discreet and wise as thou art: Thou shalt be over my house, and according unto thy word shall all my people be ruled: only in the throne will I be greater than thou. And Pharaoh said unto Joseph, See, I have set thee over all the land of Egypt. And Pharaoh took off his ring from his hand, and put it upon Joseph's hand, and arrayed him in vestures of fine linen, and put a gold chain about his neck; And he made him to ride in the second chariot which he had; and they cried before him, Bow the knee: and he made him ruler over all the land of Egypt. And Pharaoh said unto Joseph, I am Pharaoh, and without thee shall no man lift up his hand or foot in all the land of Egypt. And Pharaoh called Joseph's name Zaphnathpaaneah; and he gave him to wife Asenath the daughter of Potipherah priest of On. And Joseph went out over all the land of Egypt. (Gen 41:38–45)

Pharaoh immediately recognized the superior qualities of the discerning Joseph; his excellence in wisdom, and the Spirit that motivated him, and without hesitation appointed him to the second-highest office in the entire land of Egypt. He also gave him a wife and she was the daughter of the noble priest Potiphera.

As Joseph had predicted, Egypt produced bountifully for seven continuous years. During those years of abundance, Joseph collected all the food produced and stored it in the cities. In each city, he stored the food grown in the fields surrounding it. Joseph stored up huge quantities of grain, like the sand of the sea. It was so much that he stopped keeping records because it was beyond measure. Here is a godly economic principle for economists and governments. When times are good, we save for when the economy's performance is poor or reach crisis stage. Governments, in particular, need to have savings for critical times such as debt crises and production crises and all other crises. Even when times are tough, we must be sure to save a little something for rainier times.

There is another principal that we can adopt from Joseph's experience. Agriculture, our oldest profession, is a great method to secure economic prosperity. In Barbados, for example, when sugar was king, Barbados prospered. Currently, too many acres of land are left idle, without a harvest, without contributing to our economic growth. While unemployment is high and the treasury is low, some of our citizens waste away their lives on the block, without seeking any form of legal remuneration. We have been taught to stay away from the hardship of agriculture because its work is too burdensome and heavy, and in the meantime, the country and its people are suffering. Government needs to ensure that all of the country's idle lands are brought back into meaningful production without delay and by extension provide employment for those persons who are out of work. We need to have the capacity to feed our own people and at the same time, have enough overflow to feed others as well.

Well-behaved, nonviolent prisoners can sign onto supervised programmes to work in the fields in exchange for their freedom to be with their families. Such programs would reduce the cost to government of managing the prison. Of course, any breach of privilege would mean that the prisoner would have to return to prison to continue serving their full sentence. As long as the program is completed faithfully by the prisoner, he should be pardoned, and given a clean record so that he can be easily rehabilitated in the society. The state must not only exercise justice but must show mercy and pardon. Justice tempered with mercy and pardon is a foundational principle of Christianity and one for which the state (leaders of the state) will be held liable. The state must forgive and forget because this is right and pleasing in God's sight.

The seven years of abundant harvest expired and there was severe famine in the land of Egypt. "There was no food, however, in the whole region because the famine was severe; both Egypt and Canaan wasted away because of the famine" (Gen 47:13 NIV). This is the commencement of the first economic crisis known to man. Joseph, the prime minister of Egypt, had no worry. First, he trusted God and served him, as did his foreparents, Abraham, Isaac, and his father, Jacob. God responded to their faithfulness with favor. Second, Joseph acted wisely. During the years of abundance, he saved for the future, so that when the difficult economic times came, the government was in a great position to effectively manage the economic crisis.

"Joseph collected all the money that was to be found in Egypt and Canaan in payment for the grain they were buying, and he brought it to Pharaoh's palace" (Gen 47:14 NIV). The prime minister's strategy for the economy was successful. He had a seven-year supply of food that outlasted the seven-year downturn in the economy. He made the citizens of Canaan and Egypt buy the food until they had exhausted all their money. He ensured that all the money collected was deposited in the treasury located in Pharaoh's palace.

> When the money of the people of Egypt and Canaan was gone, all Egypt came to Joseph and said, "Give us food. Why should we die before your eyes? Our money is all gone. Then bring your

livestock," said Joseph. "I will sell you food in exchange for your livestock, since your money is gone." So they brought their livestock to Joseph, and he gave them food in exchange for their horses, their sheep and goats, their cattle and donkeys. And he brought them through that year with food in exchange for all their livestock. When that year was over, they came to him the following year and said, "We cannot hide from our lord the fact that since our money is gone and our livestock belongs to you, there is nothing left for our lord except our bodies and our land. Why should we perish before your eyes—we and our land as well? Buy us and our land in exchange for food, and we with our land will be in bondage to Pharaoh. Give us seed so that we may live and not die, and that the land may not become desolate." So Joseph bought all the land in Egypt for Pharaoh. The Egyptians, one and all, sold their fields, because the famine was too severe for them. The land became Pharaoh's, and Joseph reduced the people to servitude, from one end of Egypt to the other. However, he did not buy the land of the priests, because they received a regular allotment from Pharaoh and had food enough from the allotment Pharaoh gave them. That is why they did not sell their land. Joseph said to the people, "Now that I have bought you and your land today for Pharaoh, here is seed for you so you can plant the ground. But when the crop comes in, give a fifth of it to Pharaoh. The other four-fifths you may keep as seed for the fields and as food for yourselves and your households and your children. You have saved our lives," they said. "May we find favor in the eyes of our lord; we will be in bondage to Pharaoh." So Joseph established it as a law concerning land in Egypt—still in force today—that a fifth of the produce belongs to Pharaoh. It was only the land of the priests that did not become Pharaoh's. (Gen 47:15-26 NIV)

Joseph's management of the economy was simply brilliant. There was no free food for the citizens of Egypt. No welfare department existed. Every family was required to purchase their food. When the legal tender (money and animals) ran out, citizens gave up their land and became employees of the state. A 20 percent tax system was introduced which the people accepted with gratitude. When citizens did not have money or other assets with which to pay for their food, they were required to pay through sweat, blood and tears, else they would have starved to death. Joseph, the great and wise leader that he was, was able to get the Egyptians to willingly do what he wanted them to do and show him gratitude for doing it.

I am very sure that Joseph recognized the importance of wise management of the economy. People generally do not care which political party is governing the country or who the political leader is if their children are starving, if they are insecure in their homes and so on. They are interested in a properly functioning economy where they will have enough resources to meet their daily needs of food, clothing, shelter, and protection. They will rebel at the ballot box when the economy is broken. Joseph collected all the money that was found in Egypt and Canaan in payment for food and he saved it in Pharaoh's treasury for the tough periods that were sure to come.

Joseph's Family Reunion

Joseph was separated from his family for approximately twenty-two years. He was sold into slavery at the tender age of seventeen years but became second in command of Egypt at age thirty. Seven years of bountiful crops ensued, which was followed by a severe famine which affected the entire world. The famine had manifested itself for two years when Joseph was reunited with his entire family. What a pleasure that must have been when Joseph wept for joy at the sight of his brothers and later his father. God knows what plans he has for us, and we must trust God in the mist of adversity. We must not give up or despair, God is in the mist and he will deliver us from whatever situation or challenge that we face.

Our media today is rife with stories of divided families. We learn of children who are envious and jealous of each other and hate each other to death. We learn of spouses who curse and quarrel so much that their marriages end up in the divorce courts or voluntary separation. There are indeed many, many horror stories of domestic violence and murders in the family. We should not be surprised by any of this. Christ taught us:

> Do not you think that I came to bring peace on earth? No, I tell you, but division. From now on there will be five in one family divided against each other, three against two, and two against three. They will be divided, father against son and son against father, mother against daughter and daughter against mother, mother-in-law against daughter-in-law and daughter-in-law against mother-in-law. (Luke 12:51–53 NIV)

The Bible teaches:

> For a son dishonors his father, a daughter rises up against her mother, a daughter-in-law against her mother-in-law; a man's enemies are members of his own household. (Mic 7:6)

In Isaiah we read,

> By the fury of the Lord of Hosts the land is burned up, and the people are like fuel for the fire; no man spares his brother. (Isa 9:19)

In Jeremiah we read:

> Beware of your friends; do not trust anyone in your clan. For every one of them is a deceiver, and every friend a slanderer. Friend deceives friend, and no one speaks the truth. They have taught their tongues to lie; they weary themselves with sinning. You live in the mist of deception; in their deceit they refuse to acknowledge me, declares the LORD. Therefore, this is what the LORD ALMIGHTY says, See, I will refine and test them, for what else can I do because of the sin of my people? Their tongue is a deadly arrow; it speaks with deceit. With his mouth, each speak cordially with his neighbor, but his heart set a trap for him. Should I not punish them for this? declares the LORD. Should I not avenge myself on such a Nation as this? (Jer 9:4–9)

We also read in Jeremiah:

> Even your brothers, members of your own family, have turned against you. They plot and raise complaints against you. Do not trust them, no matter how pleasant they speak. (Jer 12:6)

Yet Joseph, who was loyal to the God of heaven, demonstrated such love, compassion, and forgiveness for his brothers, who were so envious and full of hatred that they sold him as a slave to Ishmaelites who were traveling to Egypt from Gilead:

> Then Joseph said to his brothers, come close to me. When they had done so, he said, I am your brother Joseph, the one you sold into Egypt! And now, do not be distressed and do not be angry with yourselves for selling me here, for it was to save lives that God sent me ahead of you. (Gen 45:4–5 NIV)

Joseph had overcome the slavery and imprisonment of Egypt. He worked in the highest positions in Potiphar's house and the prison and had become the prime minister of Egypt. But he was separated from his family for much too long and he was now in a position to accomplish his greatest spiritual feat. He had learned to forget all the trouble he experienced in all his father's household (Gen 41:51). God was yet to bestow his greatest favor on Joseph. He brought every living member of his family together in one place, and they brought all their possessions with them:

> Pharaoh said to Joseph, your father and brothers have come to you, and the land of Egypt is before you; settle your father and brothers in the best part of the land. Let them live in Goshen. And if you know any of them with special ability, put them in charge of my own livestock. (Gen 47:5–6)

Joseph was reunited with his family and were habilitated in the land of Goshen, the best land in Egypt, and those members who had special skills were offered opportunities to serve in the king's court.

WISDOM MAKES A PERSON SUCCESSFUL: THE SUCCESS OF RT. HON. FREUNDEL STUART QC, FORMER PRIME MINISTER OF BARBADOS

Freundel Jerome Stuart was born and grew up in the rural southeastern parish of St. Philip, in the one-hundred-and-sixty-six-square-mile island of beautiful Barbados, located in the most eastern part of the Caribbean. His father died tragically in a factory accident when he was the tender age of nine years old and his mother, a wonderful evangelical Christian, as a single parent, fashioned his life as best she knew how, in accordance with her faith in Almighty God, bringing him up "in the fear and admonition of the Lord." Her greatest asset was her faith and trust in the God of her salvation and she ensured that he was taught all the core values that have become the hallmark of every phase of his entire life and personality and being. She knew that if she brought him up in the right way, this parental guidance and training would remain with him forever.

His mother was a humble and intelligent maid by profession, who generally served at the rich man's table and no doubt received a mere pittance for wages, certainly the crumbs that fell from the rich man's table. I am sure that like most maids, her services were unappreciated, as was the norm in that day, and is very normal today.

Stuart's mother ensured that he received the best possible education. He received an honors degree in political science and history from one of the most reputable and wonderful universities anywhere in the world, the Cave Hill Campus of University of the West Indies, Bridgetown, Barbados. He later returned to that same institution and obtained his bachelor of laws (with honors) and master of laws in public international law. He then went on to the Hugh Wooding Law School, Trinidad and Tobago, and obtained his legal education certificate, which allowed him to practice law in Barbados and other Caribbean territories.

But the pinnacle of his education is not embedded in the importance of his academic achievements alone. His wisdom is also influenced by his early involvement in evangelical churches, where he participated in their activities, including delivering soul-winning sermons. When he was prime minister of Barbados, he attended an evangelical church service in Barbados and surprised, if not stunned, the entire congregation when he recited the entire Sermon on the Mount, verbatim, like a man possessed with the eagerness to return to the pulpit.

Throughout his youth, he spent an enormous amount of time with politicians, particularly members of Parliament, both hearing them and asking them questions. He spent much of his life among ordinary folk as well, participating in much of the discussions on many of the topics of the day and providing both leadership and mentorship roles in his community. He is an avid reader and in particular has either read or studied the attributes and work ethic of every recognized political leader from every part of the world on whom there is literary work available; the good and the bad, the ethical and unethical, the moral and immoral. He has built also on the experiences and wisdom of all persons with whom he came into contact.

After leaving grammar school, Stuart taught history and Spanish at one of the newer secondary schools in Barbados before moving on to set up and practice law from his own Harford Law Chambers. As a teacher, he was a mentor to many in and out of school. To those at school, he taught them the value of a quality education because he knew that it would help them to set and attain goals and achieve targets resulting in a higher standard of living. To those who had finished school without certification, or with minimal certification, he encouraged them to take evening classes and other courses so that they could make resolute lives for themselves.

He firmly believes that education is the most important sector in any society in any part of the world, because it produces human beings, and that everyone should work as hard as they can to achieve their goals and objectives. There is inscribed on the entrance to his law office: "There is no gain without pain." I am very sure that he was the proudest man in the world when his secretary at his law office, whom he had also mentored, graduated from law school and took over the practice of law in his own law chambers after he had set out on his political path. A wonderful result indeed. He advised one of his closest friends who had neared the pinnacle of their teaching career to study and practice law and his friend is today one of the foremost constitutional lawyers of any generation in Barbados. Needless, to say, his friend is also successful in other areas of law and was elevated to use the title "Queens Council," a lawyer well skilled in the practice of law.

Stuart started his law practice primarily as a criminal lawyer and was very successful in the courts. But this saddened and disappointed his mother, who complained that he played a significant role in setting criminals free, particularly murder-accused. She, of course, thought that his was a higher calling to the pulpit, and I am sure that he could have been an outstanding evangelist, except that God had chosen him to be the leader of Barbados at its most critical juncture in its economic history.

Core Values That Effected the Life of Prime Minister Stuart

Stuart's mother ensured that he understood the importance of faithfulness to God and people; that it was important not to steal nor lie, nor to corrupt himself, that he should rather lose friends and everything else for the sake of his conviction. He exhibited tremendous self-control, humility and personal integrity, and his upbringing determined his total dependence on God for his decision-making. The most important component of his leadership is his character, and his skills, gifts, wisdom, ethics, culture, and morality were all successfully utilized protecting the management of the affairs of his country, Barbados.

The Core Value of Wisdom

So, what about the core values, taught by his mother, which have so greatly impacted him throughout his life. These values are entirely based on godly principles found in the pure unadulterated Word of God, the Bible. One of the first noteworthy core values that his mother endowed on him was the value of wisdom; that of all things in the world, he should seek and obtain wisdom. In Prov 4:7, we learn that wisdom is the principal thing and above all else, he must ensure that he is endowed with knowledge about God, understanding God's word as presented in the Bible, and applying this knowledge and understanding to advance the cause of others. This application is called wisdom and if he lacked it, he should pray to God, who will give it generously without finding fault.

Wisdom means living right, making right choices and right decisions with the right plans, and persistently following through to a right completion. Freundel Stuart had a vision to be the prime minister of Barbados and this vision determined the discipline and purposefulness with which he prepared for life. He worked diligently on that plan, day in and day out, and he eventually became the seventh prime minister of Barbados.

The Bible teaches that "the fear of the Lord is the beginning of wisdom." Freundel Stuart did not seek to be wise in his own conceit by pursuing wisdom, which is earthly, sensual and devilish. He practiced God's wisdom which is from above, which is first of all pure, then peaceable, gentle, and easy to be entreated, full of mercy and good fruits, without partiality and without hypocrisy, and based on his relationship with Jesus and the knowledge of knowing him as Lord and Savior. I am confident that the hand of the Lord was on the life of Freundel Stuart even before he entered his mother's womb because at all times, he has affirmed the lordship and kingship of God and always appeared to be at peace with God, with himself and most times with others.

The Core Value of Contentment

Stuart's mother would have taught him that

> godliness with contentment is great gain. For we brought nothing into this world, and we can take nothing out of it. But if we have food and clothing, we will be content with that. (1 Tim 6:6–8 NIV)

An obedient and reverent attitude toward God is worth more than great riches because a man's life does not consist in the abundance of things that he owns. Furthermore, we cannot carry our money beyond the grave. The point is that we should not make creating wealth and getting rich our priority when we are going to leave everything behind. Stuart accepts that one of the keys to spiritual and personal fulfillment is contentment and that God should be first in our lives and the desires of our hearts should be Christ centered and not personal wealth.

Verses 3–5 of 1 Timothy 6 tell of arrogant arguers knowing little of the truth and "supposing that gain is godliness." Making money has become a religion. Jesus taught his disciples:

> So do no worry then, saying, what shall we eat? Or what will we drink? Or what shall we wear? For the Pagans [sinners] run after all these things; and your heavenly Father knows that you need them. But seek ye first his Kingdom, and his righteousness, and all these things will be given to you as well. (Matt 6:31–33 NIV)

> Make sure that your character is free from the love of money, being content with what you have; for he himself has said "I will never desert you nor will I ever forsake you." (Heb 13:5)

God knows already the things that we need, but we fret and fuss about those apparent attractive things that we do not need. We ought to be contented with whatever God has provided for us because a relationship with him is worth more than all the riches in the world combined. This does not mean resting on your laurels when you should be working. It does not mean becoming lazy and ineffective. It does not mean becoming too discontented, too critical or too anxious.

Christ taught his disciples: "Therefore I tell you, do not worry about your life, what you will eat or drink, or about your body, what you will wear: Is not life more important than food, and the body more important than clothes"? (Matt 6:25). Christians must ensure that they do not to fall into the sin of discontentment.

In his law practice, Stuart's principal interest was ensuring a successful result for his clients, with no regard as to whether or not he would have been remunerated. Many of his clients were unable to pay the requisite legal fees but he represented them nonetheless. He chose to represent the working class, the poor and disadvantaged in preference to obtaining big bucks from being retained by the might of noble companies, the rich and famous. I am sure that Mr. Stuart must have thought within himself, as St. Paul did:

> Not that I speak in respect of want, for I have learnt in whatever state I am, therewith, to be content. I know both how to be abased and I know how to abound: everywhere and in all things, I am instructed both to be full and to be hungry, both to abound and suffer need. I can do all things through him who strengthens me. (Phil 4:11–13)

Paul was not speaking because he needed more. This was simply an expression of humility and contentment no matter the circumstances. He was prepared to survive on the basic necessities of life.

Discontent, coveting, and love of money bring many sorrows and eventually complete destruction and perdition. We must turn away from these things and get them as far away from us as we can because: "They that will be rich fall into temptation and a snare, and into many foolish and hurtful lusts, which drown men in destruction" (1 Tim 6:9). We must not place our priority on riches but on such things as generosity, honesty, and helpfulness. When we are engrossed in the pursuit of riches, we become snared in temptations to disregard others; we become cruel and grasping, friendless and we sacrifice principle using unlawful methods to gratify our passion for gain.

The Core Value of Patience

Patience is a core value in which the Christian suffers, endures, or waits as a determination of the will and not simply under necessity. It is the capacity to accept or tolerate delay, trouble or suffering without getting angry. Stuart's mother would have taught him to:

> Rejoice in hope, be patient in tribulation, be constant in prayer. (Rom 12:12)

> But if we hope for what we do not see, we wait for it with patience. (Rom 8:25)

> For I know the plans I have for you, declares the LORD, plans for your welfare and not for evil, to give you a future and a hope. (Jer 29:11)

> Know this my beloved brothers: let every person be quick to hear, slow to speak, slow to anger. (Jas 1:19)

> And endurance produces character, and character produces hope. (Rom 5:4)

> For this is a gracious thing, when, mindful of God, one endures sorrows while suffering unjustly. For what credit is it if, when you sin and are beaten for it, you endure? But if when you do good and suffer for it you endure; this is a gracious thing in the sight of God. For to this you have been called because Christ also suffered for you, leaving you an example, so that you follow in his steps. He committed no sin, neither was deceit found in his mouth. When he was reviled, he did not revile in return; when he suffered, he did not threaten, but continued entrusting himself to him who judges justly. (1 Pet 2:19–23 ESV)

> And the Lord's servant must not be quarrelsome but kind to everyone, able to teach, patiently enduring evil. (2 Tim 2:24)

What wonderful words of comfort and advice from the God of glory. Former prime minister Stuart possesses many of the characteristics outlined in the referenced Scriptures. He suffered much and endured with patience, including the periods after taking up the mantle of parliamentarian and later as prime minister and political leader of Barbados. He did not retaliate nor did he seek vengeance. His testimony is one of faith, hope and endurance.

As leader and prime minister of Barbados, he suffered with the entire country and endured with the patience of Job, the suffering and pain of the worse recession that the world has ever known, and Barbados ever experienced. The patience, one of the fruits of the Holy Spirit, that he demonstrated, could only have been given to him by God. He has often quoted this verse of Scripture from Heb 12:1: "Therefore, since we also are surrounded by such a great cloud of witnesses, let us lay aside every weight and the sin that so easily besets us, and let us run with patience the race that is set before us."

He exhibited his patience by enduring all the difficulties and long-suffering Barbados experienced during his tenure as political leader, by seeking through fiscal and monetary policy to overcome Barbados's worst recession and by enduring trials and testing. This is God's way of perfecting our patience. His example is the Lord God, who is also long suffering toward us: "For it became him, for whom are all things, in bringing all things unto glory, to make the captain of their salvation perfect through suffering" (Heb 2:10).

We too must glory in our tribulations knowing that tribulation works patience, and patience, experience, and experience, hope. The Bible teaches: "Blessed is the man who remains steadfast under trial, for when he has stood the test, he will receive the crown of life, which God has promised to those who love him" (Jas 1:12).

God gives us the power of endurance and patience. God's ambassador of patience, Job, was rewarded double for his trouble, extreme pain and suffering.

The Apostle Paul was also God's ambassador of patience. God sent his disciple Ananias to inform his chosen instrument, Paul, how much he must suffer for the name of Jesus, and Paul's suffering was beyond imagination.

Abraham waited with patience and was rewarded with the promise.

And Christ our perfect example: "The author and finisher of our faith; who for the joy that was set before him endured the cross, despising the shame, and is set down at the right hand of the throne of God" (Heb 12:2).

In the former prime minister's case, the country and region noted that he grew by leaps and bounds and his character appears to be sanctified. The good news is that God will render to each of us who by persistence in doing well seek glory, honor, and immortality, will inherit eternal life. Freundel Stuart was patient in spirit, which is better than being proud in spirit. His self-control and alertness during this specific period, was simply amazing to say the least. Paul had this to say:

> And not only this, but we also exult in our tribulations, knowing that tribulations bring about perseverance, And perseverance proven character; and proven character hope, And hope does not disappoint because the love of God has been poured out

within our hearts through the Holy Spirit who was given to us.
(Rom 5:3–5 NASB)

And Stuart lived by this motto.

The bad news for Christians is that through many afflictions, we must enter the kingdom of God, and many are the afflictions of the righteous. The good news is that God delivers us from all our afflictions. When we are afflicted, God comforts us so that we can comfort others with similar experiences. It does not matter our perplexity nor persecution. It matters not how many times we are struck down, or how many times we are tormented by messengers from Satan, we know that God's grace is sufficient for us.

The Core Value of Forgiveness

The Lord our God is the author of forgiveness and its significance is demonstrated throughout the Scriptures. The psalmist declares:

> Thou, Lord, art good, and ready to forgive; and plenteous in mercy unto all that call upon thee. (Ps 86:5)
> But there is forgiveness with thee, that thou mayest be feared. (Ps 130:4)

God revealed himself to Moses on Mount Sinai and spoke from a cloud and said:

> The Lord, the Lord God, the compassionate and gracious God, slow to anger, abounding in love and faithfulness, Maintaining love to thousands and forgiving wickedness, rebellion and sin yet he does not leave the guilty unpunished. (Exod 34:6–7 NIV)

Jesus too emphasized forgiveness. He taught his disciples to pray:

> Forgive us our debts as we forgive our debtors. (Matt 6:12)

Paul in his Letter to the Ephesians wrote:

> And be ye kind one to another, tender-hearted, forgiving one another, even as God for Christ's sake hath forgiven you. (Eph 4:32)

Stuart's mother taught him that he must forgive all who have wronged him no matter how many times that he suffered at their hands or how grave was the nature of the wrong that was done. She taught him to be kind and tender hearted:

> Not rendering evil for evil, or railing for railing, but contrariwise blessing; knowing that ye are thereunto called, that ye should inherit a blessing. (1 Pet 3:9)

It is important that Christians clothe themselves with appropriate Christian character. Paul writes:

> Therefore, as God's chosen people, holy and dearly beloved: clothe yourself with compassion, kindness, humility, gentleness, and patience. Bear with each other forbearing with one another, and forgive whatever grievances you may have against one another: forgive as the Lord forgave you. (Col 3:12-14 NIV)

The Core Value of Generosity

Stuart's mother would have ensured that he knew verbatim Luke 6:38: "Give and it shall be given unto you; good measure, pressed down, and shaken together, and running over, shall men give into your bosom. For with the same measure that you mete, it shall be measured to you again." He would have learned that it was better to give than to receive and when he gave, it should not be repeated on the mountain top because God sees the good things that we do secretly and will reward us openly.

It is noteworthy that Stuart owned a plot of land. He gave up that land without money and without price for the erection of an evangelical church, and that church today carries out the mandate of Christ himself: to preach the good news of God's kingdom. That lighthouse is still burning and souls are yet being won into the kingdom of God while others are continuing to grow, spiritually.

I am reminded of the noble Cornelius, the first Gentile to receive the gift of the Holy Spirit. Cornelius's prayers and generous giving to the needy came up as a memorial offering before God. God rewarded him with the gift of the Holy Spirit. Stuart's reward for his generosity was that of becoming Barbados's seventh prime minister.

I am confident that Stuart was aware of Paul's exhortation to Timothy:

> As for the rich in this present age, charge them not to be haughty, nor to set their hopes on the uncertainty of riches, but on God, who richly provides us with everything to enjoy. They are to do good, to be rich in good works, to be generous and ready to share, Thus storing up treasures for themselves as a good foundation for the future, so that they may take hold of that which is truly life. (1 Tim 6:17-19 ESV)

The young Stuart had a vision that one day he would become prime minister of Barbados. In due season, in 1994, Stuart participated in electoral politics in Barbados for the very first time. In his first speech after his selection as a candidate, he said that during his political career, some of his challenges would be representation of the poor, to bring healing to those who were overcome by grief, disappointment or despair and to provide comfort for those who felt empty, depressed or downtrodden. He wanted to liberalize those were still psychologically enslaved and articulate a new vision for the people of Barbados, including his critical mission of enfranchising black businesses and small businesses, that had suffered in Barbados for so long and deserved a breakthrough in terms of their development, progress and bottom line. His view was that any programs or policies reaching his desk, his priority would be, how would this program or process be of benefit to the poor, middle class and disadvantaged in our society or alternately how would it disadvantage them?

However, enforcement of this vision was not to be, because God had a more important duty for him at the most critical period in the country's political, social and economic history. The forces and the time unpredictability of the world's worst economic recession would devastate most countries around the world, including Barbados, and had to be given immediate, concentrated and prolonged attention.

Stuart duly won a seat in Parliament in 1994 but lost it in the 1999 general elections, when his party again lost, as they had done in the 1994 elections. Stuart switched ridings in 2003 but lost his bidding as his party again lost that general elections. He was one of his party's two persons appointed to the Senate that year and served in that capacity until he was reelected to the House of Assembly in the general elections of 2008. When Stuart was appointed as a senator in 2003, one of the island's top political scientists, a professor at the University of the West Indies, opined that he would be a "handful" for all the other senators put together. He had observed and noted the depth of wisdom and knowledge endowed in this country politician, whose fired-up approach to debates the country would have discerned when he served in the parliamentary period between 1994 and 1999, and of course, his fiery political speeches at rallies throughout the country.

Stuart returned to the House of Assembly in 2008, as a member of the government team, and was appointed as deputy prime minister, attorney general, and minister of home affairs of Barbados.

Barbados's revered leader and prime minister, the Right Honorable David John Howard Thompson, became terminally ill May 2010 and passed away on October 23 that same year. Freundel Stuart acted as prime minister for the full duration of Thompson's illness and succeeded him as prime minister on October 23, 2010, when he received the support of the majority of the members elected to the House of Assembly.

It is my opinion that in the same manner that God called Joseph, Jacob's son, to be prime minister of Egypt, at a time when the world experienced its first recessionary crisis, the God of heaven called and appointed Freundel Stuart and set him apart, to be the seventh prime minister of Barbados, at a time the world would experience its worst recessionary crisis in one hundred years.

Yes, he was the son of a single maid, whom God chose to be the mother of the seventh prime minister of Barbados. The God of Israel, Barbados and the entire universe sees each of us as individual human beings whom he created for service and to worship him, and no matter what our situation, our status in society, no matter how our communities look down or up on us, it is all about God. Yes, many are called, few are chosen, and God chose to promote Freundel Stuart to the highest political office in the land:

> For promotion cometh neither from the east, nor from the west, nor from the south. But God is the judge: he putteth down one and setteth up another. (Ps 75:6–7)

Prime Minister Stuart's Handling of a Perceived Coup

Freundel Stuart was sworn in as the seventh prime minister of Barbados on October 23, 2010, and by October 2011, a leading newspaper carried an article captioned "DLP Rift," in which it alleged that eleven government members, including seven senior cabinet ministers, had affixed their signatures to a formal letter and immediately dispatching the said letter to Prime Minister Stuart requesting an "urgent" audience with him. The newspaper reported that a copy of the letter was in their possession and it stated: "Against the backdrop of growing concern among supporters of the government and our party, with respect to perceived weaknesses in our leadership of the country, and a sense of drift and inertia arising therefrom, we the undersigned elected members of the Parliamentary Group seek an urgent audience with you to discuss matters of grave concern to us as well as to chart a path forward for the retention of our party in government."[1]

As far as this so-called eager eleven is concerned, the magnitude of the situation was so grave and their concern about the implications so deep that this "urgent audience" with the prime minister was requested before he traveled on government business (within two days). (Lest peradventure

---

1. Luigi Marshall, "DLP Rift?," *NationNews* (Barbados), December 11, 2011.

he heard while he was on foreign soil that Barbados had installed its eighth prime minister and he was returning home as a depleted and depressed member of parliament.)

It appears to me that a group of political terrorists, acting from without the corridors of the government and outside the fold of the ruling Democratic Labor Party, infiltrated the minds and hearts of the ruling party, as they had done successfully some sixteen years earlier. At that time the government and the ruling party were infiltrated, divided and conquered and eventually banished to political oblivion for fourteen consecutive years.

We are reminded in God's word that we are to: "Watch out for those who cause divisions and put obstacles in your way that are contrary to the teachings that you have learnt. Keep away from them" (Rom 16:17). Fortunately, this apparent attempt was nipped in the bud, scorched by the sun and withered away like seeds planted on rocky land, without much earth to propagate roots.

I am sure that Prime Minister Stuart understood that

> no weapon formed against me will prevail and you will refute every tongue that accuses you. This is the heritage of the servants of the LORD, and this is their vindication from me, declares the LORD. (Isa 54:17)

> And we know that in all things, God works for the good of those who love him, who have been called according to his purpose. (Rom 8:28)

The psalmist David put it this way:

> They confronted me in the day of my calamity, but the LORD was my stay. (Ps 18:18)

The wisest man that ever lived looked at it another way:

> A wise man is strong and a man of knowledge increases power. (Prov 24:5)

> Wisdom strengthens a wise man more than ten rulers (or eleven) who are in a city. (Eccl 7:19)

> A wise man scales the city of the mighty and brings down the stronghold in which they trust. (Prov 21:22)

Christ himself put it best:

> No one can enter a strong man's house and plunder his goods, unless he first binds the strong man. And then he will plunder his goods. (Mark 3:27)

Prime Minister Stuart did not allow this perceived threat of a coup to get under his skin. He did not allow it to undermine him or hinder him. With the coolness and calmness of a cucumber, with the courage and strength of a lion, and with the confidence and wisdom of Solomon, he conquered the situation. According to him, he had found no evidence of an attempted palace coup against him. He reported that he was leading a hard-working, united government, carrying out the programs of the government within the context of its economic constraints.

He announced that if there was indeed an attempt to derail his government, it had clearly not worked. He argued that if there was an attempted coup, the laws of history would apply so that if the coup succeeded, the person at whom the coup was aimed would pay for it with his neck, but if the coup failed, the plotters and those who were trying to execute it would pay for with their necks.

I am confident that at that grim moment, the prime minister was comforted with the words of the Apostle Peter: "And the God of all Grace who called you to his eternal glory in Christ, after you have suffered a while, will himself restore you and make you strong, firm and steadfast" (1 Pet 5:10). When all the commotion was over, Stuart stood tall; well cemented as prime minister of Barbados and as leader of the Democratic Labour Party.

The words of the psalmist David would also have comforted him:

> Behold, he that keeps Israel will neither slumber nor sleep. The LORD is thy keeper: The LORD is thy shade upon thy right hand. The sun shall not smite thee by day, nor the moon by night. The LORD shall preserve thee from all evil: he shall preserve thy soul. The LORD shall preserve thy going out and thy coming in from this time forth, and even forevermore. (Ps 121:4–8)

He would also have been comforted with these words:

> The name of the LORD is a strong tower: the righteous runs into it and is safe. (Prov 18:10)

Prime Minister Stuart must have recognized that his party needed consensus to prevent his party from falling apart, and with a terrible crash. He succeeded in uniting the parliamentary group and the entire party, and his leadership was concreted not only in the parliamentary group and the party but also throughout the whole country. He knew that a united party will stand but a party would fall if it is divided against itself.

For him, it was better to promote peace, harmony, quiet, calm and control between others rather than discord, dissention, factions, strife and contentions. Paul wrote to Titus:

> But avoid foolish disputes, genealogies, contentions, and strivings about the law; for they are unprofitable and useless. Reject a divisive man after the first and second admonition, knowing that such a person is corrupt and sinful, being self-condemned. (Titus 3:9–11 NKJV)

Former prime minister Stuart recognized that interrelationships between members are important and he was not inclined to treat the matter as an attempted coup to destroy his leadership and his party. He approached it from a position of love rather than hate and vengeance which belong to the Lord. Love thinks no evil and that is why he thought the best of his fellow parliamentarians and would have assigned the best of motives to his action. Wisdom indeed.

Forgiveness as a Leadership Tool and as a Core Value

The spirit of forgiveness would have applied to this situation. Forgiveness here refers to the restoration of relationships that entails the removal of objective guilt, and by extension, being slow to anger, abounding in love, mercy, compassion and graciousness; bearing with and forgiving each other. The Apostle Paul wrote in his Letter to the Ephesians:

> Be kind to one another, tender hearted, forgiving one another, as God in Christ forgave you. (Eph 4:32)

Christ himself taught:

> For if you forgive people when they sin against you, your heavenly Father will also forgive you. But if you do not forgive others their sins, your Father will not forgive your sins. (Matt 6:14–15)

Christ when teaching that we should often pray, taught that whenever we pray, we should pray that God would forgive us our trespasses even as we forgive them that trespass against us. If we are to obtain God's mercy and favor, we are also to be merciful to others.

Christ outlined the correct procedures for handling wrongdoing against each other. He taught:

> If your brother or sister sins, go and point out their fault, just between the two of you. If they listen to you, you have won them

> over. But if they will not listen, take one or two along, so that every matter maybe established by the testimony of two or three witnesses. If they still refuse to listen, tell it to the church, and if they refuse to listen even to the church, treat them as you would a pagan or a tax collector. (Matt 18:15–17 NIV)

This process was presented for the church but it equally applies in the secular world and when applied, it produces a good outcome. Fortunately, these apparent matters were nipped in the bud and the potential painful outcome was avoided. That battle was won and there was no noticeable shedding of even one drop of blood.

Prime Minister Stuart would have demonstrated his spirit of love and forgiveness by retaining all ministers of the crown in their ministerial portfolios. He pursued a policy of peace and the building up of each other rather than tearing down and destroying each other. Godly wisdom again prevailed in these circumstances. The psalmist put it this way:

> He does not deal with us according to our sins, nor repay us according to our iniquities. For as high as the heavens are above the earth, so great is his steadfast love toward those who fear him; As far as the east is from the west, so far does he remove our transgression from us. As the father shows compassion to his children, so the LORD shows compassion to those who fear him. For he knows our frame; he knows that we are dust. (Ps 103:10–14)

But of course, a coup was probably just a figment of somebody's imagination, and without merit.

Foreign Exchange Controls

Barbados suffered several credit rating downgrades by international rating agencies Standard & Poor's and Moody's even amid the government's cost-cutting measures to tame a runaway deficit, and this caused economists to predict that the Barbados dollar could be devalued, while others called on the Barbados government to enter a standby arrangement with the International Monetary Fund (IMF), to help with the country's ailing economy. They believed that an IMF deal would allow government to avoid any further erosion of the balance of payments, and that a standby arrangement would allow Barbados's access to cheaper financing to help fuel growth to the economy.

It is acknowledged that an IMF standby arrangement is a facility through which member countries borrow a specified amount of money over a one-year or two-year period to overcome short-term cyclical balance of payments difficulties and support macroeconomic stabilization programs. Loan repayments are usually made within a three-to-five-year period. The performance criteria for release of the money is usually so harsh that many countries view this type of arrangement with suspicion and something to be avoided at all costs.

Fixed Exchange Rate Policy

Former prime minister Stuart was well aware that devaluation of currencies in Barbados would not improve price competitiveness but was more likely to cause high inflation and economic contraction. He stated that despite Barbados's fiscal and economic challenges, Barbados will stick with a fixed exchange rate policy. Barbados had taken the decision in 1975 to fix the exchange rate to the United States dollar and Barbados depended on it for forty years and protected it with all the vigor at its command. He said that those who blithely and glibly argue that Barbados's currency is overvalued have not yet been able to show how devaluation has improved spectacularly the situation of Barbados's neighbors who have pursued that course. He further argued that devaluation is a policy response to the disequilibrium in a country's balance of payments and quoted from Barbados's eminent economist Sir Arthur Lewis, who stated:

> Devaluation raises the cost of imports and therefore the cost of living. This provokes demand for high wages and other incomes. If they are granted, part or all the devaluation would be cancelled out by the increase in domestic costs. A country devalues if costs are out of line in export industries or the alternatives, wage subsidies are too costly for the budget. There is no point in devaluing unless this will increase the volume of exports so that the elasticity of supply of exports and the elasticity of world demand are the two factors which determine whether a country should devalue or apply import controls instead.[2]

Stuart declared that this argument is as valuable today as when it was first expressed and that the passage of time and personalities had done nothing to sully the freshness of the analytical rigor. He stated that given the position that Barbados was in, it did not justify any tampering with

---

2. W. Arthur Lewis, *Development Planning: Essentials of Economic Policy*, 6th ed. (London: Allan & Unwin, 1966), 41.

the exchange rate and that he and his cabinet would continue to make the exchange rate a matter of priority. The former prime minister recognized that "the rich rules over the poor, and the borrower is slave to the lender" (Prov 22:7), and he must have considered the prolonged hardship his fellow Barbadians would have had to endure if Barbados were to enter a standby arrangement with the IMF, and then decided that it was not worth it to cause Barbadians such pain and horror. The questions former prime minister Stuart had to answer was whether Barbados needed to adjust its tried and proven foreign exchange policy and whether Barbados was willing to become a slave to the International Monetary Fund. He had to sit down and determine what deleterious effects foreign exchange controls and an IMF arrangement would have on the society of Barbados.

Foreign Reserve Maintenance

On the other side, reserve accumulation has some impact on credit ratings and helps to improve the sustainability of the external position and Barbados's credit ratings could have been much worse if it did not maintain adequate levels of foreign reserves. Stuart defended the fixed exchange rate which was pegged to the US dollar. He noted that the fixed exchange rate had served Barbados well for over forty years and that Barbados through its policy choices will continue to make the preservation of that exchange rate a matter of continuing priority. The build-up of foreign reserves are our savings for our future purchases of goods and services that we need and that is not available in our country or it will be more efficient to purchase from abroad. In other words, having built up the foreign reserves to an amount which is greater than the twelve-week safety threshold, it would be unwise to deplete it with outlandish spending. To put this in a spiritual context: "The wise store up food and choice olive oil, but a fool gulp theirs down" (Prov 21:20).

In the meantime, the Stuart administration borrowed substantially from the Central Bank of Barbados and the National Insurance Scheme of Barbados (printed money) to sustain what many considered an overpopulated workforce. He knew that to reduce the size of employment in government would cause many families pain beyond comprehension and he too would have felt the pain in the heart of his belly, because he would have experienced that kind of infirmity firsthand, having been raised by a working-class mother, working as a maid, for below minimum wage, after his father died tragically in an accident when he was but a child. The challenge that Stuart faced as head of the cabinet of Barbados was how to reduce that debt to sustainable levels without putting families on the breadline. How to achieve the right balance of payment position in order to maintain the stability of the Barbados currency. How to keep the unemployment rate low. How to keep down inflation. How to maintain the parity of the Barbados dollar, while at the same time pursuing economic policies to bring growth to the Barbados economy. And that was a daunting but manageable task.

Stuart Scorned as the Silent Man

When his detractors could find nothing with which to accuse and smear former prime minister Stuart, a chorus was started calling him the silent man. Many believed that he should have spoken on every issue raised in Barbados. The silent "do little" man, as one specific journalist liked to call him, needed to go to Mount Hillaby, the highest part of Barbados, and shout from the top of his voice "abra cadabra" and all Barbados's economic, social, environmental and governance problems would disappear like Houdini. Everything in Barbados will be good again, and Barbadians will live happily ever after like at the conclusion of a fairy-tale movie. They believed that he was the right person to decide on all issues raised in Barbados without regards to its nature or context. Taking responsibility for all issues would have had the deleterious effect of stress, distress, serious illnesses and eventually death. In Exodus 18, Moses was spending so much energy and time hearing all the complaints of the Israelites that he could not get to very important work. Jethro, his father-in-law, recommended that Moses delegate most of this workload to others (create a cabinet) so that he could concentrate his efforts on work only he could do. In the governance of a country, there will naturally be many disputes, many questions of interpretation for decisions, and so many key and important things that require action, that it would be impossible for a single person, who despite their best efforts, would be able to faithfully complete. Prime Minister Stuart recognized that there were ministers in his cabinet and officers in the public service who were abundantly capable of making proper decisions, and that delegating duties and responsibilities relieved him of some of the burden, while at the same time improved the quality of the governance. To do everything would have been an unwise utilization of energies.

The wise man Solomon teaches that, "when words are many, transgression is not lacking, but whosoever restrains his lips is prudent" (Prov 10:19). The wise man knew that too much babbling without the appropriate care and deep thought would lead to ineffective conversation, the possibility of saying things which are not true, or idle, and may lead to destructive condemnation.

The former prime minister chose to bridle his tongue, chose not to speak rashly or inconsiderably, to speak from a position of knowledge, careful forethought and sound judgment, ensuring that what he said was the truth and properly spoken, rather than unknowingly stating a falsehood or making some form of misstep. Solomon put it another way:

> He who restrains his words has knowledge and he who has a cool spirit is a man of understanding. Even a fool when he keeps silent is considered wise; when he closes his lips is considered prudent. (Prov 17:27-28)

Put differently, a wise person knows when to speak, where to speak and to whom he should speak. He has a command of himself and does not speak rashly nor hastily. And even when others consider him to be a fool, he does not betray his folly with words and therefore is considered wise. We must keep quiet if we have nothing worthwhile to say. It is better to hear, learn and then speak from a position of knowledge and power. Former prime minister Stuart has never spoken out of turn and never in contradiction nor usurpation of any of his fellow colleagues in the Cabinet of Barbados or public servants. He spoke after careful thought and when decisions had been agreed.

Job was a blameless and upright man of God who had overcome the evil one. He was a man of impeccable integrity, rich beyond comprehension and as usual if you are rich you will be well known and people will treat you with respect, dignity and prestige. But the accuser of God's faithful children, Satan, accused Job of being faithful to God only because he was rich. As a matter of fact, Christ himself said:

> Truly I say to you that with difficulty a rich person will enter the kingdom of heaven! And again, I say unto you it is easier for a camel to go through the eye of a needle than for a rich man to into the kingdom of heaven. (Matt 19:23-24)

God allowed the devil to put Job's faith to the test. The devil robbed Job of all his children, employees and all of his wealth, including his home. The devil's attack on Job did not end there. Job's physique was attacked with sores so viciously that Job was not physically recognizable. Job's wife then instructed him to curse God and die, but Job endured his suffering in silence.

Job's friends accused him of sinning against God. They believed, as we do today, that if we trust and serve God, we would prosper no holds barred.

But our faithfulness and loyalty to God may be tried, tested and proven. This was Job's response to his friends:

> Would a wise man answer with empty notions or fill his belly with the hot east wind? Would he argue with useless words, with speeches that have no value? (Job 15:2–3)

Job never deviated from his love for God and remained silent in his suffering. He recognized that God's grace was sufficient for him. Job passed the spiritual fitness test with flying colors and of course, God restored him double for everything that was taken away from him; double for his trouble:

> The Lord blessed the latter part of Job's life more than the first.
> ... Nowhere in the land were there found women as beautiful as Job's daughters. (Job 42:12–15)

Stuart learned to speak in the right circumstances. He learned this from the Master himself. According to Isa 53:7, Jesus was oppressed and afflicted but did not open his mouth. His oppressors led him like a lamb to be slaughtered and like a sheep before his shearers, but he did not open his mouth. Jesus kept his silence even when he faced his threatening accusers, including the chief priest, Pilate, and Herod.

When Stuart spoke out, we could trust his word. He could put together sophisticated speeches but it was his character that gave weight to his word. He lived his life in such a way that when he spoke, his words were heavy, but his silence was heavier than his words. His character produced a very heavy silence, a strong inner life that exhibited integrity and honor.

While reviewing the success of former prime minister Freundel Stuart, we can think of this passage of Scripture taken from the first letter of St. Paul to the church at Corinth:

> For ye see your calling, brethren, how that not many wise men after the flesh, not many mighty, not many noble, are called: But God hath chosen the foolish things of the world to confound the wise; and God hath chosen the weak things of the world to confound the things which are mighty; And base things of the world, and things which are despised, hath God chosen, yea, and things which are not, to bring to nought things that are: That no flesh should glory in his presence. But of him are ye in Christ Jesus, who of God is made unto us wisdom, and righteousness, and sanctification, and redemption. (1 Cor 1:26–30)

Stuart, His Government, and His Party Are Deposed

Then came May 24, 2018. The day of reckoning for Freundel Stuart and his Democratic Labour Party government. That was the day of the general election in Barbados. The Democratic Labour Party, under the leadership of Prime Minister Freundel Jerome Stuart suffered the worst electoral defeat in the history of Barbadian politics. They did not win a single seat of the thirty seats in the House of Assembly of Barbados.

As a leader, Stuart knew who he was, but many did not understand his philosophy. It was a bit sad that intellectual Barbadians were looking for a charismatic personality, a person who appeared to be eloquent in speech, a person with a dynamic personality, and one with scholastic excellence, openness and flamboyance, talkativeness, with an extroverted personality. Stuart has all these, but these don't qualify a person for leadership. Leaders are persons that blossom and produce the fruits of their hidden potential in extraordinary circumstances. Leaders prove to themselves and others that they are trustworthy, respectable, and credible, and have their priorities settled.

We can safely conclude that Stuart was a principled politician. Unfortunately, some politicians are power hungry, while others have defects such as low-esteem, poor self-concept, and try to make up for it by attempting to grab power and position. Some politicians are concerned about the next elections only, and are preoccupied making promises without purpose. Great leaders are concerned with the next generation. They think about what effect history will have on yet unborn children. They think about heritage and destiny.

Stuart does not believe that leadership is a product of natural endowment and all others are to be servants. Neither does he believe that it is a product of a person's birth trait and if you don't have it you become a servant. Some of us still believe that to be a leader you need white or fair pigmentation, thin lips and pointed noses. His success should not be judged based on the accolades or lack thereof from call-in programs, the media, etc., but should be judged on what God instructed him to do and how effective and efficient he completed those tasks. He should not be judged on how he preserved history, but on how through him, history was made. He should not be judged on how he preserved and protected traditions, but on how he made traditions. He should not be judged on whether he was married to the past, but on whether he was able to contribute to the future. He should not be judged on intellectual capacity, although he obtained outstanding qualifications from the University of the West Indies, but should be judged on his values, high standard of moral ethics, that is, his character. His character is his destiny.

Theodore Roosevelt said that "character in the long run is the decisive factor in the life of an individual and of nations alike." A person's character is all that they have. No person should sell their character for any price. They should not make deals or compromises with their character, but should walk away from everything that will negatively interfere with their character, because without character every other aspect of leadership is at risk. Leaders will not be remembered by their compromises but by what they stood for. Far too many "better-offs and higher-ups" collapse because they violated their character. Too many underhanded things are done in the darkness of night, when everyone else is sleeping, no one is watching, and when they think that no one would find out. We will build trust when we pursue with all our passion the direction of character.

Leadership requires following your own convictions, depending on your self-image, self-worth and self-esteem, and not on the popular interests. Stuart's focus was passion, purpose, and the people's interest. They were certain principles that he would not violate, and they were standards in life that he did not break. He allowed no one to define him nor determine his limitations. He was always true to himself. He believed in the untested and the untried, that is, if it was not done before, it does not mean that it could not be done. Those who were looking to control Stuart were grievously mistaken. Great leaders are uncontrollable because it is difficult to break their faith and position, and they stand out. They do not follow tradition; they destroy boundaries and ask questions that you cannot answer. They make you angry because they are true to themselves and are no one else's clone.

It is reported that on that destructive night, that fateful night of May 24, 2018, Stuart stood with courage, strength and humility as he waited at the ghost town of his party's headquarters for the election results. He was there alone, except for his longtime trusted friend and not more than one or two others, who stood in empathy and solid support with him in his moment of agony and pain, to face the exuberant media. There were no politicians from his party left standing when the nails were being driven into the hands and feet of the existing government. It is not that easy when your team is so severely beaten and left on the Jericho Road for dead. But dead they were not. Badly beaten and bruised, yes, but sufficiently alive to allow for full recovery. How quickly they rise from the agony of defeat will depend on whether they have the will to live by taking the appropriate medicine, even if it is bitter medicine.

Stuart, the godly man that he is, stood tall and accepted all blame for his party's demoralizing and demeaning loss. In so doing, he also silently accepted the blame for all the strikes, go-slows, and recurring marches which became the new order of negotiating for the unions. He accepted the blame for all the foreign materials found in the piping system of the South Coast Sewage Plant, which caused its malfunctioning and resulted in sewage flowing on to the streets. He accepted the blame for all the litigation that was taking place, for example at the proposed new Andrews Sugar Factory, the new Hyatt Hotel, and the Barbados National Terminal Company Limited. Simply put, he took ownership of everything consequential. And so, he walked away with his integrity intact. His honesty, and as one editorial put it, "His uncompromising commitment to correctness and lawfulness has never been questioned."[3]

And so, his legacy of moral uprightness, a leaders' most important asset, will live until the end of time.

---

3. Kaymar Jordan, "This Is the House That Mr. Stuart Burnt," *Barbados Today*, editorial, May 30, 2018.

Chapter 9

Prosperity through Obedience

"If they obey and serve him, they will spend the rest of their days in prosperity and their years in contentment [pleasantries]" (Job 36:11). Obedience is defined as compliance with a law, order or request, or submission to an authority. God is our supreme authority and he has proclaimed a set of rules, statutes, laws, ordinances, judgments and covenants that all mankind is required to obey. We are given the choice of obedience to God with everlasting rewards or disobedience to God with eternal consequences. Sin is defined as disobedience to God's laws and often our disobedience to God stands in the way of our prosperity and will prevent us from receiving our eternal reward of being with our Lord forever when he returns to this world for his glorious church. The Bible teaches us that if we obey him, we will spend our life in prosperity and contentment.

OBEDIENCE BRING FOOD SECURITY

In Isaiah 1, through his noble prophet, God called out the nation of Israel for their sins and wickedness. He compared them to the people of Sodom and Gomorrah, on whom, because of their impiety and wickedness, he imposed the divine judgment of fire and brimstone. These cities were particularly known for their homosexuality, false security, greed, idolatry, gluttony, drunkenness, and refusal to reverence God. While they refused to be obedient to God's message and continued in sin, they remained isolated from

God, and his favor was withdrawn from them, although he was unwilling to abandon them completely.

The multiplicity of their sacrifices was unacceptable to God and their prayers became an abomination. God implored them to stop committing evil deeds and be sanctified. Then they could reason with him. Their sins were like scarlet and he promised to make them white like snow, and though they were as crimson, he would make them as wool. God called on the people of Judah to show willingness and obedience so that they may eat of the good of the land: "If you are willing and obedient, you shall eat of the good of the land" (Isa 1:19).

This is God's promise to us as well that when we obey his word, he will be our Jehovah Jireh. The psalmist put it this way: "He shall be like a tree planted by the rivers of water that bringeth forth its fruit in its season, whose leaf also shall not wither; and whatever he does shall prosper" (Ps 1:3). In Psalm 23, we learn that God allows us to lie down in green pastures and restores our souls. He prepares a table before us in the presence of our enemies. He anoints our head with oil and our cup overflows. Goodness and mercy will also follow us for all our lives.

The story is told about Jesus when he taught a multitude from Simon Peter's boat at the Sea of Galilee. When he had finished teaching the crowd, he instructed Peter to launch his boat into the deep waters and let down his fishing nets so that he could catch some fish. Peter told the Master that he and his other fishing colleagues had worked all night and caught no fish: "Nevertheless," Peter said, "at your word, I will let down the net" (Luke 5:5). Peter obeyed our Lord and let down his net and it happened. A great miracle took place. There were so many fish in the nets that the they began to break. They called their fellow fishermen in the other boat and filled both boats with so much fish that the boats began to sink. Peter, James and John were astonished at the large catch that resulted from obedience to our Lord and Savior, Jesus Christ. Prosperity definitely comes from obeying God.

OBEDIENCE GUARANTEES LONG LIFE

The Bible teaches us that there will be lifelong benefits and peace from obeying God's instructions: "My son, do not forget my law, but let your heart keep my commands. For length of days and long life and peace they will add to you" (Prov 3:1–2).

We also read that "the fear of the Lord leads to life and he who has it will abide in satisfaction. He will not be visited with evil" (Prov 19:23). Here is the deal. We must read, mark and inwardly digest God's Holy Word. We must write his words on the tablet of our hearts and we must be obedient to his word. When we are obedient to his Word, we will reap the benefits of long life, peace, and satisfaction, and we will be protected from the torment of evil Satan. We do not have to spend our last dime trying to extend our physical life by one day. We need only be obedient to God.

In accordance with Eph 6:1–3, children are advised to obey their parents in the Lord because this is right. They must give honor to their parents because this is the first commandment with the promise of well-being and long life.

OBEDIENCE ENSURES PROSPERITY AND GOOD SUCCESS

"This book of the law shall not depart out of your mouth, but you shall meditate therein day and night, that you mayest observe to do according to all that is written therein: for then thou shall make thy way prosperous, and then thou shall have good success" (Josh 1:8). Joshua was second in command to Moses, and he took over the leadership of Israel after Moses had passed away. The Israelites sojourned in the wilderness for forty years before Joshua triumphantly led them into the land that God promised them.

Joshua was an outstanding military leader who was careful to trust and obey God for victory for the people of Israel. As long as Israel remained obedient to God, they were ensured victory over their enemies. After their successful battle of Jericho, the Israelites were responsible for collecting all the silver and gold, and vessels of bronze and iron, and deliver them into the treasury of the Lord, for they were to be consecrated to the Lord. But the Israelites disobeyed God by taking the accursed thing from Jericho, which God had instructed them not to take: "Israel has sinned, and they have transgressed my Covenant which I commanded them. For they have taken some of the accursed things, and have both stolen and deceived; and they have also put it among their own stuff" (Josh 7:11). Obedience brings victory and disobedience results in defeat at the hands of the enemy. As a result of this act of disobedience the Israelites were defeated at the battle of Ai. It is important to note that one person's faithfulness to God can result in the success of a nation, and contrariwise, another person's sin can lead to the defeat of an entire nation.

"He who opens his ear to instruction, and commands that they turn from iniquity. If they obey and serve him, they will spend their days in prosperity, and their years in pleasures" (Job 36:10–11). Job was a prosperous agriculturist who loved and obeyed God. He was faultless, righteous and served God and did no wickedness. God was so pleased with Job's worship that he boasted about it. Satan then put Job's faithfulness to God to the test. He took away all Job's possessions and killed all his employees and children. Job then worshiped God, declaring that the Lord giveth and the Lord taketh away and blessed be the name of the Lord.

Finally, Satan afflicted Job with leprosy from the crown of his head to the sole of his feet. The affliction was so severe that Job took a piece of pottery to scrape his flesh. His friends visited him to comfort him, but they did not recognize him from a distance. His wife advised him to give up on God and die, but his response was that if we accept prosperity from God, we must also be willing to accept misfortune. One of Job's friends accused him of sinning against God. Job responded by saying: "As for me, I know that my redeemer lives, and at the last day he will take his stand on the earth" (Job 19:25). Job appreciated his wealth, but that was not his priority. He looked forward that one day, he would meet and greet his living Redeemer. He was keen on the eternal prosperity of his soul. For Job's faithfulness and obedience, God prospered him with twice as much as he had before his affliction. God's favor was on him more in the latter part of his life than in the earlier part of his life. Sometimes Christians are afflicted and struck down. We know that our resurrected Lord lives and will deliver us from all our distresses.

OBEDIENCE ALLOWS GOD TO CHOOSE US

In times of crisis, God always looked for someone to stand in the gap and lead his people:

> The people of the land have practiced oppression and committed robbery, and they have wronged the poor and needy and have oppressed the sojourner without justice. I have searched for a man among them who will build the wall and stand in the gap before me for the land so that I would not destroy it; but I found no one. (Ezek 22:29–30)

Ezekiel was called to stand in the gap for God. He chose to obey God and illustrated his message on one occasion by lying on his side for three hundred and ninety days, during which he ate one eighth-ounce meal per day cooked over manure; he shaved his head and beard; and could show no sorrow at the passing of his spouse. As God's watchman for the house of Israel, he preached God's judgment against idolatry, challenging the people to turn from their sins to serve the true and living God. He also preached

God's message of hope and his faithfulness. It was Ezekiel who was led by the Spirit to prophesy to the valley of dry bones that restored them to life.

If we do not own Christ as Savior, we too, like the valley of dry bones, are spiritually dead, but God promised to restore us, to restore the church, and to restore our nation to life again.

Moses stood in the gap. He took off his sandals so that he could stand on holy ground. Then led the people of Israel from the oppression of slavery.

Joshua stood in the gap. He too took off his sandals and stood in a holy place before leading the children of Israel into the promised land of Canaan.

Isaiah stood in the gap. He had a vision in which he saw the Lord, high and lifted up. He heard when the seraphim cried to each other and said: "Holy, holy, holy is the Lord of Hosts; the whole earth is full of his glory."

This led Isaiah to confess:

> Woe is me, for I am undone! Because I am a man of unclean lips and I dwell in the midst of a people of unclean lips. For my eyes have seen the King, the Lord of Hosts. Then one of the Seraphim flew to me, having in his hand a live coal which he had taken with the tongs from the altar. And he touched me with it, and said: Behold, this has touched your lips; your iniquity is taken away, and your sin is purged. (Isa 6:3–7)

It was Isaiah who prophesied how the King of kings and Lord of lords would grow up; how he would be despised and rejected by us; that he would bear our griefs and our sorrows and would eventually die for our sins and our healing.

Jeremiah stood in the gap. God chose him and sanctified him before he was born to be his messenger. God touched his mouth and said: "See, I have set you over the nations and over the kingdoms, to root out and to pull down, to destroy and to throw down, to build and to plant" (Jer 1:10).

John the Baptist stood in the gap. He was preordained by God to be the forerunner (Mal 3:1) to our Lord and Savior, Jesus Christ. He was the greatest prophet who ever lived. Christ said: "I tell you, among those born of women there is no one greater than John" (Luke 7:28). His uncompromising message was repentance from sin because God's kingdom was near.

GOD HONORS THE REQUESTS OF HIS BELIEVERS

Jesus left Bethany and was on his way back to Jerusalem. He was hungry. He saw a fig tree which was growing by the side of the road and hoped to eat some fruit from the tree. Jesus was disappointed that there were no fruits on the tree and cursed the tree by commanding that no fruits grow again on that fig tree. By the next morning, the tree had withered away. When his disciples saw what happened, they were filled with admiration and astonishment as they wondered how the fig tree dried up so soon. Jesus responded by telling them:

> Truly I tell you, If you have faith and do not doubt, not only will you do what was done to the fig tree, but even if you say to this mountain, be lifted up and thrown into the sea, it will happen. If you believe you will receive whatever you ask in prayer. (Matt 21:21–22)

Faith is of critical importance for the believer whenever he approaches God's throne of mercy and grace to make known to him our requests and supplications. Whatever is asked will be granted, provided that we have no doubts of any kind in our hearts.

A remarkable story of faith is recorded in Luke 7. After Jesus had preached to great multitudes from the mountain, he visited Capernaum with the multitude following him. While Jesus was there, a centurion's faithful and dear employee was very sick and ready to die. The centurion heard about Jesus and believed in him. He sent elders of the Jews to him with a specific and fervent request, that Jesus would urgently come and heal his servant. Jesus acceded to the centurion's request and accompanied the elders to the centurion's house.

When Jesus was near the house, the centurion sent friends to deliver a second message to Jesus. Recognize that the centurion addressed him as "Lord." He humbly declared his unworthiness to be in the presence of Jesus, although he believed in the power of Jesus. This is what he said:

> Wherefore neither thought I myself worthy to come to thee; but only say the word, and my servant shall be healed. For I am a man set under authority, having under myself soldiers, and I say to one, Go, and he goeth, and to another, Come, and he cometh; and to my servant, Do this, and he doeth it. (Luke 7:7–8)

Jesus marveled at him and told the crowd that this was the greatest faith that he had seen in all Israel.

In the gospel according to St. John, Jesus told his disciples: "If you remain in me and my words remain in you, ask whatever you wish, and it will be given you" (John 15:7). Christians will not receive from God by doing good deeds, being honest and trying to do what is right. Christians must be part of the attachment to Christ and his word like a branch that is attached to a tree. With the Christ-centered experience, all efforts to receive from God will be fruitful.

Christ also taught us that we must

> ask, and it will be given to you, seek and you will find, knock and the door will be opened to you. For everyone who asks, receives; he who seeks finds; and to him who knocks, the door will be opened. (Matt 7:6–8)

Christ has this simple lesson for us. We must ask and God will give. When we make our requests, we must believe that he will grant them. We must ask in faith because whatever is not of faith is sin. There must not be the slightest doubt in our hearts because when we doubt, we are like the wave on the sea which is driven with the wind and tossed. When we believe God and trust him where we cannot trace him, we can expect great and mighty results. Christ promised that if we believe him, we will receive whatever we ask in prayer, but we must ask because when we ask, we receive, when we seek, we find, and when we knock, doors are thrown wide open.

The Apostle John repeated our Lord's message. In 1 John 3, we read:

> Beloved if our hearts do not condemn us, we have this confidence before God. And we will receive from him whatever we ask, because we keep his commandments, and do what is pleasing in his sight. (1 John 3:21–22)

There must be no condemnation in our hearts. We are condemned when we do not believe in him, in his power to supply our needs and fill our prescriptions. We must recognize that when we are obedient to his commandments, and please him, whatever we ask him for, he will give it to us. John further states:

> These things have I written unto you that believe on the name of the Son of God; that ye may know that ye have eternal life, and that ye may believe on the name of the Son of God. And this is the confidence that we have in him, that, if we ask any thing according to his will, he heareth us: And if we know that he hear us, whatsoever we ask, we know that we have the petitions that we desired of him. (1 John 5:13–15)

John is stating categorically that he is writing to believers whose testimony is that they have eternal life. We must approach God fearlessly, with a clear, pure conscience, and full of confidence. We must not ask with the wrong motives or wrong desires or with pleasurable intent because we are unlikely to get a positive response from God. Our requests must be in accordance with his will and we can claim victory that God has complied with our request; that there is tangible evidence that we have already received what we asked for.

"Be anxious for nothing, but in everything, by prayer and petition, with thanksgiving, present your requests to God" (Phil 4:6). Anxiety is failure to trust God and his power and our doubts concerning what he taught us in his word. That doubt or lack of faith in God is a sin because anything that is not of faith is a sin, and without faith, it is impossible to please God. Christians spend too much time worrying and less time praying, believing and thanking. We worry about our homes, about our jobs, about our schools, our circumstances. Paul's advice is to quit worrying and through prayer, lay all on God's altar of compassion and mercy and faithfulness.

When we pray, we must always remember to thank God for satisfying our requests in advance of receiving them. Faith is the substance of what we pray for and although we cannot see it, God has already given it to us. It is already in our possession and we must thank God because he is good and his mercies endure forever. He has done excellent things including taking our sins in his body on the cross. He has given us peace that surpasses all our understanding. Indeed, we should thank and praise him for bringing us through every situation, seen and unseen, and for answering our prayers of faith.

OBEDIENCE ENSURES GOD'S INHERITANCE

> By faith Abraham, when he was called to go out into a place which he should after receive for an inheritance, obeyed; and he went out, not knowing whither he went. By faith he sojourned in the land of promise, as in a strange country, dwelling in tabernacles with Isaac and Jacob, the heirs with him of the same promise: For he looked for a city which hath foundations, whose builder and maker is God. (Heb 11:8–10)

What tremendous faith. It must be repeated that without faith it is impossible to please God. God spoke to Abraham and advised him to leave his home country, his family and his father's house and go to a land that he would show him. God promised to make him a great nation, bless him, make him famous, make him a blessing, bless them that blessed him, curse those who cursed him, and in him, all the families of the earth would be blessed.

Abraham believed and obeyed God and went to the land which God gave him as an inheritance. He lived in the land by faith, but confidently looked forward to an eternal home in a city whose designer, builder and ruler is God. Abraham looked in hope for that eternal inheritance and all God's people, also look in hope to inheriting this home with Abraham:

> And I saw a new heaven and a new earth: for the first heaven and the first earth were passed away; and there was no more sea. And I John saw the holy city, new Jerusalem, coming down from God out of heaven, prepared as a bride adorned for her husband. And I heard a great voice out of heaven saying, Behold, the tabernacle of God is with men, and he will dwell with them, and they shall be his people, and God himself shall be with them, and be their God. And God shall wipe away all tears from their eyes; and there shall be no more death, neither sorrow, nor crying, neither shall there be any more pain: for the former things are passed away. And he that sat upon the throne said, Behold, I make all things new. And he said unto me, Write: for these words are true and faithful. And he said unto me, It is done. I am Alpha and Omega, the beginning and the end. I will give unto him that is athirst of the fountain of the water of life freely. He that overcometh shall inherit all things; and I will be his God, and he shall be my son. (Rev 21:1–7)

We notice that Abraham looked forward to this eternal home. He anticipated this inheritance, a city designed and built by God, whose ruler is God and which was promised before time began. Our blessed Lord and Savior, Jesus Christ, died on the cross of Calvary, that whoever believe on him will not perish but have eternal life in the New Jerusalem. Abraham was confident in what he hoped for and was assured about what he did not see.

God's people of faith, such as Abel, Enoch, Noah, Abraham, physically died:

> These all died in faith, not having received the promises, but having seen them afar off, and were persuaded of them, and embraced them, and confessed that they were strangers and pilgrims on the earth. For they that say such things declare plainly that they seek a country. And truly, if they had been mindful of that country from whence they came out, they might have had opportunity to have returned. But now they desire a better country, that is, an heavenly: wherefore God is not ashamed to be called their God: for he hath prepared for them a city. (Heb 11:13–16)

This world is not our home, we are just passing through. We will not live here for a long time and we must not become attached to the world's desires and possessions that we will leave behind when we die.

God has indeed prepared an inheritance, a city for all who would believe on his name. This is a better country, a heavenly one. The patriarchs died without experiencing the fruit of their faith, and we should not be discouraged if everything is not as we want them to be here on earth. Jesus has words of encouragement for us:

> Let not your heart be troubled: ye believe in God, believe also in me. In my Father's house are many mansions: if it were not so, I would have told you. I go to prepare a place for you. And if I go and prepare a place for you, I will come again, and receive you unto myself; that where I am, there ye may be also. (John 14:1–3)

Abraham and the other patriarchs have laid the foundation for us as Christians to build on. We are all God's fellow workers, God's field, and God's builders. In accordance with his grace, we are wise master builders who build on the foundations that different wise master builders have laid. We must, however, build on this foundation with extreme care without interfering with or changing one iota of the foundation that was already laid:

> For other foundation can no man lay than that is laid, which is Jesus Christ. Now if any man build upon this foundation gold, silver, precious stones, wood, hay, stubble; Every man's work shall be made manifest: for the day shall declare it, because it shall be revealed by fire; and the fire shall try every man's work of what sort it is. If any man's work abide which he hath built thereupon, he shall receive a reward. If any man's work shall be burned, he shall suffer loss: but he himself shall be saved; yet so as by fire. (1 Cor 3:11–15)

The foundation of our personality, life and being is Jesus Christ. Everything we do must fit into his plan and design. The work which we perform on this foundation must be fireproof because our work will be tested by fire to determine whether or not we will be rewarded.

On three occasions, in Revelation 22, the very last chapter in the Bible, we are taught that Jesus will come quickly: "Behold, I am coming quickly, and my reward is with me, to give to each person according to what he has done" (Rev 22:12). The Son of man will come in his Father's glory with his angels, and he will reward each one of us in accordance with what we have done. Unfortunately, some of us will come up empty-handed because we did not have the right work ethic and generally were shirkers. The harvest is plentiful and ready to be reaped. Let us significantly increase our work force, our workload and our work ethic, and ensure that many more souls are won into the precious kingdom of God.

REWARDS IN THE NEW JERUSALEM

The Bible teaches:

> What will it profit a man if he gains the whole world, yet forfeits his soul? Or what can a man give in exchange for his soul? For the Son of man will come in his Fathers glory with his angels, and then he will repay each one according to what he has done. (Matt 16:26–27)

Wealth in this present world does not matter when Christ returns to reward his people. In any event, you will physically die and leave it all behind for the use of others. It is pointless trying to accumulate all the wealth in the world without regard for the condition of your valuable soul. We need to take our eyes off the temporary and focus on the eternal. What will you give in exchange for your soul? I implore you to give your soul over to the control of Christ today in exchange for the eternal rewards that he has stored up in heaven for you.

Christ has given instructions that we hold on firmly to what we have, our faith in him, so that no one takes our crown (Rev 3:11). Our life's experiences are not so important, and neither is our physical strength. We must hold on steadfastly to our salvation, ensuring our crown is not taken away from us.

St. Paul's advice is echoed in these words:

> Brothers, I do not consider myself yet to have laid hold of it. But one thing I do: Forgetting what is behind, and straining towards what is ahead. I press on toward the goal to win the prize of God's heavenly calling in Christ Jesus. (Phil 3:13–14)

Paul knew that despite his best efforts for the sake of the kingdom of God, he had not yet attained the prize. There are some things in our past that make us wonder whether we will ever be able to stand on the podium and receive our reward. Paul advises us not to look back, but to strain every sinew in our bodies, keep our eyes focused on what we have to do to step onto the prize-winners podium when Jesus present his rewards. The race is not won until we cross the finish line.

What are some of the rewards that Christ has in his safe in heaven for us?

THE IMPERISHABLE CROWN

> Know ye not that they which run in a race run all, but one receiveth the prize? So run, that ye may obtain. And every man that striveth for the mastery is temperate in all things. Now they do it to obtain a corruptible crown; but we an incorruptible. I therefore so run, not as uncertainly; so fight I, not as one that beateth the air: But I keep under my body, and bring it into subjection: lest that by any means, when I have preached to others, I myself should be a castaway. (1 Cor 9:24–27)

Paul is comparing the discipline of striving to win a prize at the Olympics, for example, with striving to win the prize at the end of the Christian's physical life's journey. Athletes who win medals at the Olympic Games often testify of the grueling training they endured for years, sometimes as much as eight or ten hours per day of rigorous physical training, to ensure that their bodies are rightly conditioned to undertake the event. They work with coaches who work out any perceived flaws in their techniques in order to gain advantage over the other competing athletes. They work with dieticians to ensure that they eat and drink the right meals and have the right weight. They check every label on every product to ensure that what they consume is not prohibited by the law of the event. Then the big event comes. The top athlete's prize will be a gold medal, the second prize is a silver medal, and the third prize winner receives a bronze medal. All the other athletes go home empty-handed.

There is bad news for the prize winners. The prize is perishable. It will not last. Someone may even steal the medal before you return to your dwelling house. Moth and rust may corrode your medal and your medal is useless to you after you die. It must also be mentioned that all other competitors would go home without the benefit of some sort of prize. So sorry for your disappointment, after all your hard work, you go home empty-handed and are listed in the column "also ran."

The Christian is running a race, but to win an imperishable crown, and all in the race are certain to win this victor's crown, which is our heavenly reward, if we endure to the end of the race and cross the finish line. This crown is an everlasting crown that cannot be stolen and no moth or rust can corrupt it. Peter defined this as an inheritance incorruptible and undefiled and which does not fade away. Paul said that if you are to wear this crown, then like an athlete, you are required to put in the hard work and be constantly on the lookout for possible pitfalls from the enemy of your souls, the devil. As we travel along this Christian journey, we are sure that there will be hardships to overcome and endure. Christ insists that if we want to follow him, we must deny ourselves and take up our crosses on a daily basis, and follow him:

> Saying, The Son of man must suffer many things, and be rejected of the elders and chief priests and scribes, and be slain, and be raised the third day. And he said to them all, If any man will come after me, let him deny himself, and take up his cross daily, and follow me. For whosoever will save his life shall lose it: but whosoever will lose his life for my sake, the same shall save it. (Luke 9:22–24)

We must endure all suffering for the sake of the gospel of Christ. As Christians, we must be imitators of Christ and obey his commands to the point of death.

Paul said that he "fights," but our fight is not against flesh and blood, but against the rulers, against the authorities, against the powers of this world's darkness, and against the forces of evil in the heavenly realms. Paul said that he disciplines his body and brings it under subjection so as to put to death the deeds of the body. We must abstain from fleshly lusts because these wage war against the soul. If any part of our bodies is used as an offense to God, we are to get rid of it because it is better to enter heaven without some parts of our bodies, than to be thrown into the unquenchable, fiery abyss of hell. We must pursue righteousness, godliness, faith, love, patience, and gentleness. We must fight the good fight of faith so that we can hold on to eternal life and at the end of it all, obtain the victor's imperishable crown.

CROWN OF RIGHTEOUSNESS

The athlete competing in the 100 meters at the Olympic Games must get on his own mark, get ready to run the race and then start the race after the starting gun signals that the race should begin. He must then run in his own predetermined lane until the race is finished. If he violates any of the competition rules, he is disqualified, and it does not matter that he was the first to cross the finish line. Paul informed Timothy: "Similarly, if anyone competes as an athlete, he does not receive the victor's crown unless he competes according to the rules" (2 Tim 2:5). Christians are competing in a race that is run in accordance with predetermined rules which must be strictly adhered in order to avoid disqualification from the victor's crown.

Paul was also a participant in this very tough race. He knew that Christians will have to endure long suffering, perseverance, persecutions and afflictions (2 Tim 3:10–12), and he prepared himself for the task. He was stoned and left for dead; he was beaten with rods three times; he was whipped with thirty-nine lashes, five times; he was attacked by an angry mob; and he received many death threats. Yet, he persevered. He did not give up. He wanted to stand in the winner's podium. Paul recognized that he would have to endure hardships as a good foot soldier of the cross of Jesus Christ (2 Tim 2:3; 2 Cor 11:22–33), and in his struggles he was shipwrecked three times; he was arrested and held for two years without bail and without a trial; he was even bitten by a viper. In 2 Cor 12:7–10, we learn that Satan had burdened Paul with a thorn in his flesh. He pleaded with the Lord three times for deliverance from Satan's torment, but God's response was: "My grace is sufficient for you, for my strength is made perfect in weakness."

Paul recognized his need to be humble, and instead gladly boasted in his infirmities, and took pleasure in all the reproaches, needs, persecutions and distresses for Christ's sake, so that the power of Christ may rest on him, that despite his weaknesses, then he could be strong in Christ.

Paul was a very faithful soldier of the cross, and he recognized that he was near the end of life's race. As he approached the finish line, he considered the race he was about to complete and gave this testimony:

> I have fought the good fight, I have finished the race, I have kept the faith. Finally, there is laid up for me the crown of righteousness, which the Lord, the Righteous Judge will give to me on that Day, and not to me only but also to all who loved his appearing. (2 Tim 4:7–8)

What a great testimony of affliction and endurance! At the end of the race, it would be worth it all. He will one day step forward and receive his crown of righteousness from the righteous presenter, the Righteous Judge, Jesus Christ. The judgment of Christ is fair and balanced. It is beyond reproof. It is final. There are no appeals. The way Paul started the race is not important. It is how he finished the race that is important. He remained loyal, faithful and deeply rooted in his relationship with his coach, Jesus Christ, and is assured of the crown of righteousness.

Paul acknowledged that the crown of righteousness was not for him only, but for all those who love Christ's appearing. So, what is our status in this heavenly race? Is our fight the good fight of faith? Are we on course to complete the race within the documented guidelines or do we even know the guidelines? Our citizenship is in heaven, and we must run this race with patience, even as we eagerly await the return of our Savior. We too will have to endure hardships, persecutions, affliction and pain, but if we faithfully complete the race, we too will be rewarded with our crown of righteousness. It is a tough race but we must never give up.

THE UNFADING CROWN OF GLORY

> Feed the flock of God which is among you, taking the oversight thereof, not by constraint, but willingly; not for filthy lucre, but of a ready mind; Neither as being lords over God's heritage, but being examples to the flock. And when the chief Shepherd shall appear, ye shall receive a crown of glory that fadeth not away. (1 Pet 5:2-4)

The Apostle Peter was very privileged to witness the miracle of the revelation of the glory of Christ on the Mount of Transfiguration. Jesus went up on the mountain to pray with Peter, James and John. While Jesus was there, the appearance of our Lord's face was altered. His face shone like the sun; his robe became white as light such that there is no laundry detergent on earth or anywhere else in the universe that could have made them whiter; a bright cloud overshadowed them and a voice spoke from the cloud: "This is my beloved Son in whom I am well pleased, hear him."

Peter spoke from a position of knowledge and experience and was therefore in a strong place to speak of the unfading crown of glory. He addressed fellow elders of the church; those officers who provide supervision, protection, discipline, and instruction in righteousness to fellow believers. In 1 Pet 5:1–5, Peter urged the elders to be the shepherds of God's flock that came under their charge; to recognize that they are caring for God's flock, that they must be willing to serve out of eagerness; they must not be greedy for money and they must be examples of believers in words and actions. When the elders shepherd the flock as prescribed, when the Chief Shepherd appears, he would reward them with the crown of glory that will never fade away; that will maintain its recognizable glory and splendor.

In Acts 6, the story is told of how the members of the early church at Jerusalem donated money to the church to help the needy members of the congregation. The church grew very quickly so that it became impossible for the apostles to perform the functions of preacher, teacher and prayer warrior, while at the same time performing the full-time task of distributing the money collected by the church for the needy. Stephen, a man of full of faith and the Spirit of God, was one of seven men chosen to manage this ministry of the poor, and he also preached the gospel of Jesus Christ to all persons. His message was strong and powerful and stirred up hatred and scorn for him among the Jews.

They eventually arrested him and the great council of rulers indicted him falsely for speaking blasphemous words against the temple and the law of Moses. Stephen was requested to respond to the charges that were made against him. As he spoke, they stared at him but could not resist the wisdom and the Spirit by which he spoke. They saw that his face was shining as though it was the face of an angel. He preached to them beginning from the time that the God of glory appeared to Abraham and the success stories of the Israelites like Joseph, Moses and the prophets. He reminded them that despite the goodness of God, the people of Israel had been unfaithful to God. Stephen preached that the people of Israel persecuted the prophets and then murdered Jesus and by their rejection of him, they were partakers in his murder. When they heard Stephen's preaching, they were cut in their hearts, and gnashed their teeth at him:

> But Stephen, full of the Holy Spirit, looked up to heaven and saw the glory of God, and Jesus standing at the right hand of God. Look, he said, I saw heaven open and the Son of Man standing at the right hand of God. (Acts 7:55–56)

Stephen also had the opportunity to see the glory of God. What we know is that where the glory of God exists, changes occur. As the glory of God shone on Stephen, his countenance changed. His face shone like it was the face of an angel.

When Moses came down from Mount Sinai after being in the presence of God, his face shone:

> And he was there with the Lord forty days and forty nights; he did neither eat bread, nor drink water. And he wrote upon the tables the words of the covenant, the ten commandments. And it came to pass, when Moses came down from mount Sinai with the two tables of testimony in Moses' hand, when he came down from the mount, that Moses wist not that the skin of his face shone while he talked with him. And when Aaron and all the children of Israel saw Moses, behold, the skin of his face shone; and they were afraid to come nigh him. (Exod 34:28–30)

I believe that the elders of the church will be easily recognizable when the Chief Shepherd appears and rewards them with the unfading crown of glory. Their countenances will change and their faces will be like a shining light. God's glory will shine on them and through them. These elders would probably have been ministers of the new covenant of the Spirit that gives life. We too can be ministers of the gospel of Christ. We can minister in many ways. Anyone who works for the advancement of the gospel of Christ will be considered as ministers worthy to be rewarded with the unfading crown of glory.

CROWN OF REJOICING

> Now the tax collectors and sinners were all gathering around to hear Jesus. But the Pharisees and the teachers of the law muttered, "This man welcomes sinners and eats with them." Then Jesus told them this parable: "Suppose one of you has a hundred sheep and loses one of them. Doesn't he leave the ninety-nine in the open country and go after the lost sheep until he finds it? And when he finds it, he joyfully puts it on his shoulders and goes home. Then he calls his friends and neighbors together and says, 'Rejoice with me; I have found my lost sheep.' I tell you that in the same way there will be more rejoicing in heaven over one sinner who repents than over ninety-nine righteous persons who do not need to repent." (Luke 15:1–7 NIV)

Jesus has set the example of the way believers ought to live. Too often, we look with scorn on prostitutes, drunkards, drug addicts, the homeless, persons suffering with such diseases as HIV and AIDS. We go to wits end to avoid contact with such persons in order to avoid the stigma of association, and probably would "sink up" if we were seen gathering with such persons.

Do you think, for example, that Christian pastors, priests or evangelists would be comfortable attending an event advertised for lesbians and gays? How would he respond to his photograph "big up" on the television screen and in the leading newspapers about his attendance at such an event? Is it not a fact that most of us, including our church leaders, prefer the comfort zone of our churches rather than any type of stigma? After all, the Jews have no dealings with Samaritans! But maybe, just maybe, some of our church leaders are unashamedly practicing gays or maybe lesbians and are not careful about the doctrine of Christian principles.

Jesus made the headlines after he called Matthew from his prominent position of tax collector to be his disciple. Matthew invited Jesus, other tax collectors and others to a sumptuous celebratory banquet. It was not cool to hang out with tax collectors and sinners and the law professors and Pharisees complained about this occurrence. In the story of St. Luke 15:1–7, Jesus reinforces his message to preach the good news of the gospel to those sinners who have not yet been converted. All the tax collectors and sinners came to hear Jesus preach, and again the scribes and the Pharisees complained that Jesus ate with tax collectors and sinners. And what about the woman of Samaria that Jesus met at the well of Sychar? Jesus had a conversation with this woman and it resulted in a whole town being saved from their sins.

Christ's message to all of us is that he did not come to call the righteous, but sinners to repentance. They that are whole do not need a physician, but those who are sick. We are instructed to go into the highways and hedges and compel those that are lost to come into Christ's banqueting house where his banner over them is love.

The story of the lost sheep is a timely reminder that we are to make a very special effort to find the backsliders. Jesus is teaching that if a church has a hundred members and one leaves the congregation, that as shepherds of the entire flock, we should leave the ninety-nine that are safely in God's fold and go after the one who has left the safety his house and may encounter the wiles of the devil. There is rejoicing in heaven over one sinner that repents than over ninety-nine who have already repented and are in the safe arms of Jesus.

Our commission is to seek the lost and compel them to be part of Jesus' flock. When we have done so successfully, then our reward will be the crown of rejoicing. The crown of rejoicing is the crown for soul winners:

> For what is our hope, or joy, or crown of rejoicing? Is it not even you in the presence of our Lord Jesus Christ at his coming? (1 Thess 2:19)

Jesus himself put it this way:

> For the Son of Man will come in his Father's glory with his angels, and then he will repay each one according to what he has done. (Matt 16:27)

CROWN OF LIFE

"Blessed is the man who perseveres under trial, because when he has stood the test, he will receive the crown of life that God promised to them who love him" (Jas 1:12). The crown of life is for persons who have been victorious in their Christian living and have made it all the way through the gates of the pearly white city, that John saw coming down from heaven.

The Christian journey is not an easy one. It has its tests and temptations. Christ himself said that if we will be his followers, we have to put aside selfishness, take up our crosses and follow him. He said that we would be reviled, persecuted, falsely accused, and hated by the world. There will be obstacles from close family members, friends, and enemies alike, and we must be willing to give up our own lives for his sake.

The three "Hebrew Boys," Shadrach, Meshach, and Abednego endured such a test. They refused to worship the golden image set up by King Nebuchadnezzar and incurred his rage. They chose instead to take a stand for their Living God, the Lord God Almighty, although they were aware that the king would impose the death penalty for their act of disobeying his commands. Sure enough, they were convicted and condemned to death in the fiery furnace which was heated seven times hotter than it ought to have been. You guessed right; God was with them and delivered them from their troubles, as he would be with us and set us free from every evil confrontation that we may encounter. The Bible teaches that we must be faithful, even to the point of death, and we will be given a crown of life. We must be willing to give up our lives for the sake of the good news of salvation.

One of the pillars to obtaining the crown of life is endurance. We must not give up no matter what the test or challenge. Jesus teaches that when we endure to the end, we will be saved (Matt 24:13). Christ again taught:

> I know thy works, and tribulation, and poverty, (but thou art rich) and I know the blasphemy of them which say they are Jews, and are not, but are the synagogue of Satan. Fear none of those things which thou shalt suffer: behold, the devil shall cast some of you into prison, that ye may be tried; and ye shall have tribulation ten days: be thou faithful unto death, and I will give thee a crown of life. (Rev 2:9–10)

Christ is reminding us that he is on top of the situation. He is aware of the good deeds that we are doing. He is in control of our tribulation, lack of physical wealth, and our sufferings. We must not worry about our perceived poverty because we are in fact rich. We must be faithful unto death and he will reward us with the crown of life. It is noteworthy that these promises were made to Abraham and his seed. For all of us who are baptized into Christ, we have clothed ourselves with Christ. There is neither Jew nor Greek, slave nor free, male nor female, for we are all one in Christ Jesus. If we belong to Christ, then we are Abraham's seed, and heirs according to the promise. In other words, all persons who are called after the name of Christ are entitled to all the benefits of the promises of Abraham and will receive crown of life.

Let me be clear. When you step on that winner's podium to receive your reward, there will be no disqualification and all protests will be in vain. Christians, small and great, will stand before God Almighty at that great white throne, and they will have to give account of the works that they performed on their Christian journey. God will open the Book of Life where he recorded all our activities and we will be judged from the performance reports recorded therein: "And whosoever was not found written in the book of life was cast into the lake of fire" (Rev 20:15).

ELIJAH WAS OBEDIENT

When morally bankrupt Ahab was king of Israel, he provoked God to anger because he was more wicked than all other kings of Israel. Ahab married Jezebel, the daughter of the king of the Zidonians, and she imported hundreds of Baal prophets to the land of Israel. She opposed the true and living Almighty God and set out to utterly destroy all his prophets. She exhibited tremendous influence over her husband, King Ahab, and together they became the vicious enemy of Elijah, the great prophet of the Old Testament.

Elijah appeared out of obscurity to be used by God to change the idolatrous character of Israel and influence believers down through the ages. The Apostle James tells us that Elijah was an ordinary man, like all of us. There were times in his life when he exhibited weaknesses and failures; he was discouraged and was afraid, but in the mist of it all, he trusted and obeyed God, and God chose him to preach his messages of warnings and judgments to restore Israel's lost faith in him. So, Elijah confronted the wicked Ahab with words of judgment: "As the LORD God of Israel liveth, before whom I stand, there shall not be dew nor rain these years, but according to my word" (1 Kgs 17:1). Elijah prayed earnestly and specifically that it might not rain and it did not rain for three and a half years. He prayed for rain to fall again and heaven opened and God showered the blessings of rain on the earth again (Jas 5:17–18).

God told the fugitive from the pursuit of Ahab, Elijah, to leave where he was and go into hiding at the brook of Cherith and while he was there, the brook provided drinking water for him, while God himself commanded the ravens to providentially provide food for him. Of course, Elijah obeyed God and went to the Brook of Cherith where God provided the promised sustenance for him and protected him (1 Kgs 17:2–5).

Since no rain was falling because of Elijah's prayer, the land was parched dry and the water at the Brook Cherith dried up. God was not finished with his faithful prophet. Again, the LORD spoke to Elijah, and told him to move on from the brook and go Zarephath, where he would be sustained by a widow. Once again Elijah obeyed God and went to Zarephath where a window provided for his physical needs. God fulfilled his promise to take care of the needs of his obedient servant. Jesus taught that all who hear and obey the word of God would be blessed. God promised the Israelites blessings for obedience to him. He promised to make them more important than the other nations of the world; to make their land prosperous, to provide security for them, to bless their children, their crops and livestock. He promised them that their obedience would benefit them in terms of long life and prosperity (Deut 28; Deut 5).

Spiritual and Eternal Prosperity of Elijah

The Dead Is Raised

What spiritual blessings did Elijah receive from his tolerance, long suffering, faithfulness and obedience to God? We have already noted that Elijah prayed that rain would not fall until he called it down from the skies and that happened. We also noted that God provided food security throughout the three-and-a-half-year period of drought, and also physical protection for Elijah from the wicked King Ahab and his idolatrous wife, Jezebel. Specifically, at Zarephath, God used a mere one-meal amount of flour and oil and miraculously sustained Elijah, the widow, and her son for as long as the drought lasted. "Some-time later the son of the widow who owned the house became ill. He grew worse and worse, and finally stopped breathing" (1 Kgs 17:17 NIV). Elijah recognized the anguish of the widow and felt compassion for her. He took the deceased body of the little body to the upper room where he was accommodated. Elijah was now properly in his closet, alone with God, where he exercised his faith in him, fervently praying that the child may be returned to the land of the living. Yes, God answers the prayer of his obedient children. The LORD returned the child to life. It was a miracle that was never witnessed at anytime before.

Elijah demonstrated his faith in God by confronting Ahab with the message of God's judgment that there would be a period when no rain would fall. He proved that God was a provider and sustainer by his exploits at Cherith and Zarephath. He had seen evidence of the power of the fervent prayer of a righteous man because God answered his prayers with respect to rain and his prayer about the widow's deceased son.

God Answered by Fire

The time had come again for Elijah to confront and expose Ahab's wickedness, destroy the powerless false god, Baal, and its false prophets, and restore the kingdom of Israel to worship the true and living God of the universe. God conveniently organized a meeting between Elijah and Obadiah, who was a faithful believer in God, but served in Ahab's palace. Obadiah had offered protection and provision to one hundred of God's prophets and now it was his job to set up Elijah's reunion with Ahab. The meeting was set up and it was agreed that all the children of Israel would meet Elijah to witness a showdown at Mount Carmel, with the four hundred and fifty prophets of Baal and the four hundred prophets of Asherah, who ate at Jezebel's table. "Elijah went before the people and said: How long will you waver between two opinions? If the LORD is God follow him; but if Baal, follow him" (1 Kgs 18:21 NIV).

Elijah had a wonderful idea. The prophets of Baal were to sacrifice an ox on wood and put no fire under it and Elijah would do the same. The God who answered by fire is the true and living God. The prophets of Baal prepared their ox and called on Baal from morning until midday, but Baal never answered them. Elijah poked fun at them declaring that Baal was probably engaged in some other activity; perhaps gone aside; probably traveling, or even sleeping. I dare say that he was as dead as a doornail. They shouted with loud voices and cut themselves with swords and lances but Baal did not answer them because he could not. A mere dummy object made with human hands will not respond because it cannot hear, see, feel nor answer. After all, it is just an idol just like the motor vehicle which we put before God; the same as our business fortune which causes us to forget God; it is the same idol as the fame that gave us false pride to the extent that we no longer depended on God.

It was then Elijah's turn. He called the people near to him. He repaired the broken-down altar of the Lord, and built a trench around it large enough to hold two measures of seed. He then arranged the wood, cut the ox in several pieces and laid it on the wood on the altar for sacrifice to Almighty God. He then drenched the altar with water three times:

At the time of sacrifice, the prophet Elijah stepped forward and prayed:

> Lord, the God of Abraham, Isaac and Israel, let it be known today that you are God in Israel and that I am your servant and have done all these things at your command. Answer me, Lord, answer me, so these people will know that you, Lord, are God, and that you are turning their hearts back again. (1 Kgs 18:36–37 NIV)

This was an event organized by God and carried out by the righteous, resolutely obedient prophet of God. The result of this fervent prayer with humility, was instantaneous:

> Then the fire of the Lord fell and burned up the sacrifice, the wood, the stones and the soil, and also licked up the water in the trench. When all the people saw this, they fell prostrate and cried, "The Lord—he is God! The Lord—he is God!" (1 Kgs 18:38–39 NIV)

God's power prevailed and the Israelites worshipped God again, but all the false prophets were killed. Are we in the center of God's will? Do we worship false gods? How effective is our prayer life? Are our lives an example such that it will lead others to follow Christ. Now is the time for change to make a difference to the kingdom of God.

Elijah—the Fastest Human Being Ever!

In 2011, Justin Gatlin ran a wind-assisted 9.45 seconds, over a distance of 100 meters, the fastest time ever recorded for a human being on earth or mars. This was 0.13 seconds faster than Usain Bolt's 9.58 seconds world record of the 2009 Olympic games. In horse racing, the fastest time recorded is 20.57 seconds in Grantville, Pennsylvania, over a distance of 402 meters (2 furlongs) on May 14, 2008. In 1 Kings 18, the Bible records the story of the prophet Elijah, who for a distance of between seventeen and thirty miles, from Mount Carmel to Jezreel, outran King Ahab's chariot of horses.

Elijah had prayed that there be no rain and for three-and-a-half years there was neither rain nor dew on the earth. After the destruction of Baal and Queen Jezebel's false prophets, Elijah prayed for rain. His servant Elisha, after examining the skies seven times, reported that there was a cloud formed over the sea as big as a man's fist. Elijah knew that an abundant amount of rain was about to fall and instructed King Ahab to get into his chariot and ride from Mount Carmel to Jezreel before the heavy rain stopped him along the way. The power of the Lord anointed Elijah and he, "Mr. Energetic," outran the chariot of horses all the way to Jezreel. What a performance! In whatever we do, we can trust the Lord to bring us through successfully. We do not need performance-enhancing drugs, astrology, spiritualists, or satanism, God has promised to look after our needs if we would trust and obey him.

Elijah Receives His Eternal Inheritance Early

> For if we believe that Jesus died and rose again, even so them also which sleep in Jesus will God bring with him. For this we say unto you by the word of the Lord, that we which are alive and remain unto the coming of the Lord shall not prevent them which are asleep. For the Lord himself shall descend from heaven with a shout, with the voice of the archangel, and with the trump of God: and the dead in Christ shall rise first: Then we which are alive and remain shall be caught up together with

them in the clouds, to meet the Lord in the air: and so shall we ever be with the Lord. (Thess 4:14–17)

God sent his only begotten Son, our Lord, to this sin-cursed earth to redeem us back to himself and to offer us eternal life. We simply have to believe and obey the gospel and Christ will return to meet his chosen people in the air, so that we can be with him for all eternity: "And it came to pass as they still went on, and talked, that, behold, there appeared a chariot of fire, and horses of fire, and parted them both asunder, and Elijah went up by a whirlwind to heaven" (2 Kgs 2:11). Elijah satisfied his covenant of obedience and servitude to God and God did not hesitate. He immediately sent his chariot for him and took him alive to heaven to be with him forever and ever. Of course, when Jesus was transfigured on the high mountain, Elijah and Moses appeared with Jesus sharing in that moment of glory.

Jesus will come again for a people who by their righteous living are prepared to meet him and are steadfastly looking forward to his second coming. What about you? Are you prepared to meet our Lord when he returns, or are you yet worshipping mammon? How long will you be halted between two opinions? Jesus is knocking at your door. Will you take that call or will you go to the back door and answer the devil's call? Please do not turn the Savior away from your heart.

Elijah—an Ordinary Man

The life of Elijah is a stark reminder that our righteousness will not exempt us from fear, pain and affliction. Elijah was a man with passions like us. He was courageous to confront the wicked King Ahab, who killed many of God's prophets and led the Israelites to worship the false God, Baal. He feared for his life after he destroyed Baal and its four hundred and fifty prophets, causing the Israelites to return to worship the true and living God. Jezebel had again threatened to take his life so he escaped to Beersheba about one hundred miles south of Jezreel. He humbled himself when he accepted the very last meal from the poor, hungry, widow of Zarephath which she was about to prepare for her son and her. He also was very humbled whenever he approached God in prayer. Elijah was moved with compassion when the widow's son died and he immediately sought God's intervention in restoring the little boy's life. And of course, Elijah suffered despair. Jezebel was informed by her husband, King Ahab, that Baal and all its prophets were destroyed by Elijah's sword and she sent a message to him informing him that he would be dead by the end of the following day. He was afraid for his life and ran to Beersheba and then much further into the wilderness, where he sat alone under a juniper tree: "And he requested for himself that he might die; for I am not better than my fathers" (1 Kgs 19:4). The great Elijah was just an ordinary human being who became a very powerful spiritual leader of Israel, and is a perfect example for all of us to emulate. What is the nature of our relationship with Christ?

Chapter 10

Prosperity through Tithes and Offerings

TO ROB GOD BY WITHHOLDING THE TITHE

Will a man rob God? Yet ye have robbed me. But ye say, Wherein have we robbed thee? In tithes and offerings. Ye are cursed with a curse: for ye have robbed me, even this whole nation. Bring ye all the tithes into the storehouse, that there may be meat in mine house, and prove me now herewith, saith the Lord of hosts, if I will not open you the windows of heaven, and pour you out a blessing, that there shall not be room enough to receive it. (Mal 3:8–10)

THE TITHE DEFINED

The tithe is a tenth of anything. In other words, out of every $10.00 that you earn, the first dollar is "holy unto the Lord" (Lev 27:30–32). It is to be separated, consecrated, and dedicated to the Lord, and you are not to touch it. Tithing is an act of worship. The tithe is then to be used to support God's work (Acts 4:32–35). It is to be used for those who are employed in the work of the kingdom of God (1 Cor 9:14; Gal 6:6; 1 Tim 5:17). The tithe is to be used to assist the poor Christians of the church, the elders of the church, the afflicted fatherless and widows (Rom 15:26; 1 Cor 16:1–2;

Acts 11:27–30; Jas 1:27). It is to be used for the upkeep of the priest, pastor, evangelist, etc. (Num 18:21–24; Deut 14:22–27).

God said he would rebuke the devourer for the sake of someone who tithes, according to Malachi's report of what God said to his people (Mal 3:11). He promised that if they participated in his system, their crops would not fail, nor would their herds have miscarriages. The crops for many of us today are projects, jobs, careers, businesses, professions, etc. The devourer is the devil who eats up your prosperity. The devourer is what happens when every time you get something, it has to be paid out for something else. Something is always eating up what God is giving you or what you should have. The devourer is causing you not to prosper or flourish as you should.

A major question that Christians ask as they begin to put their financial house in order is: "Do I tithe before or after my bills"? Many people would tithe after all their other financial obligations are met and then tithe from the remaining money if any is left over:

> Thou shall take of the first of all fruits of the earth, which thou shall bring of thy land that the Lord thy God giveth thee, and thou shall put it in a basket, and shall go unto the place which the Lord thy God shall choose to place his name there. (Deut 26:2)

> And now I have brought the first fruits of the land, which thou, O Lord, hast given me. And thou shall set it before the Lord thy God, and worship before the Lord thy God. (Deut 26:10)

> When thou hast made an end of all thy tithing of all the tithes of all thine increase the third year, which is the year of tithing, and has given it unto the Levite, the stranger, the fatherless, and the widow, that they may eat within the gates and be filled. (Deut 26:12)

The process of bringing the firstfruits to God, before paying the bills, is called tithing. God's word says that you must tithe first before you do anything else with your fruits (income). Tithing establishes a new relationship between you and God. The treasure house of God is now open to you. If you put God first as he says to do, surely, he will bless.

WHAT DOES BLESSED MEAN?

The word *blessed* in Hebrew means to have the benefits of peace. If whatever you have is not bringing you peace, it is not a blessing from the Lord. Also, in the Greek language of the New Testament *blessed* means happiness, to be satisfied, to be healthy, to have wholeness, to have soundness, to have riches, prosperity, and more than enough. If you tithe and make offerings after all the bills are paid, you are leaving yourselves at the mercies of the bills and your tithe and offerings will be subject to and under the control of the bills. If you tithe first and give a generous offering, your bills come under the control of your tithe and offerings.

Malachi 3:10–11 speak of open windows of heaven for tithing and uninterrupted harvests for your offerings. As long as you have bills, always keep them in their proper place behind the tithe. Put God's business first and foremost and he will put your business first. First things must come first. If you want to receive from God, you must first begin to give. The Bible teaches this principle over and over again throughout the entire book. Luke 6:38 says to give first, then it will be given to you: "Give and it shall be given unto you, good measure pressed down, and shaken together and running over, shall men give into your bosom. For with the same measure that you mete, withal it shall be measured to you again."

Malachi 3:10 says to tithe first, then God will open the windows of heaven and pour out a blessing on you: "Bring the whole tithe into the storehouse, that there may be food in my house. Test me in this says the Lord Almighty and see if I will not throw open the flood gates of heaven and pour out so much blessing that you will not have room [enough] to receive it."

SOWING AND REAPING

God's system of tithes and offerings, honest wages (which he spelled out in Deuteronomy), and doing a day's work for a day's pay is founded on the principal of sowing and reaping. You plant a seed, but receive a harvest. The seed is multiplied back to you several times: "Be not deceived, God is not mocked, for whatsoever a man soweth that shall he also reap" (Gal 6:7). The one who sows to satisfy his sinful nature, from that sinful nature will reap destruction. An agriculturist who plants yams, reaps yams. If he plants corn, he reaps corn. If he sows stingily, he will reap a scanty harvest. The focus is on money as a means through which to accomplish a good life for you and God's work being carried forward. This principle underlies every area of human life, not just in finances. The consistency between what one sows and what one reaps is also valid in the spiritual realm. If we sow to the flesh, we will reap death and decay. If we sow to the Spirit, we will walk in the Spirit, be led by the Spirit, live by the Spirit, and harvest everlasting life. Walking in the Spirit calls for fresh committed determination each day.

"Remember this: whoever sows sparingly will also reap sparingly, and whosoever sows generously will also reap generously" (2 Cor 9:6 NIV). Paul wrote to the church at Corinth which was a very rich church. They were sending a gift to a church in a poor city and made plans to collect a big offering for this poor church that was experiencing financial difficulties. Our problem is that we give God what we can spare from what is left over. God will return to us what he can spare. Generosity has more to with our attitude of giving than the amount of money that we give. When you struggle and feel guilty with respect to your giving, you are not generous. Generosity takes place when you recognize that when you give generously, you will also reap generously. "Each man should give what is desired in his heart to give, not reluctantly nor under compulsion, for God loves a cheerful giver" (2 Cor 9:7 NIV). Do you feel under pressure to give to the ministry of the Word of God, and do not feel compelled to give to the needy? Give with joy unspeakable because God loves a cheerful giver:

> And God is able to make all grace abound to you, so that in all things and at all times, having all you need you will abound in every good work. (2 Cor 9:8 NIV)

When you are generous, God will give you generous ideas that when put into practice will bring generous outcomes. He will give you gifts of business and investment creativity that will result in growth in all areas of your life. God's grace, God's gift to you, is a guarantee to you that in all things and at all times you will have more than what you need. It does not matter what your situation is right now. It does not matter the crisis. It does not matter if you have or not, you will be prosperous because you are going to be a generous giver and God is going to positively respond to your generosity.

HISTORY OF TITHING

Tithing was practiced 430 years before the law of Moses. In Heb 7:1–11, we see that Abraham paid tithes for himself before the dispensation of the law. He also paid them for Levi, who lived under the dispensation of the law. In fact, Abraham tithed for all posterity—for his natural children (seed)and for his spiritual children (seed) who now live in the dispensation of grace: "And if ye be Christ's, then are Abraham's seed, and heirs according to his promise" (Gal 3:29). The obligation of tithing reaches across the prelaw dispensation, the dispensation of the law and the dispensation of grace.

If you are going to receive the optimum in your life, you must not overlook the basic building blocks of biblical prosperity. It is absolutely necessary that you follow the biblical plan of tithing. Tithing is not an option. The tithe is something you literally owe to God. God says that if we do not tithe, we are committing robbery. He says we owe him the tithe and we pay it because he commands it. By faithfully bringing the tithe to him, we establish our basic honesty and obedience.

Leviticus 27 clearly says the tithe belongs to the Lord:

> And all the tithe of the land, whether of the seed of the land, or of the fruit of the tree, is the Lord's: it is holy unto the Lord. And if a man will at all redeem ought of his tithes, he shall add thereto the fifth part thereof. And concerning the tithe of the herd, or of the flock, even of whatsoever passeth under the rod, the tenth shall be holy unto the Lord. He shall not search whether it be good or bad, neither shall he change it: and if he change it at all, then both it and the change thereof shall be holy; it shall not be redeemed. (Lev 27:30–33)

If you don't tithe, God says you are a robber. If you know your neighbor is a robber, you would not leave your windows open. Instead you would close and lock them to keep the thief out. The same is true of God. When we fail to tithe, we are stealing from him so he closes the windows of financial blessings. Tithing is the first step toward living under an open heaven for God's promises to open heaven over the tither. The opposite is also true. Failing to tithe will close the windows. When God said: "Ye are cursed with a curse" (Mal 3:9), Malachi was speaking of the self-imposed penalty (curse) for violating the spiritual principle of tithing. God says that there is a penalty for withholding the tithe. Heaven closes over the violator. The blessings stop flowing. The many things God wants to do for that person does not come to pass.

The Tithe Belongs to God

"All the tithe of the land, whether of the seed of the land, or of the fruit of the tree, is the Lord's, it is Holy unto the Lord" (Lev 27:30). Everyone God spoke to in this verse had worked hard in cultivating and reaping the harvest. However, God plainly says 10 percent of the increase belongs to him. The Bible is clear when it forbids the person who works to produce the harvest, from eating God's portion (10%). It is set apart as holy. In every sense of the word, it belongs to God.

We must be careful not to desecrate what is holy to our God. In Daniel 5, we learn of how Belshazzar, king of Babylon, set himself against the Lord of heaven by using the sacred goblets from his temple for his own entertainment and the entertainment of his wives, concubines and nobles. He did not honor God with his worship but instead worshipped the lifeless objects of gold, silver, bronze, iron, wood and stone. We all know about the human hand that God sent to write on the wall the consequences of that violation. God numbered the days of his reign as king of Babylon and brought it to an end. He was weighed in the balances and found wanting. And his kingdom was divided and given to the Medes and Persians. The very night of desecrating God's holy property, Belshazzar lost his life.

The Early Church Tithe

"And here men that die receive tithes, but there he receiveth them, of whom it is witnessed that he liveth" (Heb 7:8). The author of Hebrews wrote this verse thirty-five years after the death of Christ. That put tithing well within the New Testament age. In the book of Hebrews, the author spoke of the time Abraham gave tithes to Melchizedek (Gen 14). He explained who Melchizedek actually was. Then he made a most significant statement. The writer says the New Testament saints were paying tithes at that very moment (AD 65) (Heb 7:8).

We must understand two words from Heb 7:8 so that we can totally grasp their significance. They are the words *here* and *there*. The word *here* is a translation from the Greek word *hode* which means "in the same spot." The writer was saying: Here in this same spot where I stand, men who die receive "present tense" tithes. This verse was probably written thirty-three to thirty-five years after the death of Christ. The reference in Hebrews means that it was a common practice for Christians to pay tithes in the early New Testament churches.

The word *there* is the Greek word *ekei*, which speaks of another time and another place. Priests and others who receive tithes will die, except for Melchizedek, of whom the Scriptures testify that he is alive. It is therefore the responsibility of every Christian to tithe. Tithing is for our day but this remains one of the most violated commandments. Melchizedek taught Abraham that the God of heaven is the Most High God and that he should put nothing nor no one ahead of him. He learned that God created the heaven and the earth and everything and everyone that are in them and is the source and protector of everything and everyone.

Let us try to understand what tithing is, what tithing means and why we must tithe. A person who joins the Royal Barbados Police Force, together with all recruits who become attached at that time, before them and after them, have to go through a period of initial basic training. This training is designed to prepare them for police work and any tasks eventually requiring the services of the police force, for example, riot control. Specifically, you are trained to be disciplined. You must obey the commands of all the training instructors and superior officers the moment the command is given. There can be no hesitation. Whatever the instruction, whatever you thought of that instruction, you cannot argue or disagree, you have to accept the command and do as you are instructed, when you are told and how you are told. You have no rights. Someone controls you. The basic training received prepared recruits for all situations of crisis which may occur in their career. When given a command, you would have been properly disciplined to act as per command, without hesitation, because your lives and/or the lives of others depended on immediate action on command.

Tithing is about obeying God's command. It is from the heart that we tithe. It is with the tithe that we worship God. We must always bear in mind that it is God who created all things. God took absolutely nothing and created everything. God commanded the universe to come into existence from what was not visible. We create nothing. Everything that is in the world was created by God and for God. We take God's creation and make other things and then boast, falsely, of our creative genius. We took what God created and restructured it or manufactured it, using the wisdom that God gave to us.

God created everything and therefore owns everything. He is the creator and possessor of heaven and earth (Gen 14:19). The earth and everything in it; the world and all who live in it, belongs to God because he founded it upon the seas and established it upon the waters (Ps 24:1–2; 1 Cor 10:26; Ps 50:12; Ps 89:11; Isaiah 42:5). God has given mankind responsibility and authority over everything he created, but this dominion is not ownership.

The Bible Sanctioned 10 Percent

When we tithe, we invest 10 percent of what God has given to us into his kingdom. We can see when we compare:

> Now consider how great this man was, unto whom even the patriarch Abraham gave the tenth of the spoils. And verily they that are of the sons of Levi, who receive the office of the priesthood, have a commandment to take tithes of the people

according to the law, that is, of their brethren, though they come out of the loins of Abraham. (Heb 7:4–5)

In both passages of Scripture, the writer identified the same event. In the first passage we are told that Abraham gave to Melchizedek. He said that Abraham gave tithes of all. When the same event was described by the author of the Hebrews, it was revealed that Abram gave a tenth of the plunder.

TITHING UNDER THE NEW COVENANT

> Woe unto you Scribes and Pharisees, hypocrites! For ye pay tithes of your spices—mint, and anise and cumin. But you have neglected the more important matters of the law—justice, mercy and faithfulness. You should have practiced the latter, without neglecting the former. (Matt 23:23)

Many "religious" people say tithing is not under the new covenant but only for the Israelites. Although Jesus obviously accepted tithing, they say his life among the Jews, the remnant of Israel, was still under the old covenant laws. The fact is that tithing was instituted under Abraham (Gen 4:20). If we are going to accept that Abraham's true promised seed was Jesus, making the Abrahamic blessing also ours today as Paul wrote in (Gal 3:29), then we must accept that the tithes go with the Covenant and not the Mosaic Law, given 430 years later (Gal 3:16–25).

There are principles in the Bible which are "perpetual truths," from Genesis to Revelation, and tithing is one of them. Tithing under the New Testament is different because we are "Spirit led" and not "law led." That does not mean that God's laws were done away with. Jesus specifically said they were not and never would be (Matt 5:18). He fulfilled all of the law; therefore, it is now written in our hearts, not on stone tablets (Heb 10:16).

Under the new covenant, tithing starts at 10 percent. God wants to bless some Christians and take them to a higher level, so he has been dealing with them about giving more than 10 percent. But 10 percent is just the starting gate. God's system is to support the church and make sure you are blessed. Out of every $10.00 you earn or receive you owe God $1.00 before taxes or anything else: then you give an offering, a good offering that is acceptable. When you do that, God said, "I will pour you out a blessing that you will not even have room enough to receive."

Blessings

Do you know what blessings means? Have you read (John 6:5–12) about the disciples taking five loaves of bread and two fish from a young boy and giving it to Jesus to feed five thousand men plus women and children? When Jesus blessed the food and gave it back to them, the provisions were multiplied. When something is blessed, you are able to do more with it than you were able to do with it before. The people ate all they wanted and there were twelve baskets of leftovers. This was so because the boy's lunch was blessed.

A lot of people make a lot of money but are not able to do a lot with it. It is not blessed because they are robbing God with the tithes and not giving acceptable offerings so God cannot bless their incomes. You can do more with 90 percent blessed than with 100 percent cursed. Remember that if you give nothing, nothing no matter how you multiply is still equal to nothing. On the other side, some people refuse to commit their lives to God, but they give him money, the biggest checks, and pat themselves on the back, thinking that they have helped out God. You cannot substitute tithing for right living. When you are tithing, you must ensure that you are a part of the gift offered to God, so that he may receive you as well as the gift.

God said all the way through the book of Hebrews that Christians have a better covenant than the Abrahamic covenant; not a different one but an improved one. That means that what we have has more benefits, more of an advantage. It is what they had, plus more. What we have in the New Testament is better than what God promised the Israelites in the Old Testament. However, if the new one does not include financial and material blessings, which theirs did, how can the new covenant be better? If God promised to bless them, and they had prosperity, because we have a better covenant, we should have no poverty.

Under the old covenant, they offered sacrifices as atonement for their sins giving them a covering under God. Under the new covenant, we have Jesus, an eternal, once-for-all sacrifice for our sins: "But this Man, after he had offered one Sacrifice for our sins forever, sat down on the right hand of God" (Heb 10:12). The new covenant is therefore better. Under the old covenant, the Holy Spirit periodically overshadowed (anointed) prophets, priests, kings and certain people for special service as God willed. Under the new covenant, the Holy Spirit abides in all who accept Jesus. The new covenant is therefore better. Under the old covenant, only the high priest was allowed to enter the holy of holies and that only once per year. Under the new covenant, all born-again believers are part of a royal priesthood: "For ye are a chosen generation, a Royal Priesthood, a Holy Nation, a peculiar people, that ye should show forth the praises of him who have called you out of darkness into his marvelous light" (1 Pet 2:9). We are able to go to the throne of grace with boldness at anytime.

Jesus is our high priest and mediator of the new covenant: "But now have he obtained a more excellent ministry, by how much also he is the Mediator of a better Covenant, which was established upon better promises" (Heb 8:6). If the new covenant is better, that means that it must include what being blessed under the old covenant represented, plus something else, which is the spiritual blessings provided by Jesus. However, if you are only spiritually blessed, you cannot consider yourself totally blessed. If you have the natural blessings of Abraham, you are not totally blessed. Life does not consist of the abundance of things we own, only. Life must include things if we are to be blessed, bless others, and continue the Lord's work. Under the new covenant, we have a right to both.

Our love for God may be proved by something that is a major part of everyone's life, and that is our use of money. How we use money demonstrates the reality of our love for God. In some ways, it proves our love more conclusively than depths of knowledge, lengths of prayers or prominence of service. These things can be feigned, but the use of our possessions shows us up for what we actually are.

ROBBING GOD

The Bible teaches us that as Christians that we are God robbers if we do not pay our tithes and if we do not give offerings, and fully deserve the penalty for robbing God. Robbery is not a summary offence. Neither is it a misdemeanor. Robbery is a serious offence for which a heavy penalty is imposed.

The modern courts will find a person guilty of robbery if he steals and immediately before or at the time of doing so, he uses force on any person or seeks to put that person in fear of being then and there subjected to force. In other words, robbery is an aggravated form of theft. Theft is where a person dishonestly appropriates property belonging to another with the intention of permanently depriving the person to whom the property belongs of that property. One area of appropriation of property is where a person is innocently in possession of the property, i.e., without stealing it, but later assumes a right to it by keeping it or dealing with it as an owner (unlawful possession).

Robbery is committed by one person against another person. But is God a person? Yes, he is. God has emotion, intelligence and a will. The important ministry of distributing spiritual gifts is in accordance with the will of God's Spirit (1 Cor 2:11). His will is also seen in his ability to direct the activities of his servants. He is a leader who gives direction to his people, e.g., he forbade Paul to preach in Asia and Bithynia but led Paul and his party to Europe through the vision of the man at Macedonia. He knows and searches the things of God. He has a mind and is able to teach people. God guides, testifies, convinces, restrains, performs miracles and can be grieved and lied to. When we withhold any portion of the tithe, we are violently stealing from God or otherwise withholding from God property that belongs to him and using it as if we are the rightful owners. When we rob God, we become entitled to the penalties as set out in Mal 3:9.

Many Christians find it difficult to believe that a human being can actually rob God. Everything we have is from God, so when we refuse to return to him that part of what was given, we rob him. We may very well be preventing the growth of his church. In any event, spiritual workers deserve their pay and their support ought to be enough to care for their needs. If we do not pay our tithes, our pastors, priests, evangelists, and so on will have no means to support themselves and family. The result is that they will seek that means elsewhere and the spiritual growth of the church will be neglected.

During Malachi's day, the people were not giving tithes, so the Levites went to work on their farms to earn a living thereby neglecting their God given responsibility to care for the temple and for the service of worship. Malachi urged the people to stop holding back their tithes, to stop keeping from God what he deserved. Do you selfishly want to keep 100 percent of what God has given or return 10 percent of what God has given you so that God's kingdom could be advanced? The people of Malachi's day ignored God's command to give the tithe of their income to his temple. They may have feared losing what they had worked so hard to get, but in this they misjudged God. "Give and it will be given you. A good measure, pressed down, shaken together and running over, will be poured into your lap" (Luke 6:38). We must remember that the blessings God gives are not always material and all may not be experienced completely here on earth, but we will certainly receive them in our future with him.

To Rob God in Offerings

The New Testament refers to a variety of offerings:

1. The body offered to God: "I beseech you therefore, brethren, by the mercies of God, that ye present [offer] your bodies a living sacrifice, holy, acceptable unto God, which is your reasonable service" (Rom 12:1);

2. Offerings of money or material goods: "But I have all and abound: but I am full, having received of Epaphroditus the things which were sent from you, an odor of a sweet smell, a sacrifice acceptable, well pleasing to God" (Phil 4:18);

3. Sacrifices of praises to God: "By him therefore, let us offer the sacrifice of praise to God continually, that is, the fruit of our lips giving thanks to his name" (Heb 13:15); and

4. Sacrifices of doing good: "But to do good and communicate forget not: for with such sacrifices, God is well pleased" (Heb 13:16).

The Bible teaches us (Mal 1:7–8) that the people of that day sacrificed to God wrongly through:

- Expedience—being as cheap as possible;
- Neglect—not caring how they offered the sacrifice;
- Outright disobedience—sacrificing their own way and not as God had commanded.

Their method of giving showed their real attitudes toward God. As intermediaries between God and the people, priests were reflecting God's attitude and character. By accepting imperfect sacrifices, they were leading the people to believe that God accepted those sacrifices as well. But God is not pleased with our mediocre offerings. As Christians, we are often in the same position as these priests because of how we reflect God to our family and friends.

The condition of a sacrifice matters to God. He created all things, defective animals as well as the healthy ones, but does not accept gifts that are flawed. God cared about this so highly that he sent his messenger, Malachi, to speak very strongly. The imperfect sacrifices of the priests and people demonstrated the content of their heart. The people were not sincere. To sacrifice a perfectly healthy animal looked to them like a waste and they considered the work of preparing their gifts properly to be a foolish use of time and energy.

Malachi confronted this attitude with the law of God which clearly demanded unblemished sacrifices and sincere hearts:

> If the offering is a burnt offering from the herd, he is to offer a male without defect. (Lev 1:3)

> If someone's offering is a fellowship offering, and he offers an animal from the herd, whether male or female, he is to present before the Lord an animal without defect. (Lev 3:1)

> Do not sacrifice to the Lord your God an ox or a sheep that has a defect or flaw in it for that would be detestable to him. (Deut 17:1)

Malachi confronted people with God's judgment for their actions. God was perfectly aware of what they were doing and the condition of their hearts. No sacrifices at all would have been better than second rate and insincere ones. The people were not giving "sacrifices." They were merely doing what was convenient, just enough to appear to obey God. Then they would pat themselves on the back for being right.

But though God's people had broken their covenant with him, God remained true to his promises (Isa 53). He did not shrink from sending his only Son to a cruel death on the cross. Jesus was the true unblemished sacrifice to which the Old Testament sacrifices pointed:

> For such an high priest became us, who is holy, harmless, undefiled, separate from sinners, and made higher than the heavens; Who needeth not daily, as those high priests, to offer up sacrifice, first for his own sins, and then for the people's: for this he did once, when he offered up himself. For the law maketh men high priests which have infirmity; but the word of the oath, which was since the law, maketh the Son, who is consecrated for evermore. (Heb 7:26–28)

Jesus was perfect, free from all sin. Through his sacrificial death, salvation was provided for all our sins. The Lord demonstrated his sincere love for us because he sacrificed the very best to save us (John. 3:16).

Offering Our Bodies to God

"I beseech you therefore, brethren, by the mercies of God, that ye present [offer] your bodies a living sacrifice, holy, acceptable unto God, which is your reasonable service [this is your spiritual act of worship]" (Rom 12:1). Paul is encouraging Christians to present their bodies as a living sacrifice, meaning that they should use their bodies to serve and obey God. We are to consecrate and offer ourselves wholly and completely to the true and living God. As Christians, we are to give our bodies selflessly and completely over to God. Our bodies are the temple of the living God and his Spirit dwell in our bodies. We should set apart our bodies for God's use and service.

In 1 Thess 5:23, Paul prayed that our whole spirit, soul and body, be preserved without sin until the coming of our Lord Jesus Christ. He prayed that Christians would be sanctified in all aspects of their lives. Every part of a Christian's life should testify that it is set apart for service to our holy God. In other words, we are to consecrate our bodies to the Lord by giving permission to the Holy Spirit to be in complete control. Sin should not reign in our bodies to obey its passions by presenting the members of our bodies to sin as instruments for unrighteousness but as instruments of righteousness.

Paul writing to the Corinthians said: "I keep control of my body and bring it into subjection, lest that by any means, when I have preached to others, I myself be a cast away" (1 Cor 9:27). Paul practiced and subjected his body to tremendous sufferings, discipline, and control, as a living sacrifice, so that he could finish his course of serving Christ until he meets him at the rendezvous of the portals of glory.

At the end of his Christian experience here on earth, Paul testified:

> For I am now ready to be offered, and the time of my departure is at hand. I have fought a good fight, I have finished my course, I have kept the faith: Henceforth there is laid up for me a crown of righteousness, which the Lord, the righteous judge, shall give me at that day: and not to me only, but unto all them also that love his appearing. (2 Tim 4:6–8)

Paul had obtained warrants of arrest from the high priest to go to Damascus to continue his persecution of the church. It did not matter to Paul whether there were men or women serving the Lord Christ, Paul's mission was to arrest them, handcuff them and take them to Jerusalem for trial. Paul was stopped in his tracks. He met the man on the middle cross, Christ Jesus himself, who refocused his mission. He was now to be the Ambassador for Christ and the standard bearer for the Gentile Christians, and also for the Jews.

And it was Paul's turn to endure hardships, pain and imprisonment; to struggle against the evil within himself and within the world; to endure the hardship as a good soldier of the cross; to spread the gospel all over the world; to answer the case of the gospel before Felix and Agrippa, and to content with false doctrines within the church. Paul endured several cases of dangers and indignities but in all these things, he was more than conqueror through Jesus Christ who loves us all.

Paul considered himself the least of all apostles but knew that he had labored harder that all of them. He was imprisoned more often, with countless beatings that left him at death's door. Five times in his preaching experience he received thirty-nine lashes from the Jews; three times he was beaten with rods. He was stoned, shipwrecked three times, drifted while at sea, was in danger from rivers, the sea, robbers, Jews, Gentiles and those false so-called brothers in the church. Paul endured many sleepless nights. There were many occasions when he was both hungry and thirsty and there were occasions when he was nakedly exposed to the elements. There was even a time when the governor under King Aretas guarded Damascus so that they might arrest him, but God provided an escape route for him through a window in the wall.

It can therefore be said, without fear of contradiction or rebuttal, that Paul lived a complete life in Christ Jesus which he lived according to God's purpose. He performed beyond the call of duty and experienced a tremendous sense of peace, contentment and fulfilment in his personal life. He was contented with every situation his new life in Christ threw at him. He was brought low but he also abounded. He suffered hunger but he also had plenty.

When God called him home to paradise to be with him, Paul had done all that he could do and there was nothing left for him to do that he had not already done. He had carried the cross daily for Christ. He experienced death daily for the cross of Christ. Here is Paul's writings to the Romans:

> Therefore, brethren, we are debtors, not to the flesh, to live after the flesh. For if ye live after the flesh, ye shall die: but if ye through the Spirit do mortify the deeds of the body, ye shall live. (Rom 8:12–13)

The foundation of our Christian society is marriage between male and female. It is the sacred constitution of the Christian. Paul wrote:

> Be not deceived: neither fornicators, nor adulterers, nor effeminate, nor abusers of themselves with mankind, Nor thieves, nor covetous, nor drunkards, nor revilers, nor extortioners, shall inherit the Kingdom of God. (1 Cor 6:9, 10)

The Bible teaches that deceivers were at work in ancient Corinth. They are similarly at work in our churches today as they were at ancient Corinth. Many of us deny the sinfulness of sexual sins. We say that sexual activity between consenting adults is permissible and perhaps commendable whether or not we are married, but we are dead wrong.

ADULTERY

Adultery may be defined as sexual intercourse between a married person and another person of the opposite sex who is not their spouse. We are instructed in 1 Corinthians 7, that every person should have their own spouse. In Genesis 39, adultery is defined by Joseph, Jacob's son, as "great wickedness and sin." In Leviticus 20, adultery was a capital offense punishable by death. God does not and will not sanction acts of adultery. Peter has advice, which can also be rightfully applied to the lives of all married persons. He said:

> Forasmuch then as Christ hath suffered for us in the flesh, arm yourselves likewise with the same mind: for he that hath suffered in the flesh hath ceased from sin; That he no longer should live the rest of his time in the flesh to the lusts of men, but to the will of God. (1 Pet 4:1–2)

Paul was teaching at Ephesus when he heard of one very serious case of immorality among the Christians. A person should not have sexual intercourse with his father's wife. An elderly father's young second wife had an affair with her husband's son and the church members did nothing about it. They thought it was none of their business. The Apostle Paul said it was their business and that he must be put out of the church. Immorality diminishes the spiritual maturity of the church. The church cannot be one powerful witness for God and righteousness if a notorious sinner is recognized and accepted as a member in good standing. In 1 Cor 5:1, Paul wrote concerning this deplorable action: "It is reported commonly that there is fornication among you, and such fornication as is not so named among the Gentiles, that one should have his father's wife."

John the Baptist was martyred for teaching the same doctrine. He preached that it was immoral for Herod Antipas to sleep with Herodias, his brother's wife (Matt 14:3–12).

Paul teaches from Hebrews 13 that marriage is honorable in all, and the bed undefiled, but whoremongers and adulterers God will judge. In the Old Testament the penalty for adultery was death (Deut 22:22; Lev 20:10).

The Bible records the judgment which the Israelites experienced when they camped in or near the territory of Moab. The women of Moab not only seduced the Israelites to sleep with them, but joined them in worshipping false gods (Num 25:1–9). The guilty Israelites were executed and a plague killed thousands more, leaving a death toll of between 23,000 to 24,000 persons. The Apostle Paul cautions: "Neither let us commit fornication, as some of them committed and fell in one day three and twenty thousand"

(1 Cor 10:8). Once the marriage has taken place, the married couple should not defraud each other of sexual intercourse, but may consent to postpone intercourse for a while for purposes of prayer and fasting. They should come together again so that they would not be tempted by Satan to commit sexual sins.

As Christians, our belief and practice regarding marriage, is that it is a legal and spiritual union or contract made by a man and a woman to live as husband and wife. One man and one woman come together to form the union and not two or three or four or five. Christians believe in the permanency of marriage, that from the moment the marriage vows are exchanged, and the license signed, it is for better or for worse, for richer or for poorer, in sickness and in health, to love and to cherish, until death takes one of the partners, and that this is in accordance with God's holy ordinance. We certainly endorse the idea of married couples loving, caring, comforting and honoring each other. We cannot opt out of the marriage simply because our economic fortunes have depreciated, or because one of the partner's health has deteriorated or for any cause.

Divorce, however, is permitted, but certainly not encouraged, if one spouse has been unfaithful. Jesus put it this way, "Whoever shall put away his wife, except it be for fornication, and shall marry another, committeth adultery, and whoso marrieth her which is put away doth commit adultery" (Matt 19:9). Remember that infidelity is the one and only biblical reason given whereby a person can divorce and remarry without violating God's laws relating to adultery. It seems therefore that if the adulterer remarries, he or she will be breaking God's laws relating to adultery while the guiltless spouse can remarry and would not be breaking God's laws.

It is very embarrassing that the rate of divorce among Christians is approximately the same as that of the secular world. We must therefore constantly examine and reexamine our lives to ensure that we still have a right relationship with God and also do everything at our command to ensure that we have good and lasting relationships with our spouses.

There are instances when couples will feel compelled to separate or divorce; for example, if one or both partners are violent to the extent that one or both partners can receive serious or fatal injuries. When this separation occurs then the partners should remain unmarried or be reconciled to one another (1 Cor 7:7–12).

An important aspect of Christian living is the act of confession and the act of forgiveness. We need to confess our faults to each other, especially in the marital relationships, so that both partners can work together to resolve any issues. No, we do not know what your partner did to you but it is your Christian responsibility to forgive each other, so that the marriage can be brought back on track. If you do not forgive, your Father in heaven will not forgive you.

Remember that as Christians, if we are to follow in the footsteps of Christ, we must "deny ourselves and take up our crosses daily and follow him." That is to say that our Christian journey will not be easy and we will have to work very hard, every day, to ensure that we have an exciting and enduring marriage.

FORNICATION

Fornication may be defined as sexual intercourse between a man and a woman and neither are married. If one of the participants were married, the married person would be committing adultery, while the unmarried person would be a fornicator. Paul, in 1 Corinthians 7, has instructed us that if we are to avoid fornication, then it is acceptable for a man and woman to get married to each other and not to burn with sexual desire. It is important to understand that each man must have his own wife and each woman must have her own husband. Paul wrote:

> Flee fornication. Every sin that a man doeth is without the body; but he that committeth fornication sinneth against his own body. What? know ye not that your body is the temple of the Holy Ghost which is in you, which ye have of God, and ye are not your own? For ye are bought with a price: therefore glorify God in your body, and in your spirit, which are God's. (1 Cor 6:18–20)

Many persons who call themselves Christians are involved in common-law marriages; they live together like husband and wife without completing their marriage vows and legal documentation. They conclude that a good "sleep with" is better than a bad marriage. This is a common practice accepted in our societies as normal but does not measure up to God's word. The common-law relationships will not receive God's blessings, approval and sanctification:

> Now concerning the things whereof ye wrote unto me: It is good for a man not to touch a woman. Nevertheless, to avoid fornication, let every man have his own wife, and let every woman have her own husband. (1 Cor 7:1–2)

Paul here advocates that we should abstain from even touching a woman and I dare to say that women should also refrain from touching men. There are many unwanted and ungodly outcomes when we start touching and worse yet, when we start fondling. Paul's advice is simple but wise: do not touch. Touching and fondling breathes trouble and trouble does not set up like rain. There are many unwanted pregnancies and many homes are broken by sexual infidelity which usually commence with a simple touch. Additionally, there are many sexually transmitted diseases, such as herpes, AIDS, gonorrhea, and syphilis, that destroy the body, break up homes, and destroy friendships, as well as lower productivity in the workplace.

One of the more popular spots in Corinth was the temple of Aphrodite, where persons would pay a fee and participate in the temple sacrifice with a sumptuous feast and entertainment. Then they could spend the night with one or more of the priestesses who served in the temple for the pleasure of the worshippers. Christian standards of sexual morality were alien to the citizens of Aphrodite's town. While our modern-day evangelical churches are not overcome with orchestrated and organized worship, blended with sexual activity for the pleasure of church members, there is definitely too much sexual immorality in the church.

The body is not for fornication but for the Lord and the Lord for the body. Our bodies are members of Christ and it is not right for us to take our members of Christ and join it to a harlot. Our bodies are the temple of the Holy Spirit who dwells in us and whom we have from God. We have a responsibility to glorify God in our bodies.

The Scriptures teach us that no fornicator, nor adulterer, nor homosexual shall inherit the kingdom of God and we must offer our bodies to God as living and holy sacrifices.

HOMOSEXUALITY

The Bible teaches: "Thou shall not lie with mankind, as with womankind: it is abomination" (Lev 18:22). The Bible is clear. There is absolutely no doubt on God's standard for our Christian living. The male must not have sexual intercourse with another male person. This sinful action is a detestable practice. The practice of male homosexuality was such a serious offence that God himself ordered the death penalty for the parties found guilty of this sinful, abominably wicked and shameful evil (Lev 20:13). God does not and will not change. He is the same yesterday, today, and forever. God says that homosexuality is abomination, then the Christian must accept that it is abomination and take a stand for God and with God on this issue.

Homosexuality is viewed as a perfectly natural, normal and acceptable sexual experience. That is not what the Bible teaches. Paul lists ten kinds of offenders who will not inherit the kingdom of God and four of them are sexual sins or sins against the body. There was a time when our moral standard was based on the teachings of the Bible. These are days when legislators are going to parliament and enacting laws that permit a man to marry a man and a woman to marry a woman contrary to God's teaching as outlined in the Bible. The supreme courts and courts of final appeal around the world are also giving effect to homosexual unions, and lesbian unions, and there are many civil rights leaders who think legislation with regard to heterosexual marriages discriminates against the gay community. God says it is a sin and he is willing to forgive the evils that we have committed against our own bodies. The psalmist said:

> For thou hast possessed my reins: thou hast covered me in my mother's womb. I will praise thee; for I am fearfully and wonderfully made: marvelous are thy works; and that my soul knoweth right well. My substance was not hid from thee, when I was made in secret, and curiously wrought in the lowest parts of the earth. (Ps 139:13–15)

The time is right now for every God-fearing person to take their heads from between their legs, get on the Jesus train, and say to the world that homosexuality is wrong, and that all sexual activity outside of marriage is sinful. God made us and he knows what is best for us and we ought to obey God rather than man:

> Wherefore God also gave them up to uncleanness through the lusts of their own hearts, to dishonour their own bodies between themselves: Who changed the truth of God into a lie, and worshipped and served the creature more than the Creator, who is blessed for ever. Amen. For this cause God gave them up unto vile affections: for even their women did change the natural use into that which is against nature: And likewise also the men, leaving the natural use of the woman, burned in their lust one toward another; men with men working that which is unseemly, and receiving in themselves that recompence of their error which was meet. (Rom 1:24–27)

There is no clearly discernible excuse for a woman to have sexual relationships with another woman nor a man to have sexual relationships with another man. God has not prevented them from engaging in their acts of uncleanness through lust from the deep recesses of their hearts. He has given us the freedom, the power to dishonor our own bodies between ourselves. He has allowed us to worship created things rather than God, who created all things. He has allowed us to reject the God-ordained sanctity of marriage and choose unnatural sexual relations between ourselves. He has allowed us to change God's truth and turn it into a lie.

The result of our unnatural episodes in this physical life are various types of sexual diseases (HIV/AIDS, herpes, syphilis, gonorrhea, intestinal parasitism, gay bowel syndrome, HPV with its accompanying anal cancer, throat cancer, penile cancer, cervical, or lung cancer, hepatitis and various types of zoonosis). Then there is the experience of spiritual death and unless we repent of our wicked ways, we will experience eternal death. "Be not deceived: neither fornicators, nor adulterers, nor effeminate, nor abusers of themselves with mankind, Nor thieves, nor covetous, nor drunkards, nor revilers, nor extortioners, shall inherit the Kingdom of God" (1 Cor 6:9, 10). Effeminate describes female impersonators engaged in male homosexuality. "Abusers of themselves with mankind" is a general term for male homosexuals. Paul makes no excuses for any of these. He made it clear that they shall not inherit the kingdom of God. Christians must speak where the Bible speaks and remain silent where the Bible is silent.

> And turning the cities of Sodom and Gomorrha into ashes condemned them with an overthrow, making them an ensample unto those that after should live ungodly; And delivered just Lot, vexed with the filthy conversation of the wicked: (For that righteous man dwelling among them, in seeing and hearing, vexed his righteous soul from day to day with their unlawful deeds;) The Lord knoweth how to deliver the godly out of temptations, and to reserve the unjust unto the day of judgment to be punished: But chiefly them that walk after the flesh in the lust of uncleanness, and despise government. Presumptuous are they, selfwilled, they are not afraid to speak evil of dignities. (2 Pet 2:6–10)

God created man in his own image, after his own likeness. God determined that man should not be alone. God decided that man should have a helpmeet. God decided that a man will leave his parents and be joined together with his wife as one flesh. A woman also leaves her parents and becomes one flesh with her husband. Marriage between male and female is honorable and the bed is undefiled. God must be at the center of all marriages. Before we fall in love or commence a relationship, the Holy Spirit, who abides in our hearts, ought to be our guide and director and an active participator with regard to our choice for marriage. Marriage is a lifelong covenant between a man and a woman, until separated by death. The Christian must distance himself from all sexual relationships outside of marriage; that is to say, marriages that are not and will not be sanctified by God. God blessed Adam and Eve and gave instructions to increase and multiply the population on the earth. Same-sex unions cannot produce God's desired outcome.

Sexual relations outside the bond of marriage should be frowned on and stamped out everywhere. It must not be part of the church nor the Christian life:

> Knowing this, that the law is not made for a righteous man, but for the lawless and disobedient, for the ungodly and for sinners, for unholy and profane, for murderers of fathers and murderers of mothers, for manslayers, For whoremongers, for them that defile themselves with mankind, for men stealers, for liars, for perjured persons, and if there be any other thing that is contrary to sound doctrine. (1 Tim 1:9–10)

The sinner can make his way to the foot of the cross and receive God's forgiveness. It is for this purpose that Jesus came into this world.

> For what the law could not do, in that it was weak through the flesh, God sending his own Son in the likeness of sinful flesh, and for sin, condemned sin in the flesh: That the righteousness of the law might be fulfilled in us, who walk not after the flesh, but after the Spirit. For they that are after the flesh do mind the things of the flesh; but they that are after the Spirit the things of the Spirit. For to be carnally minded is death; but to be spiritually minded is life and peace. Because the carnal mind is enmity against God: for it is not subject to the law of God, neither indeed can be. So then they that are in the flesh cannot please God. (Rom 8:3–8)

DRUNKENNESS

Drunkenness is defined as the loss of control of oneself because of excessive drinking of alcohol. The Scripture clearly presents drunkenness as a sin for which the guilty must bear personal responsibility. Proverbs 23:29–35 describes the physical and psychological effects of drunkenness. A drunken person will have intense sorrow or misery, or affliction or misfortune. The drunkard will exhibit foolish or meaningless chatter. He "will see strange sights," his mind will "imagine confusing things," he will be like one sleeping on the high seas, his head will be spinning, he will be beaten but he won't feel it. In the end, it "bites like a snake and poisons like a viper." To put it differently, alcohol abuse destroys clear and effective thinking. It spins life out of control.

There are so many people who, under the influence of alcohol, beat their spouses and anger their family and friends, break the law in its various forms, and also encourage others to do so. They are many violent incidences, horror stories of beating, wounding and murder because of persons under the influence of alcohol that will blow our minds. Drunkenness destroys a person's capacity to perform with the required efficiency. These persons spend more and more on alcohol and less and less time managing their homes, employment and businesses. The results of drunkenness include divorce, job losses, traffic accidents, family breakups, and death. The Bible teaches us that drunkenness is a sin and that no drunkard will inherit the kingdom of God.

Wine is a gift from God. We learn as far back as Gen 27:28 that among the blessings that God provided for Jacob was the gift of wine. Isaac was old and knew that death was imminent. He called the heir of the inheritance, Esau, his firstborn son, and requested him to prepare that special meal with the intention that after he had eaten, he would pronounce that special blessing on him. Jacob, Isaac's second son, deceived his blind father and received God's blessing which Isaac intended for Esau. Among the blessings Jacob received from God, through Isaac, was the gift of wine: "Therefore God give thee the dew of heaven and the fatness of the earth and plenty of corn and wine" (Gen 27:28).

Jesus' first miracle was to turn a large quantity of water into wine and he himself drank wine: "John came neither eating nor drinking, and they say, he hath a devil. The son of man came eating and drinking, and they say a friend of publicans and sinners" (John 11:18–19; Luke 7:33–34).

When a person accepts Jesus as Lord and Master of their life, they become married to Christ and he is their bridegroom. In any household, the groom is expected to be the breadwinner. He customarily provides for the entire household. The country of Israel was not different. God, the bridegroom of the land of Israel, provided them with their land flowing with milk and honey as an inheritance. Israel rebelled against their bridegroom, the Lord God of heaven and earth, and worshipped and served the false god Baal. They omitted to give God the thanks and praise due to him, forgetting that it was the Lord who had given them the power to get wealth. God provided the oil and the wine and the corn:

> For she did not know that I gave her corn, and wine, and oil, and multiplied her silver and gold, which they prepared for Baal. Therefore will I return, and take away my corn in the time

thereof, and my wine in the season thereof, and will recover my wool and my flax given to cover her nakedness. (Hos 2:8–9)

Wine can be used as medicine. In Luke 10, Jesus told how the Good Samaritan used wine and oil to dress the wounds of the man who was robbed and injured while he was traveling from Jerusalem to Jericho. Paul, in 1 Tim 5:23, advised him to use wine to assist in the proper functioning of his bowels and his infirmities. In 2 Sam 16:2, Ziba advised King David that the wine was to be used to revive those soldiers expected to faint while traveling through the wilderness.

Wine was used as a sacrifice offering to God. The Israelites were required to offer the fourth part of a *hin* (a hin is 5.7 liters) of wine for a drink offering on the holy altar as a sweet savor to the Lord (Exod 29:40; Lev 23:13).

God told Moses that when a person, man or woman, shall separate themselves to make the vow of a Nazarite and to separate themselves unto the Lord: "He shall separate himself from wine and strong drink, and shall drink no vinegar of wine, or vinegar of strong drink, neither shall he drink any liquor of grapes, nor eat moist grapes, or dried" (Num 6:3).

In acknowledging that the God of heaven is their Lord, the Israelites did not drink wine nor strong drink during the forty years that they sojourned through the wilderness, on their way to the promised land (Deut 29:5–6).

In accordance with Judges 13, the Israelites were in bondage to the Philistines for forty years because of the evil they had done in the sight of the Lord. There was a man from Zorah, named Manoah, whose wife was barren, and had no children. The angel of the Lord visited her and gave her the good news that she would become pregnant with a son. The woman was strictly forbidden from indulging in wine or other strong drink or eating anything unclean because the child (Sampson) would be separated for God's purpose from his birth, to commence the deliverance of God's chosen people, Israel, from slavery to the Philistines.

Wine is God's gift to us. We abuse God's gift of wine to us when we drink too much, and become intoxicated, which results in serious consequences. If you do have a glass of wine, it should be as part of your meal, so that your bowels may function in the right way, and for some types of illnesses and injuries. We can also have a little alcoholic beverage because it brings joy and gladness to our hearts, but Christians must not be brought under its power.

We must make every effort to do what leads to peace and to mutual edification, but must not offend other Christians or encourage them to sin against their conscience. It is better not to eat food nor drink alcoholic beverages if it will cause a person to stumble while walking along this Christian journey.

The Bible teaches us in Isaiah 28 that woe would come to the drunkards of Ephraim, and to the drunk priests and prophets of Judah:

> But they also have erred through wine, and through strong drink are out of the way; the priest and the prophet have erred through strong drink, they are swallowed up of wine, they are out of the way through strong drink; they err in vision, they stumble in judgment. For all tables are full of vomit and filthiness, so that there is no place clean. (Isa 28:7-8)

Drunkenness will bring us misery, sorrow, distress, setbacks and all sorts of difficulties and troubles.

Noah's drunkenness brought shame to his family (Gen 19:20-27), while Lot's drunkenness resulted in an incestuous relationship with his two daughters (Gen 6:19-20). Drunkenness leads to debauchery, which is the unrestrained indulgence of immorality and sensuality: that is to say corruption, sexual misconduct, depravity, all of which are violations of God's holy law. In Luke 15, Jesus told the parable where the prodigal son traveled to a distant country and wasted all his financial resources in debauchery and excess. When he ran out of money, he satisfied his basic physical need of hunger with pig food.

The Bible teaches us that drunkards lack wisdom:

> Wine is a mocker, strong drink is raging, and whosoever is deceived thereby is not wise. (Prov 20:1)

In Proverbs 31, we are advised that heads of governments should not participate in the drinking of alcoholic beverages because they should be sober to enforce the law, ensuring that victims get proper justice. The writer says that strong drink is for those persons who are preparing for sudden death, or those who are in a sad and miserable state. It is for those persons who are poor and seeking to forget that they are poor.

There are some persons who indulge in the strong substance, and when they awake in the morning, they continue using the substance throughout the day and way into the night or until they become intoxicated: "What sorrow for those who are heroes at drinking wine and boast about all the alcohol they can hold" (Isa 5:22). Drunkards willfully make woe and sorrow for themselves. It causes Christians to sin against God. It causes us to quarrel, to fight, and to hate. It causes us to speak with vain babblings. A drunkard has no virtue nor honor and is definitely hell bound because no drunkard will enter the kingdom of God.

Long-term drinking can terminally damage the liver, pancreas, brain or heart. It can distort hearing, affect our vision, cause cancers, impair our judgment, affect our emotions, and eventually result in physical death. The Bible teaches that our bodies are the temple of the living God and that it is God's dwelling place and that we should offer it to him as a living sacrifice, holy, acceptable to him, which is our reasonable service. We must honor God with our bodies.

Isaiah prophesied that when Christ returns, he will prepare a feast and serve well-aged wines to his church: "And in this mountain shall the LORD of Hosts make unto all the people a feast of fat things, a feast of wines on the lees, of fat things full of marrow, of wines on the lees well refined" (Isa 25:6).

Jesus himself sanctified the cup of wine as "the new covenant in my blood" when, on the eve of his death, he sat at the feast of the Passover with his disciples. He desired to eat the Passover with them before he voluntarily gave his life on the cross for our sins, and promised that he would not drink of the fruit of the vine, until the kingdom of God shall come. Jesus took the cup and told the disciples: "This cup is the new testament in my blood which is shed for you."

Like his disciples, we should also look forward to Jesus bursting those glorious clouds, rapturing the church, and drinking of the choice fruit of the vine from the cup that bears his blood that was shed for us. We should be truly anticipating sitting at the table with the triumphant Jesus when the kingdom of God comes.

GLUTTONY

"For the kingdom of God is not meat and drink, but righteousness, and peace, and joy in the Holy Ghost" (Rom 14:17). A glutton is a greedy person who appears to have a voracious appetite, and is devoted to eating and drinking, in excess. It is really great when a person can boast of having such a wonderful appetite, but this appetite also put our ability to control ourselves on trial. We have to keep our eating habits under control in the same manner as we keep drinking habits and other unwelcome habits under control. Eating must never control us. We must not eat just because the food is available.

Some people are of the view that the chief error of gluttony is that it only pertains to food. Some people can't have enough toys, television, entertainment, sex or company. It is about the excess of anything. There are at least three other forms of gluttony; wanting more pleasure from something than it was made for; wanting it exactly our way; demanding too much from people (excessive desire for people's time and presence).

In Leviticus 11, God gave Israel a listing of foods that they should not eat, such as pork, shellfish, many types of seafood, scavenger birds, and many other animals and insects. These commands were intended to separate and distinguish Israel from other nations, as a nation who served the true and living God. When God created the world, everything he created was good and the one restriction on food was the "tree of knowledge and evil." Eating from that tree resulted in death.

Jesus explained to his disciples:

> Are ye so without understanding also? Do ye not perceive, that whatsoever thing from without entereth into the man, it cannot defile him; Because it entereth not into his heart, but into the belly, and goeth out into the draught, purging all meats? And he said, That which cometh out of the man, that defileth the man. For from within, out of the heart of men, proceed evil thoughts, adulteries, fornications, murders, Thefts, covetousness, wickedness, deceit, lasciviousness, an evil eye, blasphemy, pride, foolishness: All these evil things come from within, and defile the man. (Mark 7:18–23)

In Acts 10, the Lord told the Apostle Peter in a vision: "What God had cleansed, that call not thou common."

The Apostle Paul wrote:

> Now the Spirit speaketh expressly, that in the latter times some shall depart from the faith, giving heed to seducing spirits, and doctrines of devils; Speaking lies in hypocrisy; having their conscience seared with a hot iron; Forbidding to marry, and commanding to abstain from meats, which God hath created to be received with thanksgiving of them which believe and know the truth. For every creature of God is good, and nothing to be refused, if it be received with thanksgiving: For it is sanctified by the word of God and prayer. (1 Tim 4:1–5)

Romans 14:1–23 teaches that some of us will be weak in the faith and prefer to eat vegetables only. We should not have disputes over that position because God our Savior accepts them and we should accept them as well. We are not to despise each other or judge each other if one person eats meat and another vegetables only, because God accepts all of us.

We must put no stumbling in our brother's way to make him lose faith in God. There is nothing unclean of itself if it is accepted with thanksgiving, because it is sanctified by the word of God and prayer:

> He that eateth, eateth to the Lord, for he giveth God thanks; and he that eateth not, to the Lord he eateth not, and giveth God thanks But why doth thou judge thy brother? Or why doth thou set at naught thy brother? For we shall all stand at the judgment seat of Christ. For it is written, as I live saith the Lord, every knee shall bow to me, and every tongue shall confess to God. So then every one of us should give account of himself to God. Let us therefore judge one another no more: but judge this rather, that no man put a stumbling block or an occasion to fall in his brother's way. I know and am persuaded by the Lord Jesus, that there is nothing unclean in itself: but to him that esteemeth anything to be unclean, to him it is unclean. But if thy brother be grieved with thy meat, now walkest not thou charitably. Destroy him not with thy meat, for whom Christ died. (Rom 14:6b, 10–15)

There is the possibility of losing our inheritance:

> Lest there be any fornicator, or profane person, as Esau, who for one morsel of meat sold his birthright. For ye know how that afterward, when he would have inherited the blessing, he was rejected: for he found no place of repentance, though he sought it carefully with tears. (Heb 12:16–17)

In Genesis 25, we learn that Esau came home from work and was so hungry, he felt that he would die if he did not have food immediately. He then sold his birthright to his younger brother, Jacob, for a morsel of meat: "Then Jacob gave Esau bread and pottage of lentils; and he did eat and drink, and rose up, and went his way: thus, Esau despised his birthright" (Gen 25:34).

In a Jewish family, the firstborn son inherits special privileges, advantages and honor. It was a very important and sacred thing and it was through this birthright that God had made an everlasting covenant with Abraham that he would be the father of all nations and it was through this lineage that the Messiah of the world would come. Esau's birthright included family privileges and both material and spiritual benefits. He regrettably gave up all of the family privileges, and material and spiritual benefits, so that he could gratify his physical needs.

Paul called it profanity because Esau foolishly squandered his life and spiritual blessings on a bowl of pottage, not appreciating the true value of his birthright. He was not interested in spiritual matters nor matters of the heart and holiness, but treated the birthright with scorn. He wanted to satisfy his physical need for food, and he ate and drank and went on his way without a care in the world as to the long-term consequences of his error. His punishment was that he found no place for repentance, though he sought it carefully, with tears (Gen 25:30).

The Bible teaches us:

> Be not among wine bibbers, riotous eaters of flesh. For the drunkard and the glutton shall come to poverty: and drowsiness shall clothe a man with rags. (Prov 23:20–21)

> And put a knife to thy throat, if thou be a man given to appetite. (Prov 23:2)

We should look to the middle man of the cross, Jesus our Lord, and not make our belly our god or glory in our shame.

In 1 Samuel, the two sons of Eli, the priest, made the sacrificial meat to be cooked in one way rather than God's way when they sought after sauces and seasonings in order to satisfy the taste and flavor of the food, because they were worthless men who did not know God (1 Sam 2:12). "Wherefore the sin of the young men was very great before the Lord: for men abhorred the offering of the Lord" (1 Sam 2:17). Eli's sons not only gluttonously satisfied their taste buds, but also gratified their sexual desires with the congregation of the tabernacle. The penalty for their sin was that they died, but worst, the ark of the Lord was taken by the Philistines.

As saints of God, we should pay special attention to how we utilize the resources that God has given to us, whether that be material, spiritual or place of honor. Let us not waste our resources on such unimportant things as sexual gratification, and other fleeting pleasures. Rather, let us use our time, abilities, capabilities and resources to advance the kingdom of God and his righteousness. We must make the right choices at all times because wrong choices can have severe life-altering consequences. God knows our needs and will satisfy them according to his riches in glory.

One of the principal sins of Sodom was that of overeating: "fullness of bread" (Ezek 16:49). As Christians, we are only allowed to eat enough and not more. We are not allowed to eat in excess but must have control of our appetites at all times because overeating can make us sick: "Hast thou found honey? Eat so much as is sufficient for thee, lest thou be filled therewith, and vomit it" (Prov 25:16).

Gluttons will become poor. Daniel and his friends Shadrach, Meshach and Abednego refused to eat the king's food which was offered to idols instead of in thanksgiving to God. They were totally committed to God and did not bow to the pressure which confronted them nor compromise their relationship with God. They made the wise decision to negotiate rather than rebel against the Babylonian authorities. Daniel suggested a ten-day experiment with water and vegetables instead of the king's royal diet of meat and wine:

> At the end of ten days it was seen that they were better in appearance and fatter in flesh than all the youths who ate the king's food. So, the steward took away their food and the wine they were to drink, and gave them vegetables. (Dan 1:15–16)

ILLEGAL DRUGS

Illegal drugs are about tasting, feeling and sensing something that your soul begins to emotionally enjoy and the spirit reflects on. When we use it too often, its cravings are deposited in our hearts and soon its use becomes an uncontrollable habit, which can only be completely obliterated by replacing it with good habits. The Bible teaches: "He that hath no rule over his own spirit is like a city that is broken down, and without walls" (Prov 25:28). Although illegal drug use is not specifically mentioned in the Bible, its impact on the drug user and society far exceeds the evil of alcohol abuse. The addictive nature of some drugs is so powerful that a single episode can hook a person for life. Furthermore, the irreversible damage to the organs of the body and the mental capacities makes illegal drugs extremely dangerous. The greatest danger is the all-consuming control of one's life, constantly interrupting one's focus on work and destroying personal relationships and spiritual well-being. We are taught that our minds must be prepared for action and we must have a sober spirit.

Beyond the personal toll of drug addiction is the disastrous burden placed on families, friends, society and the work environment. History has recorded so many famous persons who have died before reaching the age of forty years old and their deaths were related to such things as overdose of heroin, cocaine and other illegal drugs, suspected suicide, and obesity. The Bible teaches that "there is a way which seems right to a man, but its end is the way of death" (Prov 14:12).

Alcohol and illegal drug use are well-documented factors of domestic violence, road and work rage, child abuse, suicide and a variety of other socially destructive behaviors. Alcohol and illegal drug addiction present a crisis threatening to destroy the very fabric of our society. The Bible teaches:

> Let us walk honestly as in the day; not in rioting and drunkenness, not in chambering and wantonness, not in strife and

envying. But put ye on the Lord Jesus Christ, and make no provision for the flesh, to fulfil the lust thereof. (Rom 13:13–14)

The point is that the body is the temple of God; it is his dwelling place. We must not put substances in our bodies to destroy it. We must keep it as clean and as healthy as possible so that God will be comfortable living at home and would not have to resort to the stables of Bethlehem for comfortable accommodation.

The news media across the United States of America reported that former presidential candidate Mrs. Carly Fiorina choked up at one time and appeared to blink back tears as she recounted the long and painful journey of her stepdaughter's death, who passed away in 2009, after battling drug and alcohol addiction. She was responding to a question about drug abuse. She stated:

> When someone is addicted, you watch them disappear before your very eyes. You watch the—I call them the demons of addiction, because that is what it looks like—they are overcome by the demons of addiction. In our daughter's case, she simply did not have the strength to go on.
>
> We must invest more in the treatment of all mental illnesses, including addictions. I realize as long as we went through the long painful journey with Lori Ann, I met so many families going through this, but I did not realize honestly what an epidemic this has become. The reason I'm running for president, is because I don't want to see hope fading from anyone's eyes. And while there is nothing as devastating as drug addiction, it is also true that I see so many people now in this nation that lack hope. . . . I know the look people get when they achieve their God-given potential. For me that look is fuel. My husband, Frank and I, buried a child to drug addiction.
>
> We must invest more in the treatment of drugs. We are misleading young people when we tell them marijuana is just like having a beer. It's not.[1]

There is nothing that one can add to these very clear and deeply passionate words from the former presidential candidate, and governments across the world can use this experience in their efforts to combat this deadly disease.

The state alone must not shoulder the responsibility for bringing relief and comfort to these physically and spiritually afflicted persons in our

---

1. Jonathan Eastley, "Emotional Fiorina Opens Up about Step Daughter's Death," *The Hill* newspaper, September 18, 2015.

society. The church, the business community and each one of us as individual Christians are responsible for every lost soul and we will have to give account to God for the deeds done in our lives, whether they are good or evil. We will either hear *well done thou good and faithful servant* or we can hear that *in as much as you have not done it for the least of my brethren, you have not done it for me, depart from me, I do not know you.*

TOBACCO

"Having therefore these promises, dearly beloved, let us cleanse ourselves from all filthiness of the flesh and spirit, perfecting holiness in the fear of God" (2 Cor 7:1). While smoking and chewing tobacco do not impair one's judgment nor carry many of the related side effects of alcohol and illegal drugs, tobacco has proven to be a primary health concern. Yet persons year after year are becoming hooked on the habit, being deceived by associating smoking with maturity and popularity. For many years we were warned of the dangers of smoking, even to the point of forcing tobacco companies to place warnings on their products. But these warnings were not taken seriously until we succumbed to the casualties of lung cancer and addiction to tobacco. Nonsmokers also became victims of diseases caused by inhaling secondhand smoke.

In recommending abstinence from the substances that destroy the body, the Christian is called upon to a higher standard of self-control and self-denial in respect of those things which bring no benefit to his physical and spiritual well-being. Christians must realize that there is a pressing need for a pure testimony before the world. The Apostle Paul advises:

> Therefore, I urge you, brothers and sisters, in view of God's mercy, to offer your bodies as a living sacrifice, holy and pleasing to God—this is your true and proper worship. Do not conform to the pattern of this world, but be transformed by the renewing of your mind. Then you will be able to test and approve what God's will is—his good, pleasing and perfect will. (Rom 12:1-2 NIV)

"Do you not know that your body is a temple of the Holy Spirit, who is in you, whom you have received from God? You are not your own. You are bought with a price. Therefore, honor God with your body" (1 Cor 6:16). The truth is that God will not dwell in a smoky nor smoking temple. The smoke will make him take cover. Let us keep his temple holy and make his stay comfortable.

> Let not sin therefore reign in your mortal body, that ye should obey it in the lusts thereof. Neither yield ye your members as instruments of unrighteousness unto sin: but yield yourselves unto God, as those that are alive from the dead, and your members as instruments of righteousness unto God. (Rom 6:12, 13)

The Christian should value his body as a sacred place where God dwells and should realize that by the Spirit's presence and power, he can be helped against that which destroys his body, God's resting place, his temple. I am confident that God will not abide in a smoked-out temple.

OFFER SPIRITUAL SACRIFICES

"You also, like living stones, are being built into a spiritual house to be a holy priesthood, offering spiritual sacrifices acceptable to God through Jesus Christ" (1 Pet 2:5). Peter is here describing the church as God's living, spiritual house, with the living stones being Israel. He then applied the image of "stone" to Christ showing that the church does not cancel the Jewish heritage but fulfills it. Christ is the foundation and cornerstone of that living, spiritual house and each Christian is as a stone.

Paul portrays the church as a body with Christ as the head and each Christian as a member. Christ has formed us into a body, into a group of individuals who are united in one purpose and in one love for one another and for the Lord. The one body is the church. It is designed to work smoothly, in coordination, without friction. If a believer stumbles, other Christians are there to pick him up and help him to resume his walk with God. We are to respond with forgiveness and not fury. If a Christian sins, there is restoration through the church:

> Brothers, if someone is caught in a sin, you who are spiritual should restore him gently. (Gal 6:1)

> But speaking the truth in love, may grow up into him in all things, which is the head, even Christ: From whom the whole body fitly joined together and compacted by that which every joint supplieth, according to the effectual working in the measure of every part, maketh increase of the body unto the edifying of itself in love. (Eph 4:15, 16)

If a Christian sins, Jesus is the Advocate who restores him to a condition of holiness when he repents of his wrongdoing. However, as Christians, we must also be our brother's keeper, and help each other in our time of distresses.

Chapter 11

The Christian Perspective of Wealth

The Christian perspective of wealth is derived from the Scriptures. There are many times in the Old Testament that God gave riches to his people. Solomon was promised riches and became the richest of all the kings of the earth (1 Kgs 3:11–13; 2 Chr 9:22). David said that wealth comes from God: "Wealth and honor come from you; you are the ruler of all things" (1 Chr 29:12). Abraham (Gen 17–20), Jacob (Gen 30–31), Joseph (Gen 41), King Jehoshaphat (2 Chr 17:5) and many others were blessed by God with wealth. However, they were a chosen people with earthly promises and rewards. They were given a land and all the riches it held.

It is not a sin to be rich. But the possession of material wealth in whatever amount, carries with it the responsibility for proper use.

The New Testament emphasizes God's riches in us: "That you may know the hope to which he has called you, the riches of his glorious inheritance in the saints" (Eph 1:18). It sets out a different standard for Christians. The church was never given land or the promises of material wealth. Paul states that God has blessed us in the heavenly realms with every spiritual blessing in Christ. Christ spoke of the seed of God's Word falling among thorns, and showed how the deceitfulness of riches chokes the word, making it unfruitful. These references to earthly riches in the New Testament are not positive images. Jesus told his disciples that it is hard for those who have riches to enter the kingdom of God. He told them that no servant can serve two masters because either he will hate one of them and love the other or he will be loyal to one of them and despise the other. We cannot serve God and money at the same time. Wealth is again presented as a negative influence on spirituality and one that can keep us from serving God in Spirit and in truth.

We have often shown contempt: "For the riches of his kindness, tolerance and patience, not realizing that God's kindness leads you toward repentance" (Rom 2:4). Paul states in Rom 9:23 that God might make known the riches of his glory on the vessels of mercy, which he had prepared beforehand for glory of both Jews and Gentiles whom he has called. In Eph 1:7, he reminds us that "in him we have redemption through his blood, the forgiveness of sins, in accordance with the riches of God's grace." Paul, while acknowledging God's mercy, praised God for "the depth of the riches of the wisdom and knowledge of God! How unsearchable are his judgments, and his paths beyond tracing out?" (Rom 11:33).

God actually wants to show off his riches in us in heaven because he "hath raised us up together, and made us sit together in heavenly places in Christ Jesus: That in the ages to come he might shew the exceeding riches of his grace in his kindness toward us through Christ Jesus" (Eph 2:6–7).

Paul's prayer for you is that "out of his glorious riches he may strengthen you with power through his Spirit in your inner being" (Eph 3:16). He reminds us that "God will meet all your needs according to his glorious riches in Christ Jesus" (Phil 4:19). This statement was written by Paul because the Philippians had sent sacrificial gifts to take care of his needs.

Paul gives a specific warning to the rich: "Command those who are rich in this present world not to be arrogant nor to put their hope in wealth, which is so uncertain, but to put their hope in God, who richly provides us with everything for our enjoyment" (1 Tim 6:17). Paul is teaching us that God richly provides everything that we need for our enjoyment. When we receive from him, we should be generous to the needy and should not be arrogant because our cupboards are so full. He advised that they should trust in God for their security and not to put their trust in the uncertainty of perishable riches:

> Go to now, ye rich men, weep and howl for your miseries that shall come upon you. Your riches are corrupted, and your garments are motheaten. Your gold and silver is cankered; and the rust of them shall be a witness against you, and shall eat your flesh as it were fire. Ye have heaped treasure together for the last days. (Jas 5:1–3)

We need money for our proper existence. However, our riches will have no value when Christ returns for his church. Our effort should not be on the accumulation of earthly treasures that will gather moth and corrosion but on the valuable lasting treasures of the kingdom of God.

In Revelation 18, we learn that those in charge of the economic system will mourn at the fall of the great and strong city of Babylon. This fall is likely to occur when many of the rich and powerful countries of the world unite under the influence of Satan. Its leaders are political leaders and the merchants who will worship money and power, will promote unrestrained luxury and pleasure designed to exercise power over the masses of the people. In Babylon, money is king and will be treated as being more important than God because the divine principles of God will be rejected for commercialism and materialistic pleasures. It will control leaders, people and nations.

Babylon will promote the philosophy that happiness, significant security and fulfilment are attained by the abundance of things that a person possesses. This commercial system seduces the unbelieving world into materialistic stupor so that the world will become drunk with their passion for the pleasures of this city. Commercial activity will not be designed and inspired by God. Rather it is a corrupt system that is being destroyed by God through this judgment to prepare for the coming kingdom of the Lord.

The Babylonian system is also a system of sorcery and deception orchestrated through a world conspiracy involving merchants or superrich magnates in charge of the commercial system through multilateral corporations. The system poisons the minds of its citizens and deceive them through such things as Satanism, medicine, drugs, sorcery and a variety of propaganda. In Babylon, there will be an increase in crime, violence, poverty and no power of choice for individuals to make decisions. The blood of murdered saints shows up in this city and moral values are perverted.

"In one hour, such great wealth has been brought to ruin"! (Rev 18:17). The symbol of the entire wealthy and evil world system will be destroyed suddenly, violently, catastrophically and completely. This destruction of the antichrist's political and economic power is a fatal blow for his commercial and economic empire. The abundance of jewelry, clothing, furnishings, cosmetics, food, travel and souls of men will exist no more.

And then the mourning for the loss of the luxuries and pleasures of Babylon begins. Political leaders of the earth, merchants and the superrich, seamen and luxurious travelers, persons bewitched by her fornication, and those who participated in her sensual pleasures will mourn. The kings of the earth and political leaders, merchants who were flattered into idolatry by being arbitrary and tyrannical over their subjects, all those who rejoice in the success of the church's enemies, and they that have indulged in her pleasure and pride will also mourn.

God warns his believers to extricate themselves from this evil system and avoid God's righteous judgment on that empire indulging in sinful and arrogant self-indulgence. The Bible teaches us:

> Be ye not unequally yoked together with unbelievers: for what fellowship hath righteousness with unrighteousness? and what communion hath light with darkness? And what concord hath Christ with Belial? or what part hath he that believeth with an infidel? And what agreement hath the temple of God with idols? for ye are the temple of the living God; as God hath said, I will dwell in them, and walk in them; and I will be their God, and they shall be my people. Wherefore come out from among them, and be ye separate, saith the Lord, and touch not the unclean thing; and I will receive you. And will be a Father unto you, and ye shall be my sons and daughters, saith the Lord Almighty. (2 Cor 6:14–18)

"For the love of money is the root of all evil, which while some coveted after, they have erred from the faith, and pierced themselves with many sorrows" (1 Tim 6:10). God does not condemn anyone for having riches because he is the source of riches, but he gives grave warnings to those who seek after them more than they seek after him and trust in them more than they trust in him. His greatest desire is for us to set our hearts on things above and not on things on this earth. Paul wrote: "I can do all things through Christ who strengthens me" (Phil 4:13).

There was heresy in the early church which taught that everything in the world of matter is evil and that good existed only in the realm of the spirit. Some Christians regarded money as evil and not money only, but all goods and possessions, including the food we eat and the body itself:

> Not everything which goeth into the mouth defileth a man, but that which cometh out of the mouth, this defileth a man. . . . But those things which proceed out of the mouth come forth from the heart, and these, defile a man. . . . For out of the heart proceed evil thoughts, murders, adulteries, fornications, thefts, false witness, blasphemies. (Matt 15:11–19)

Jesus is saying that nothing you put into your mouth is evil. Wealth is not evil. Evil exists in the heart only.

THE RICH YOUNG RULER

The purpose of the parable of the rich young ruler (Mark 10:17–31) is to reveal heart attitudes toward money, and to warn of affection toward money and not to persuade followers to sell their possessions.

> Now when Jesus heard these things, he said unto him, Yet lackest thou one thing: sell all that thou hast, and distribute unto the poor, and thou shalt have treasure in heaven: and come, follow me. And when he heard this, he was very sorrowful: for he was very rich. And when Jesus saw that he was very sorrowful, he said, How hardly shall they that have riches enter into the kingdom of God! For it is easier for a camel to go through a needle's eye, than for a rich man to enter into the kingdom of God. (Luke 18:22–25)

This ruler sought reassurance. He wanted to be sure he had eternal life. Jesus' question to him who came and called him "good Teacher" was, in essence, "Do you know who I am?" The man did not catch the implications of Jesus' reply. The man was right in calling Jesus good because he is indeed God. The man's wealth made his life comfortable and gave him power and prestige. When Jesus told him to sell everything he owned, he was touching the very basis of his security and identity. The man did not understand that he would be even more secure if he followed Jesus than he was with all his wealth.

Jesus is really asking Christians to get rid of anything that has become more important than God. If our basis for security has shifted from God to what we own, it is better to get rid of those possessions. Money represents power, authority, and success, and often it is difficult for wealthy people to realize their needs and their powerlessness to save themselves. The rich in talent or intelligence suffer the same difficulty. Unless God reaches down into their lives, they will not come to him.

THE RICH FOOL

The rich man in the parable of the rich fool (Luke 12:13–34) exhibited three characteristics. First, he was a fool or one who could not discern spiritual truths and thus his priority on money and material possessions were wrong. Second, he forgot he was a servant, that God owned his life and could demand it back that night. Third, he was a pauper with no eternal investments. We must not allow temporary security to cloud our thankfulness to God.

A good harvest is not in itself a sign of divine favor. Jesus himself said that God makes his sun to rise on the evil and the good, and sends rain on the just and unjust (Matt 5:45). The agriculturist could not start a warehouse rebuilding program after he had reaped his crops. There was going to be a storage problem and this was foreseen by this man. He was alert to any situation involving his work and welfare. He tore down the old warehouses so that greater storage facilities could be provided. He acted quickly and decisively to avert losses and maximize profits. We have to admire his industry, foresight and general ability. But his motivation was self-centered and based on greed. He was not thankful to God for the health, ability and capability he had been given. He did not thank God for the outstanding harvest provided. It appears that his only interest was his own comfort, entertainment and self-indulgence.

When Jesus warned of making the acquiring of wealth one's top priority in life, he opposed accepted thought both then and now that wealth is the source of happiness. How often must that deception be exposed before we will believe in Jesus? Having wealth did not satisfy the rich man in Jesus' parable, but he thought that having more wealth would do just that. In our modern times, many wealthy persons never feel that they have enough. This rich man had wealth but not life. He had all that money could buy, but not that which God gives freely. God gives purpose, security, and assurance of victory over one's problems, and he has given us eternal life through his Son, Jesus Christ.

"But God said unto him, thou fool, this night thy soul shall be required of thee: then whose shall these things be, which thou has provided" (Luke 12:20). The industry, foresight and prosperity of this man were elusive and unreal. They would all vanish with his death, which God told him would occur that very night. He had made no provision for eternal possessions. He only thought of enjoying a self-centered life, and not a Christ centered life. He laid up for himself treasures on earth and none in heaven. The agriculturist spoke of taking his "ease" of self-indulgence, and thought of no one else who may have need. He died before he could begin to use what was stored in his big barns.

Planning for retirement and preparing for life in the latter years of one's existence on earth is wise, but neglecting life after death is completely disastrous. When you accumulate wealth only to enrich yourself, with no concern for helping others, you will enter eternity empty handed. We need to think beyond earth's bound goals and use what we have been given for the sake of God's kingdom.

"So is he that layeth up treasure for himself, and is not rich toward God" (Luke 12:21). In the Sermon on the Mount, Jesus taught that we are to lay up treasures in heaven. Jesus teaches that those who feed the hungry, give drink to the thirsty, visit those who are sick and in prison and clothe the naked will inherit the kingdom of God. James defined "pure religion . . . before God" as visiting orphans and widows (with a view of helping them), and keeping oneself unspotted from the world (living a life without committing sin). Saint John taught that any person who loves God will be compassionate to those in need. God blesses the poor in Spirit and admonishes us to worship him in spirit and in truth. God loves a cheerful giver. We are not just to give a pittance, but make wise investments in the kingdom of God. When we give generously, we are laying up a priceless treasure in heaven that will endure forever. Our treasure is our wealth, i.e., what we possess. It includes our money, time, interest, attention and effort.

THE SHREWD MANAGER

In the parable recorded in Luke 16:1–16, Jesus uses an unrighteous person to clearly demonstrate what righteousness is. Each Christian is a steward of God to whom he has given dominion over the entire world. The world does not belong to us. It belongs to God and he has put us in charge of it to manage it in a way that pleases him.

God has given us our lives to manage also, but our lives and everything in our possession do not belong to us. They belong to God and we have to manage our lives in a way that pleases him. God expects us to act faithfully and wisely with his resources, with whatever, and how much he gives us to manage:

> Let a man consider us, as servants of Christ and stewards of the mysteries of God. Moreover, it is required in stewards that a man be found faithful. (1 Cor 4:1–2)

He does not expect us to be idle while on the job or to perform our tasks with eye service as men pleasers, but to perform our tasks as if the he was present whether or not this was the case. God also expects us to maximize our abilities and capabilities: "As every man has received the gift, even so minister the same one to another, as good stewards of the manifold grace of God" (1 Pet 4:10).

In this parable, the master became aware of the steward's mishandling of the company's assets and the steward knew that he was about to lose his job. The steward then brilliantly used his master's resources to make provision for himself at the present time and also secured the future for himself. He used his position of trust to negotiate business deals for his benefit (corruption). He discounted the debts of the business associates, by as much as 50 percent in some cases, in return for their friendship and generous future considerations for himself when he was no longer employed: "So the master commended the unjust steward because he had done shrewdly. For the sons of the world are more shrewd in their generation than the sons of light" (Luke 16:8). Notice that Jesus commended the manager's brilliant planning for life after work in the employ of the master rather than condemn his unrighteous actions.

Jesus is also teaching us that ungodly people in this world know how to secure the most from the ungodly things of this world that they do not even own. In the same manner, Christians should seek to get the most from the spiritual things that God has made available to them. Instead of misusing our resources, we should ensure that we contribute to the development of the kingdom of God. The steward still had to give account of his work performance as we do. As Christians, we have to defend our performance before God in due course:

> For it is written; as I live says the Lord, every knee shall bow to me, and every tongue shall confess to God. So then, each of us shall give account of himself to God. Therefore, let us not judge one another anymore, but rather resolve this, not to put a stumbling block or a cause to fall in our brother's way. (Rom 14:11–13)

> Men will give account on the day of judgement for every careless word they have spoken. (Matt 12:36)

> For God will bring every work into judgement, including every secret thing, whether good or evil. (Eccl 12:14)

> So, do not be afraid of them. For nothing is concealed that will not be uncovered, or hidden that will not be made known. (Matt 10:26)

> Therefore, judge nothing before the proper time; wait until the Lord comes. He will bring to light what is hidden in darkness and will expose the motives of men's hearts. At that time each will receive his praise from God. (1 Cor 4:5)

> You have placed our iniquities before you, our secret sins in the light of your presence. (Ps 90:8)

Jesus is teaching that Christians are to be friendly to those people who are either rich or in a position of authority who can help us in the church and in our time of need: "And I say to you, make friends for yourselves by unrighteous mammon, that when you fail, they might receive you into an everlasting home" (Luke 16:9). We must lay up eternal treasures in heaven where moth and rust do not corrupt and it cannot be stolen. We build our treasure where our heart is.

We must be careful to use the resources in our trust in the right way. God wants us to be faithful in little and in much:

> He that is faithful in that which is least is faithful also in much: and he that is unjust in the least is unjust also in much. If therefore ye have not been faithful in the unrighteous mammon, who will commit to your trust the true riches? And if ye have not been faithful in that which is another man's, who shall give you that which is your own? (Luke 16:10–12)

The parable of the shrewd manager (Luke 16:1–13) teaches the Christian three principles. First, shrewdness with money can achieve eternal goals. The unjust steward recognized that he would lose his employment and carefully considered what would be his challenge for the future. He grabbed his opportunity and shrewdly put his confidence in the future and not the present. This was an outstanding outcome, although fraudulent, because it recognized the importance of a secured future.

Second, stewardship of money has eternal consequences or benefits that reveal our true priorities. Christians spend too much time focusing on mammon and not on God. We worship our achievements in academia, in sports, in our employment, our businesses, our promotions, our vehicles, our houses, our leisure, and less and less time on worship of God. We treat so many items as gods, devaluing family relationships, and engaging in unchristian activities, while at the same time paying very little attention to the true God of heaven.

We must recognize that fame and fortune are temporal. We brought nothing into this world and can take nothing out. We must bind up every opportunity to assist fellow believers, to help spread the gospel, and give to the poor. There are eternal consequences for our actions and inactions. We must use what God has entrusted to us on earth to secure our future in heaven with him.

Third, stewardship of money prevents bondage to money. Sometimes we borrow money from the bank to build a house. The bank willingly lends us the money but as part of the agreement for the loan, we sign a mortgage document to secure the funds from the bank. The bank hold the title deeds in their possession and we are allowed to have uninhibited freedom to use the property, provided that we adhere to the mortgage covenants. We are in possession of the house keys and the bank retains title until the terms of the agreement are completely satisfied.

God holds the title deeds to everything in our possession. He has a priority claim on everything that we call our own. And there are terms and conditions attached to how we manage these resources. God will always uphold his part in the covenant and as long as we manage these resources in accordance with to the terms of the covenant, we will have the freedom to use them.

THE PARABLE OF THE LABORERS IN THE VINEYARD / THE COMPLAINING WORKERS

The parable recorded in Matt 6:1–20 is the story of a farmer who hires laborers at different times during the day and each employee was paid the same contractual price for participating in the work during the contractual period no matter what time of the day the employee started the performance of his task.

The terms and conditions of employment, including salary, were agreed on before work commenced. The person who worked the full twelve hours agreed on one denarius while the other employees agreed on a fair wage. The farmer found an idler at 5 p.m. and inquired: "Why stand ye here idle"? They had an excuse. No one bothered to hire them. We want to be hired at a certain wage or in a certain type of location or business with certain conditions. The farmer was unhindered by their excuse and hired them to work in the vineyard. If you are a Christian and standing idle, there is plenty of work for you to do in God's vineyard because: "The harvest truly is plenteous, but the laborers are few" (Matt 9:37).

We must

> lift up our eyes and look on the fields; for they are white already to harvest. And he that reapeth receiveth wages, and gathereth fruits unto life eternal: that he that soweth and he that reapeth may rejoice together. (John 4:34–35)

There must be no delays. There is coming a time in our lives when the harvest will end and God's heavenly rest will begin. But we must do the work of our Father in heaven while it is day because the night will come when no man can work.

The workers were duly paid at the agreed time and the expected then happens. Employees who started at six in the morning lodged their complaint. There are at least three complaining attitudes in this parable. We often hear and read of so many persons who worked and never received a paycheck, or received their check late. We never receive our payment late with God. He is never too early nor too late, but always on time. There was justice for the workers who were hired first:

> But when the first came, they supposed that they should have received more; and they likewise received every man a penny. And when they had received it, they murmured against the goodman of the house, Saying, "These last have wrought but one hour." (Matt 20:10–12)

There was definitely hopeful anticipation on the part of the employees who worked the full twelve hours bearing the heat of the day. They expected additional reward for their faithfulness but their unrealistic, unjustified expectations were unfulfilled.

The workers were disappointed and lodged a complaint directly to the owner himself. The owner was being charged with injustice. This was the sin of envy for even if they did not receive more in their pay package, they would have been satisfied if the other employees received less than the owner paid. Christians must be careful not to allow envy to minimize their blessings and lose the spirit of gratitude and praise toward God. It may cause us into dangerous habits of covetousness and lust of the eyes. The employee's envy of the grace the owner had shown toward others led them to complain that he was evil. We that have small and petty minds have problems understanding the wholesome generosity of others.

In vv. 13–16, the generosity of the owner of the vineyard was explained. It was pointed out that the owner had lived up to his part of the contract by paying the denarius for the day's work. Justice was done and so the complaint was about the owner's generosity. Let us look at ourselves in the mirror. Have we ever complained about God's generosity to others compared to his generosity to us? We feel convicted that despite all the blessings we receive we deserve even more. We also believe that others are receiving blessings that they never worked for and of course, do not deserve.

God's gifts are determined by grace, not our merit, and we should be thankful for every demonstration of his grace, whoever the recipient is. The owner had a legal and moral right to discharge his resources in accordance with his own good will. We must take pride in our long and faithful service for the King of kings and Lord of lords, but must be prepared to share our reward equally with those who have done less and be full of joy that we can do so.

When we have finished our work here on earth, we will receive a home in heaven, not out of any goodness of ours, but because our Lord is full of mercy, compassion, and generosity. Let us therefore not be envious because he is also good to others: "So the last shall be the first, and the first last: for many are called but few chosen" (Matt 20:16).

Notice that in the parable, all the workers were called, that all responded to the call, and worked to the end of the day, and all received their reward. The one stumbling block from being chosen was the envy shown by those employees who had worked the longest. Remember that we may work for the kingdom of God, but may not be among his chosen ones:

> Not everyone that saith unto me, Lord, Lord, shall enter into the kingdom of heaven; but he that doeth the will of my Father which is in heaven. Many will say to me in that day, Lord, Lord, have we not prophesied in thy name? and in thy name have cast out devils? and in thy name done many wonderful works? And then will I profess unto them, I never knew you: depart from me, ye that work iniquity. (Matt 7:21–23)

We must be careful with how we seek to achieve a standard of excellence in accordance with the wealth of this world and which is not important at all in the kingdom of God, and in fact, maybe a hindrance, as it was in this case. Let us give up all for the sake of the kingdom of God because all our efforts and our sacrifices will not be in vain but will indeed be rewarded. Our rewards will not be measured according to the world's material standards.

BEWARE OF COVETOUSNESS

To covet is to wish to have possessions that belong to others and enjoy it as if it is our very own. Coveting comes with the desire to possess a thing because it looks good and is beautiful to our eyes. Covetousness also arises from a desire to better ourselves, for example, through a desire for authority already vested in another, for selfish means. It means indulging in thoughts that lead to actions named in other commandments. Coveting includes envy, which means that we resent that others own what we don't have. We are not allowed to have appetites and desires of a corrupt and selfish nature. The assets that we possess in this manner make us happy just for a little while. Real happiness and contentment are supplied by God and God alone.

The tenth and final commandment which the Lord gave to Moses on Mount Sinai is recorded in Exod 20:17: "Thou shalt not covet thy neighbor's house, thou shalt not covet thy neighbor's wife, nor his manservant, nor his maidservant, nor his ox, nor his ass, nor anything that is thy neighbor's." God speaks to us in several ways. He speaks to us through his Spirit, through our consciences, through vision, through his written and spoken word, etc. Sometimes he speaks with a majestic display of power and at other times, he speaks with a still small voice. God chose to give the commandments from Mount Sinai, by speaking directly to Moses, who was the conduit through whom the people of Israel and the world would receive the message, intended to guide us to a life of practical holiness.

Jesus told his disciples that covetousness comes from within the heart and makes us impure. The Bible gives several examples of evil desires leading to more sin. In the battle Israel versus Jericho, God commanded the Israelites to destroy the entire city of Jericho, except for Rahab and her family, who had provided refuse and later a way of escape for the spies from Israel who were planning the war against Jericho. The Israelites were instructed to take nothing from Jericho because everything there was devoted to destruction. Furthermore, if any person took any of the spoils from Jericho, Israel became liable to destruction and trouble.

Achan desired silver, gold and a beautiful Babylonian garment, and he stole them despite knowing that they had been devoted to the Lord. Not only was he killed as a result of his coveting, but his sons, daughters, oxen, asses, and sheep also died. Even his tent was buried with them (Josh 7:18–26). It also led to the death of thirty-six innocent Israelite soldiers and their defeat in the war at Ai (vv. 1–5).

Achan was disobedient to God's instructions and coveted a beautiful robe, gold and silver. As sure as night follows day, be sure Achan's sin would have found him out because God has placed our iniquities always before him: "Our secret sins in the light of his countenance" (Num 32:23; Ps 90:8). For his covetousness, Achan and his entire family received the death penalty, and all his possessions were destroyed. Achan's covetousness contaminated the whole nation of Israel causing them to lose the war of Ai. When God's people sin, remember it will have a deleterious effect on others. Our disobedience to God will result in suffering for us and others. When we are greedy, our greedy actions bring trouble to our family and friends.

Achan, like many of us, did not believe that God's way was the best, and so he disobeyed God, stole his property, and then tried to cover up his sins by hiding the stolen property. The Bible teaches us:

> He that covereth his sins shall not prosper: but whoso confesseth and forsaketh them shall have mercy. (Prov 28:13)
> If we confess our sins, he is faithful and just to forgive us our sins, and to cleanse us from all unrighteousness. (1 John 1:9)

God informed Joshua that the battle of Ai was lost because someone had stolen goods and hidden them in his tent. God told the people of Israel that he would not be with them until they destroyed the accursed thing. They were required to sanctify themselves because on the following day, he would point out the culprit. God could have pointed out the thief immediately, but decided on the following morning to give Achan a chance to confess, seek God's forgiveness and forsake his wrongdoing. Achan did not confess but waited for the thorough investigations to find him guilty. As Christians, we must recognize that there are consequences for sin. In this case, the nation of Israel was humiliated by a small army from Ai, losing thirty-six soldiers in the process, and Achan and his family lost their lives.

Abimelech desired the prestige of the throne, and he murdered seventy times to get it (Judg 9:1–5).

Covetousness produces lying, lusts, and murders. This is exemplified when David desired and coveted Bathsheba, another man's wife, leading him to commit adultery and then try to cover it up with murder (2 Sam 11:1–27). David was one of the greatest leaders of all Israel and a leader cannot be a covetous person, because they will not love justice and will not be merciful. A covetous leader will take bribes and will sell himself to the highest bidder. But if he hates covetousness, he will prolong and bring peace to his own life, to that of his business, his government, his country and his church. God needs people that are honest and of impeccable character in leadership positions and in every facet of life. The writer of Proverbs was able to assure us that a person who hates covetousness shall have long life (Prov 28:16).

Ahab desired Naboth's vineyard, and it led him and Jezebel to compound that sin by lying, then taking God's name in vain and committing murder (1 Kgs 21:1–19). Predatory thought leads to predatory action. The evidence is clear. Breaking this commandment sets off a chain reaction that consumes others and self before its effect dissipates. We must amputate this desire so the sin will never become an act, and then we will remain pure, as will the object of our desire. Imagination is a wonderful gift from God, but if fed dirt by the eye, the imagination can easily become impure.

> And one of the company said unto him, Master, speak to my brother, that he divides the inheritance with me. And he said unto him, man, who made me a judge or divider over you? And he said unto them, take heed and beware of covetousness: for a man's life consisteth not in the abundance of things which he possesseth. (Luke 12:13)
> Not everyone that saith unto me, Lord, Lord, shall enter into the kingdom of heaven; but he that doeth the will of my Father which is in heaven. Many will say to me in that day, Lord, Lord,

have we not prophesied in thy name? and in thy name have cast out devils? and in thy name done many wonderful works? And then will I profess unto them, I never knew you: depart from me, ye that work iniquity. (Luke 12:16–21)

Our supermarkets and other stores are overflowing with food and other merchandise of various brands and quality. Our highways are jammed with some of the most modern, luxurious and expensive automobiles. Many own luxury yachts and private aircraft. Technology has advanced beyond our wildest dreams. In the middle of all these wonderful blessings, God reminds us that a man's life is not ultimately fulfilled by the abundance of our possessions. This is because we will never own enough of the things we desire. The true value of our life is found in relationships with persons and in the quality of our faith, hope, love, joy and peace. In a relationship with our blessed Lord and Savior Jesus Christ, life can find meaning, intensity, variety and genuine, lasting satisfaction.

Luke 12:1 tells us that Jesus was at that time speaking to an "innumerable multitude of people." He was speaking of witnessing for God and trusting in his spirit in times of persecution when one of the men in the crowd interrupted his speech with a question about an inheritance. The inheritance had not been divided to his satisfaction and he solicited Jesus' help in seeing that this was properly done. Jesus refrained from listening to the details of the complaint. He recognized that the disgruntled man's primary interest was in reaping material advantage in an estate dispute. Instead of focusing on God, his heart was on the money. There are dangers involved in the habit of envying the prosperity of others. This habit may lead us to minimize our own blessings and to lose the spirit of gratitude and praise toward God. Sometimes we resent the fact that God has been generous to someone else. It is difficult for us to shake the conviction that we are deserving of God's blessings and we usually have little difficulty convincing ourselves that we are more deserving than the person who has received the blessing. We need to recognize that God's generosity is determined by grace, not our merit, and we should be happy and rejoice at every demonstration of his grace, whether or not we are the recipients.

Subject Index

Abednego, 172–73, 208–9
Abel, 163
Abimelech, 226
Abraham
    all the families of the earth blessed through, 20–21
    allowed Lot his choice of land, 21
    anticipated his inheritance, 163
    blessed by God with wealth, 213
    called by God when ninety-nine years old, 98
    died in faith, 163
    faith of, 162–63
    as the father of all nations, xiii
    gave tithes to Melchizedek, 185
    gave to Melchizedek, 187
    God's covenant with, 207
    God's promises to, 21
    Jacob receiving the blessings of, 120–21
    justified by faith and counted as righteous, 63
    laid the foundation for Christians to build on, 164
    receiving the blessings of, 18
    waited with patience, 138
Achan, 118, 225, 226
Adam, 4, 5, 14, 15
addiction, demons of, 210
addictive nature, of some drugs, 209
adoption, as God's own children, 54–55, 86

adultery, 6, 116–17, 195–97
afflictions, 67, 139
agriculture, securing economic prosperity, 127
Agrippa, 193
King Ahab, 174, 175, 226
King Ahaz, of Judah, 24
Ai, battle of, 157, 225
alcohol abuse, destroying thinking, 202
alcoholic beverage, 203, 209
all things, created by God, 25
Ananias, 72, 138
angel, at the sepulchre of Jesus, 31–32
angels of God, separating the tares from the wheat, 46
animals, unblemished sacrificed, 22
Annas, mock trial before, 28
anxiety, as failure to trust God, 162
Aphrodite, temple of, 198
apostles, waited for the baptism of the Holy Ghost, 71
appetites, 73, 75
ark of the Lord, taken by the Philistines, 208
arms of Jesus, being secured in, 90–91
Asenath, wife of Joseph, 127
asking in faith, without the slightest doubt, 161
athletes, training endured by, 166

Baal and its false prophets, destroyed by Elijah, 175–77

Babylon, 215
Barbados
  credit rating downgraded, 146
  importance of agriculture, 127–28
  location of, 113
  proclaimed God as the head of the nation, xiii
  Stuart as seventh prime minister of, 134
basic needs, satisfying, ix–x
basic training, of the Royal Barbados Police Force, 186
Bathsheba, 5–6, 117, 226
being born of water and of the Spirit, 38–39
believers
  characteristics of, 43
  God honoring the requests of, 159–62
  recognized by God as perfect, 97–100
  separating from unbelievers, 16, 43
  serving God or succumbing to the old nature, 66
Belshazzar, king of Babylon, 185
Bethel, 122
Bezaleel, 111
Bible
  as God-inspired scriptures, vii–viii
  God's word presented in, 134
  referring to our fallen nature, 66
  sanctioned ten percent, 186–87
  stories of divided families, 130–31
  teaching that all have sinned, 4
biblical prosperity, building blocks of, 184
birthright, of Esau, 119, 207
blessed, meaning of in Hebrew, 181–82
blessings
  of Abraham, 18, 120–21
  common-law relationships not receiving God's, 197
  Esau squandered, 207–8
  financial, 184
  meaning of, 188–89
  receiving, ix
blood, shed to get the skins of the animals, 22

blood of Jesus Christ
  cleansing and sanctifying the church, 97
  cup of wine sanctified as the new covenant in, 205
  redemption through, 52
  scriptures on, 30–31
bodies
  illnesses resulting from abuse or misuse of, 76
  keeping clean, 56
  offering to God, 192–94
  presenting as a living sacrifice, 190
  returned to the dust of the ground, 13
  sanctification of, 75–77
  as temples, 210, 211
body and soul, cleansing and making holy, 72
Bolt, Usain, 177
Book of Life, 104, 173
born of God, 94
borrower, as slave to the lender, 148
brand new creature, in Christ Jesus, 3
Brook of Cherith, Elijah went to, 174
brother's keeper, being, 212
burnt offering, 23
business community, role in the life of nations, xii

Caiaphas, 28
Canaan, Abraham chose the godly land of, 21
capital offense, adultery as, 195
capital punishment, cross as the cruelest form of, 30
carnal mind, as hostile toward God, 66
carnal person, dominated by self-life, 66
centurion, faith of, 160
character, importance of a person's, 153
charismatic personality, Barbadians looking for, 152
cheerful giver, God loving, 183
chief baker and butler, dreams of, 126
chief priests, seeking methods to murder Jesus, 48

SUBJECT INDEX

children
    advised to obey their parents, 157
    born spiritually dead to God, 13
children of God, 43, 46, 96
children of the kingdom, cast into outer darkness, 18
choice, power of, 9
Christ. *See* Jesus Christ
Christian growth, God's pathway for, 100–101
Christian journey, tests and temptations of, 172–73
Christian perfection, 81–105
    Christ commanding, 93–97
    defined, 81
    failing the test of, 82
Christianity, viii, 113–14, 128
Christians
    attached to Christ like a branch attached to a tree, 160–61
    becoming new creations, 85
    as beneficiaries of God's prosperity, viii
    born of water and of the Spirit, 94
    characteristics of, 3
    clothing themselves with Christian character, 140
    crucifying God afresh, 87
    defending performance before God, 220
    enduring conflicts and sufferings of life, 67
    expected to grow spiritually, 73
    as the foundation and cornerstone, 212
    involved in common-law marriages, 197
    living free from sin, 82
    loving fellow, 79
    obedience required of, 69
    overcoming Pharisee-like characteristics, 48–50
    participating in the work of the ministry, 100
    responsibilities of, 42–43
    seeking the most from spiritual things of God, 220
    setting aside all evil and accepting the word of God, 93
    spending too much time worrying, 162
    standing before God at that great white throne, 173
    treating many items as gods, 221
church. *See also* early church; perfect churches
    blood of Jesus Christ cleansing and sanctifying, 97
    as a body of Christ, 212
    at Corinth, 183
    elders of, 170
    at Ephesus, 101
    gifts Jesus gave to, 100
    as God's living, spiritual house, 212
    as God's voice in the nation, xii
    identifying laws contrary to God's holy standard, xii
    immorality diminishing, 195
    of Laodiceans, 101
    leaders preferring the comfort zone of, 171
    Paul chastised for profaning the Lord's Supper, 26
    Paul commanding to "be perfect," 94
    at Pergamos, 101
    persecution of, 193
    at Philadelphia, 102–3
    riches of no value when Christ returns for his, 214
    at Sardis, 101–2
    at Smyrna, 102
    Stuart gave land for the erection of an evangelical, 140
    at Thyatira, 101
Comforter. *See* Holy Spirit
commandments, keeping, 44, 94
commercial activity, as a corrupt system, 215
common-law relationships, 197
compassion, showing, 146
competition rules, athletes violating, 167
confession, act of, 196
consciences, 11, 67

consequences, of sin, 12, 226
consistency, between sowing and reaping, 182
contentment, core value of for Stuart, 135–36
conversion, 50, 58–61
Corinth, church at, 183
Corinthians, puffed up in imaginary wisdom, 113
Cornelius, 36, 85, 140
corrupt tree, bearing evil fruits, 92
corruption, reaping from the flesh, 74
coup, Stuart's handling of a perceived, 142–45
covenant. *See also* new covenant; old covenant
   God established with Israel, 21–22
   of God with Abraham, 207
   of Judas with the chief priests, 26
   marriage as a lifelong, 200
   obligations and benefits of, 22
cover-up, sin of, 6
coveting, 136, 224
covetous leader, 226
covetousness, 224–27
creator, God as, 24
criminal on the cross, granted mercy by Jesus, 4
cross, as the essence of God's wisdom and power, 30
crown
   of glory, 169–70
   of life eternal, 102, 172–73
   of rejoicing, 171–72
   reward of an imperishable, 166–67
   of righteousness, 99–100, 167–68
crucifixion, of Jesus, 28
cup of bitter agony, accepted by Christ in the garden of Gethsemane, 27
currencies, devaluation of in Barbados, 147
curse of the law, Christ redeemed us from, 29

daily needs, God taking care of, xi
Damascus Road conversion, of Saul of Tarsus (Paul), 61
Daniel, refused to eat the king's food, 208–9
David
   acknowledging his sin, 117
   Bathsheba and, 5–6, 226
   confessed his sin to God, 51
   confronted his sins and repented, 99
   on the LORD
      being his stay, 143
      keeping Israel, 144
      as against those who do evil, 103
   not fit to build God's house of worship, 111–12
   recognized as perfect, 99
   on wealth coming from God, 213
day's work, for a day's pay, 182
the dead
   hearing Jesus' voice and living, 53
   raised by Elijah, 175
dead church, at Sardis, 101–2
death
   consequences of, 12–19
   of Jesus, 28–31
   reigned from the moment of Adam's rebellion, 6–7
   or repentance, 37–38
debauchery, 204
debt, reducing for a country, 149
deceivers, at work in ancient Corinth, 194
decision-making, of Stuart depended on God, 134
deeds of the flesh, ensuring the death of, 74
Democratic Labour Party government, of Stuart, 152
despair, suffered by Elijah, 178
devaluation, of the currency of Barbados's neighbors, 147
devil. *See* Satan
devotion to holiness, of the Pharisees, 48
devourer, God rebuking, 181
directional change, in our way of living, 69–70
disciples, 35, 39, 41
discontentment, sin of, 136
disequilibrium, policy response to, 147

disobedience
: of Adam as sin, 15
: brought death upon all men, 5
: to God, 9, 155, 225
: resulting in defeat by an enemy, 157

divisive man, rejecting, 145
divorce, 196
"DLP Rift" article, about the eager eleven, 142
doers, of the word of God, 93
doing good, sacrifices of, 191
dominion, as not ownership, 186
doubt, 8, 11, 161, 162
drugs, illegal, 209–11
drunkenness, 201–5

early church, 84–85, 185–86, 216
earthly nature, putting to death, 68
Easter morning, events of, 31
eating habits, keeping under control, 205
economic recession, 141
economy, of Egypt as managed by Joseph, 129
education, producing human beings, 133
elders of the church, 170
Eli, the priest, sin of the sons of, 208
Elijah, 175–79
Elisha, servant of Elijah, 177
Elizabeth (wife of Zacharias), 100
employees, complaining attitudes of, 223
enduring to the end, 44, 173
enemies, loving our, 79–80
Enoch, 100, 163
envy, 223, 224
Ephesus, loveless church at, 101
Ephraim, woe to the drunkards of, 204
Esau, 119–22, 207–8
the eternal, focusing on, 165
eternal death
: avoiding the consequences of, 12
: described, 15–19
: facing the consequences of, 38
: Jesus abolished the law of, 54
: spiritual death resulting in, 200
: wages of sin as, 15, 88

eternal inheritance, 163, 177–78
eternal life
: all God's people resurrected to, 54
: God has given us, 91
: inheriting from the Spirit, 74
: Jesus offering, 37
: in New Jerusalem, 163
: rich young man wanting to inherit, 82–83

eternal possessions, rich men making no provision for, 218
evangelical churches, Stuart's early involvement in of, 133
Eve, 4–5
everlasting crown. *See* imperishable crown
everlasting life, 54
evil, existing in the heart only, 216
evil and death, choosing, 7
evil things
: coming from within, 206
: coming from within and defiling a man, 88

exultation, humility required for, 6
Ezekiel
: called to stand in the gap for God, 158
: preaching God's word of divine judgment, 103
: on a righteous man turning from his righteousness, 103–4
: on the righteous taking good care of the poor and needy, 84
: sent to proclaim God's word, 71

faith
: acting in, 11
: Christ dwelling in our hearts through, 63
: of critical importance for the believer, 160
: demonstrating, 21
: lack of, 88, 89
: transforming us to a Christian life, 55

faithfulness, 98, 125, 173
false testimony, as wicked and sinful, 125

fame and fortune, as temporal, 221
families, stories of divided, 130–31
family meeting, of Jacob, 123–24
family relationships, wisdom promoting happy, 115
family reunion, of Joseph, 130–32
famine, in the land of Egypt, 128
farmer, hiring laborers for different time periods and paying each the same amount, 222
fastest human being, Elijah as, 177
fasting, power of, when seen by God only, 49
Father in heaven. *See also* God
    forsook Jesus when he was dying on the cross, 16
    Jesus ascended to, 32
    prayer of intercession of Jesus to, 90
    will of, 91–93
favoritism, showing, 12
Felix, 193
female impersonators, 200
fiery furnace, condemned to death in, 173
fig tree, cursed by Jesus, 160
financial blessings, God closing the windows of, 184
Fiorina, Carly, 210
first fruits, tithing with, 181
firstborn son, privileges in a Jewish family, 207
fixed exchange rate policy, Barbados sticking with, 147–48
flesh
    destruction of the deeds of, 74–75
    lusteth against the Spirit, 66
    serving the law of sin, 11
fleshly lusts, abstaining from, 167
food security, obedience bringing, 155–56
foolishness, leading to disorder, 110–11
foreign exchange controls, 146–49
forgetfulness, burying sins in the sea of, 35
forgiveness
    as a core value for Stuart, 139–40, 145–46
    of God, 37, 50–52, 61, 71, 85–86
    of sins resulting from repentance, 35
fornication, 197–98
    defined, 197
    Paul on, 195, 197
    tolerated in our society, 77
foundation, Jesus Christ as, 164
fruitless Christians, cast into outer darkness, 18
fruits in our lives, produced by the Holy Spirit, 86
future in heaven, securing, 221

Gamaliel, 60
garden of Eden, 4, 20, 58
garden of Gethsemane, 27
gardener, God our Father as, 87
Gatlin, Justin, 177
generosity, 140–42, 183, 223, 227
Gentiles, 36, 61
gift of the Holy Spirit, receiving, 34–36
gifts
    of God determined by grace, 223
    God not accepting flawed, 191
    Jesus gave to the church, 100
giving, showing real attitudes toward God, 183, 191
glory, reward of a crown of, 169–70
glory of God, 11–12, 70, 170
glutton, 205
gluttony, 205–9
God. *See also* Father in heaven
    accomplishing his predetermined purposes, 111
    adoption as children of, 54–55
    answered Elijah by fire, 175–77
    breathed into us our mind, emotions and will, 78
    called Joshua, 71
    chose the people of Israel to be his own people, 20
    commanded the Israelites to destroy Jericho, 225
    concept of prosperity and abundance, ix

SUBJECT INDEX

Cornelius's relationship with, 36
covenanted to change us, 67–68
created
   everything and owning
      everything, 186, 222
   heaven and earth over a period
      of six days, 4
   man in his own image, 200
   Satan as a model of perfection,
      wisdom and beauty, 6
   us without sin in a holy state, 65
   the world by wisdom, 112–13
delivering us from all our
   afflictions, 139
demanding that we love him
   completely, 8
destroyed the entire world by
   flood, 20
determined before the foundation
   of the world to save those in
   Christ, 7
expecting us to maximize our
   abilities and capabilities, 219
forgiveness of, 37, 50–52, 61, 71,
   85–86
gave Israel a listing of foods they
   should not eat, 206
gave man the power to choose, 4
has not prevented acts of
   uncleanness, 199–200
holding the title deeds to everything
   in our possession, 222
honoring the requests of his
   believers, 159–62
informed Joshua why the battle of
   Ai was lost, 226
instructions relating to the garden
   of Eden, 4
Jacob's first-time encounter with,
   121–23
kindness leading toward
   repentance, 214
knowing
   how to deliver Christians from
      temptations, 104–5
   our character before we are
      born, 120
leading our household to serve, 9
left his throne of glory and came to
   earth as a man, 25
loved us and sent his son, 30
loving a cheerful giver, 219
making
   his sun to rise on the evil and
      the good, 218
   us worthy of his calling, 92
needing
   to completely purify us, 73
   people honest in leadership
      positions, 226
as never too early nor too late with
   his payment, 223
not abiding in a smoked-out
   temple, 211, 212
not pleased with mediocre
   offerings, 191
obedience allowing God to choose
   us, 158–59
offering our bodies to, 192–94
ordained Solomon to build his
   house before he was born, 112
as our supreme authority, 155
planned Jacob's prosperity, 119
predestinated us to be holy, 80
preparing a table before us in the
   presence of our enemies, 156
prospered Job, 158
provided
   food security for Elijah, 175
   oil and wine and corn to Israel,
      202–3
putting first in our lives, 50
remained true to his promises, 192
robbing, 189–94
sanctified
   his chosen people Israel, 68–69
   Jeremiah, 71
   Moses, 71
sending
   his chariot for Elijah, 178
   whatever we ask him for, 161
serving in the army of, 71–73
showing no partiality and
   accepting no bribes, 12
speaking directly to Moses, 225
speaking to us in several ways, 225

God (continued)
   standard of holiness, 72–73
   substituted himself for us, 30
   supplying
      our needs, x, xi
      real happiness and contentment, 224
   sustained Elijah, the widow, and her son, 175
   taking no pleasure in sin, 23
   talked to Moses from a flame of fire, 71
   tithe belonging to, 184–85
   transgression of the law of, 10
   wanting to show off his riches in us in heaven, 214
   warning believers to extricate themselves from the evil commercial system, 216
   wisdom from, 111–12
   word of
      doers of, 93
      Ezekiel proclaiming, 71, 103
      hearts and minds hardened to, 45
      understanding as presented in the Bible, 134
godliness, with contentment, 135
good and life, choosing, 7
good deeds, doing, 11, 47
good fight of faith, 167
good harvest, as not in itself a sign of divine favor, 218
Good Samaritan, used wine and oil to dress wounds, 203
good tree, bearing good fruits, 92
gospel
   of Christ, 170
   enduring suffering for the sake of, 167
   of the kingdom, 44
   obeying, 15–16
   power of, 114
   Saul of Tarsus' mission to exterminate, 60
   wisdom of God exhibited by the preaching of, 113
government
   bringing idle lands into production, 128
   head of should not drink of alcoholic beverages, 204
   needing savings for critical times, 127
   of Stuart, deposed, 152–54
government economic plan, value of, x–xi
grace
   of God, 15, 19, 55, 82
   shown by the owner toward others, 223
guilt or trespass offering, 23

happiness, as a benefit of wisdom, 115
hardships, endured by Paul, 168
health, as a benefit of wisdom, 115–16
hearts
   emotions and passions of, 78
   exposing the motives of, 220
   kingdom of God in our, 43–47
   minds and, 34, 45
   setting on things above, 216
heathen, justified through faith, 18
heaven and earth, created by pure wisdom, 112–13
hell, 16–18
help, coming only from God, x
helpmeet, for a man, 200
"here," meaning of in Hebrews 7:8, 185
heresy, teaching that matter is evil, 216
Herod Antipas, 28, 195
Herodias, 195
highways, jammed with expensive automobiles, 227
holiness
   exhibiting in daily living, 96
   Pharisees devotion to, 48
   predestination to, 80
   required to serve in God's army, 71–73
   requirement for, 62–80
   restoring a sinning Christian to a condition of, 212
Holy Ghost. See Holy Spirit
Holy Spirit
   abiding in all who accept Jesus, 188

SUBJECT INDEX

adopting us as heirs with Christ, 89
advancing the kingdom of God, 38
allowing complete authority in our hearts, 87
allowing to have dominion, 67
bodies must be controlled by, 76
came upon Mary, 24
conceived Jesus, 95
convicting us of sin and drawing us to God, 9
desiring what is contrary to the flesh, 74
executing search warrants on all things, 35
fell on all in Cornelius's house, 36
leading us to treat others the way that Jesus would treat them, 67
left Adam's spirit, 13, 14
permitting to be in complete control, 193
as the presence and power of God, 24
protecting us against the craftiness of the devil, 89
purifying us, 62–63
receiving the gift of, 34–36
redemption to receive, 56
returning us to a state of righteousness, 95
sealing us, 86–90
teaching us, 92
holy temple, our bodies as God's, 56
home in heaven, receiving, 224
homosexuality, 198–201
honest wages, spelled out in Deuteronomy, 182
honesty, establishing by bringing the tithe, 184
hope and prosperity, as God's plan for us today, vii
human beings, creation of each as unique, 112
human race, created on the sixth day, 4
human will, as man's most precious gift from God, 78
humankind, born with a sinful nature (spiritually dead), 65
humility, 6, 44

idolatry, 9, 158
illegal drugs, 209–11
image of Christ, transformed into, 64
imagination, easily becoming impure, 226
"I-Man" Pharisee, praying with himself, 49
immorality
    diminishing the spiritual maturity of the church, 195
    sexual, 6, 72, 77
    wisdom saving us from, 116–17
imperishable crown, reward of, 166–67
impiety, denying all, 55
inaction, sin of, 11
infidelity, as the only biblical reason for divorce, 196
inheritance
    Esau transferring to Jacob, 119–20
    Jesus refrained from listening to an inquiry about, 227
    obedience ensuring God's, 162–65
    possibility of losing, 207
International Monetary Fund (IMF), 146, 148
Isaac, 119, 120, 121
Isaiah
    confessed that he was a man of unclean lips, 114
    on conversion, 58
    experienced a vision of the exalted God, 114
    on Jerusalem the Holy City, 105
    prophesied of the Savior's birth, 24
    prophesied that when Christ returns he will prepare a feast and serve well-aged wines, 205
    saw the Lord sitting on his throne, 71
    stood in the gap for God, 159
Israel, 22, 68–69
Israelites
    choosing to serve the God of Abraham, Isaac and Moses, 9
    doubted God and refused to obey him, 8
    God's advice to on obedience, xiii
    God's plan of prosperity for, vii

Israelites (continued)
  meant to become a kingdom of priests and a holy nation, 8
  not drinking wine or strong drink during the forty years in the wilderness, 203
  reminded that God produces wealth, 109-0
  taking accursed things from Jericho, 157
  wrong attitudes in their hearts toward God, 88

Jacob
  blessed by God with wealth, 213
  chosen to be stronger than his older brother, Esau, 119
  conned into faithfully laboring for Laban for fourteen years, 122
  early success of, 118-24
  Esau transferring his inheritance right to, 119-20
  family meeting of, 123-24
  first-time encounter with God, 121-23
  gave up his scheming attitude, 122
  Isaac pronouncing blessings on, 120
  known by God, 120
  obeyed his father, 121
  received through Isaac the gift of wine, 202
  receiving the blessings of Abraham, 120-21
  returned home a very wealthy man, 124
James (book of), 63, 110, 174, 219
James (son of Zebedee), 27, 156, 169
Jehoshaphat, advised newly appointed judges, 12
King Jehoshaphat, blessed by God with wealth, 213
Jeremiah, 71, 159
Jericho, Joshua conquered, 118
Jesus Christ. *See also* blood of Jesus Christ
  announced his own death as penalty for the sins of the world, 25-26
  asking Christians to get rid of anything more important than God, 217
  benefits of his death, 28-31
  betrayed, rejected and condemned by his own people, 30
  birth of, 24, 95
  called Matthew from his position of tax collector, 171
  as Chief Shepherd, 169
  cleansed Paul from his sin, 72
  coming quickly, 164
  commanding Christian perfection, 93-97
  in complete control of Paul, 63
  conceived
    by divine action, 24
    by the Holy Ghost, 95
  as in control, 173
  on deceitfulness of riches choking the word, 213
  on denying ourselves, 166-67
  did not sin, 96
  died for our sins, 20-33
  emphasized forgiveness, 139
  endured the cross as our perfect example, 138
  on everlasting treasure, viii-ix
  first miracle turning a large quantity of water into wine, 202
  fulfilled Old Testament promises, 40
  gave his life for the sins of the whole world, 28, 37
  on the greatest of all God's commandments, 8
  as high priest and mediator of the new covenant, 189
  holding the keys of death and hell, 14
  kept his silence, 151
  on the kingdom of heaven, 38
  lived on this earth for thirty-three years, 25

SUBJECT INDEX

on living perfect Christian lives, 83
marveled at the faith of the
  centurion, 160
message
  concerning the kingdom of God,
    40–41
  preaching good news of the
    gospel to sinners, 171
  offering a well of living water (Holy
    Spirit), 35
  promises to overcomers, 103
  pronounced seven woes on the
    scribes and Pharisees, 48
  refocused Paul's mission, 193
  restoring sinning Christians to
    holiness, 212
  resurrection of, 31–33
  returning to meet his chosen
    people in the air, 178
  risen and ascended to his Father in
    heaven and seated at his right
    hand, 32
  sanctified the cup of wine as "the
    new covenant in my blood," 205
  saved us according to his abundant
    mercy, 74
  saw past the sins of Zacchaeus, 51
  secured in the arms of, 90–91
  on the significance of sharing with
    the needy, 84
  as the sin offering, 23
  spoke to Saul, 61
  suffered temptation but committed
    no sin, 125
  teaching
    to lay up treasures in heaven,
      218–19
    that we must be born again, 94
  tempted as we are tempted but
    refused to yield, 5
  told Zacchaeus he would be a guest
    at his house, 51
  took our judgment when he died
    on the cross, 16
  trials and torture of, 27–28
  as the true unblemished sacrifice,
    192
  as the true vine, 87

as truly God conceived by the Holy
  Ghost, 25
as the ultimate sacrifice on the
  cross for all, 24–28
as the way, the truth and the life, 79
as the wisdom of God, 114–15
Jethro, 149
Jews, anticipated a powerful political
  leader, 43
Jezebel, 174, 175, 178, 226
Joanna, 31
Job
  faith of put to the test by Satan, 150
  loved and obeyed God, 157–58
  never deviated from his love for
    God, 151
  recognized as perfect, 98
  rewarded double, 138
  rich beyond comprehension, 150
John (the Apostle)
  advising us not to sin, 93
  astonished at the large catch of fish
    resulting from obedience, 156
  on being compassionate to those in
    need, 219
  in the garden of Gethsemane, 27
  on having confidence before God,
    161
  on the Mount of Transfiguration,
    169
  new heaven and a new earth seen
    by, 70
  on purifying ourselves, 94
  saw the holy city, new Jerusalem,
    163
  writing to the seven churches of
    Turkey, 101
John the Baptist, 40, 100, 159, 195
Joseph (Jacob's son)
  adultery defined by, 195
  blessed by God with wealth, 213
  bought all the land in Egypt for
    Pharaoh, 129
  collected all the food produced in
    the years of abundance, 127
  collected all the money in payment
    for the grain and brought it to
    Pharaoh's palace, 128

Joseph (Jacob's son) (continued)
    dreams of, 124
    family reunion of, 130–32
    God called to be prime minister of
        Egypt, 128, 142
    interpreted Pharaoh's dreams, 126
    sold as a slave by his brothers, 124
    success of, 124–32
Joseph (Jesus' earthly father), 24, 100
Joshua
    as an outstanding military leader,
        157
    sanctification of, 71
    stood in the gap for God, 159
    success of, 8–9, 118
Judah, woe to the drunk priests and
    prophets of, 204
Judas Iscariot, 26, 27, 92
Jude, 82
justice, tempered with mercy and
    pardon, 128

kingdom of God
    accumulation of lasting treasures
        of, 215
    advancing, 208
    available by grace, 39
    contributing to the development
        of, 220
    defined as a process, 38
    disciples' message as, 41
    entering through many afflictions,
        139
    as eternal and secure, 39–40
    as everlasting dominion, 40
    giving up all for the sake of, 224
    message of John the Baptist as, 40
    as in our hearts, 43–47
    as Paul's message, 41–43
    praying for, 44
    as the principal theme of Jesus,
        40–41
    standard for entrance in, 47–50
kingdom of heaven, repentance for,
    38–40
kings and priests, redeemed to be, 57

Laban, 121, 122

laborers in the vineyard, parable of,
    222–24
lack of faith, in God as a sin, 162
Lamb of God, sinless, 28–29
Lamb's Book of Life, 104, 173
Laodiceans, lukewarm church of, 101
last shall be the first, and the first last,
    224
law, made for the lawless and
    disobedient, 201
law of God, 8, 191–92
lawlessness, sin defined as, 10–11
leaders
    church, 171
    covetous, 226
    God as, 190
    judging the success of, 152
    not remembered by their
        compromises, 153
    political, xii, 215
    religious, 26
leadership, xii, 145–46, 152, 153
leprosy, Job afflicted with, 158
lesbian unions, 199
Levi, sons of, 186–87
Lewis, Arthur, 147
life
    after death, 218
    conflicts and sufferings of, 67
    including abundance of things, 189
    repentance leading to, 37–38
    reward of a crown of, 172–73
    of righteousness, 63
light from heaven, encompassed Saul,
    61
light of God, 96
likeness of Christ, putting on, 68
living, according to the flesh versus
    living in accordance with the
    Spirit, 74
long life, obedience guaranteeing,
    156–57
long-term drinking, consequences of,
    205
Lord and Savior, process of accepting
    Christ as, 4
Lord's Supper, 26–27
lost sheep, parable of, 171, 172

SUBJECT INDEX

Lot, 21, 105, 200
love, covering a multitude of sins, 79
love of money, 136, 216
loving, our enemies, 79–80
Lucifer. *See* Satan
lust, 5–6

macroeconomic stabilization programs, 147
Malachi, on tithing, 190
male homosexuality, as a serious offence, 198
man, born outside a relationship with Christ, 13
Manasseh, conversion of, 59–60
mankind, 4, 14
manna, xi
Manoah, wife of became pregnant with Sampson, 203
marriage, 194, 196, 197, 200
Mary (mother of James and John), 31
Mary (mother of Jesus), 24, 95
Mary Magdalene, 31
material goods, offerings of, 191
Matthew, invited Jesus to a celebratory banquet, 171
Melchizedek, taught Abraham, 185
members of Christ, our bodies as, 76–77, 198
mental capacities, irreversible damage to, 209
merchants, worshipping money and power, 215
mercies of God, 15
Meshach, 172–73, 208–9
mind
    controlled by the Spirit of God, 11
    of God able to teach people, 190
    governed by the flesh as hostile to God, 66, 74–75
    renewing daily, 75
ministers, 170
ministry, of Jesus, 25
miracle, of becoming a Christian, 4
misfortune, accepting, 158
missionaries, scribes and Pharisees as, 50
Moab, women of, 195

money
    as an end in itself, ix
    as king in Babylon, 215
    love of as the root of evil, 46
    needing for our proper existence, 214
    offerings of, 191
    shrewdness with achieving eternal goals, 221
    use of demonstrating love for God, 189
    warning of affection toward, 217
Moody's, downgraded the credit rating of Barbados, 146
moral uprightness, as the legacy of Freundel Stuart, 154
mortgage document, securing funds from a bank, 221–22
Moses
    came down from Mount Sinai with his face shining, 170
    committed murder, 71, 114
    God revealed himself to on Mount Sinai, 139
    reestablished the covenant with God, 22
    replaced by Joshua, 118
    required to build a tabernacle, 111
    sins of, 51
    spending energy and time hearing complaints, 149
    stood in the gap for God, 159
    stood on holy ground, 114
    at the transfiguration of Jesus, 178
mother, of Freundel Stuart, 132
motives, praying with the wrong, 49
Mount Carmel, 176
Mount Horeb, 71
Mount of Transfiguration, 169
mourning, for the loss of Babylon, 215
murder
    chief priests seeking for Jesus, 48
    of Christians by Paul, 114
    Moses committed, 71, 114
    sin of, 6
    Stephen accused the people of Israel of, 170
    of Stephen by Paul, 61

nations, accepting the true and living
    God, xi–xii
Nazarites, separating themselves from
    wine and strong drink, 203
King Nebuchadnezzar, 172–73
the needy, being generous to, 214
new birth, 85, 95
new covenant, 187–89, 205
new creation, coming into existence,
    63
new divine nature, characteristics and
    attitudes of, 68
new heaven and a new earth, seen by
    John in Revelation, 70
new highway, 69–70
New Jerusalem, 163, 165
new life in Christ, 67
new man, putting on, 95
new nature, 67–68
new relationship with Christ, 64
New Testament, emphasizing God's
    riches in us, 213
Nicodemus, 38–39
Noah, 20, 98–99, 163, 204
nonsmokers, victims of secondhand
    smoke, 211
not-for-profit organizations, role in the
    life of nations, xii

Obadiah, set up Elijah's reunion with
    Ahab, 175–76
obedience
    of Abraham to God, 21
    as better than sacrifice, 23
    bringing victory, 157
    defined, 155
    establishing by bringing the tithe,
        184
    of Ezekiel, 158
    prosperity through, 155–79
    purifying our souls, 79
offerings, 190–94
old covenant, sacrifices offered as
    atonement, 188
old nature, 65–67
old sinful self, discarding, 68
Old Testament era, ended with John
    the Baptist, 40

open windows of heaven, for tithing,
    182
ordinary man, Elijah as, 178–79
outer darkness, place of, 18
overeating, 208

parable of the sower, 88
paralytic man, Jesus healed and forgave
    his sins, 47
partiality, showing, 12
passions, controlling, 75
Passover, 25
patience, 137–39
patriarchs, 43, 164
Paul. *See also* Saul of Tarsus
    on Abraham's seed and heirs, xiii
    on abstaining from evil and
        praying for sanctification, 76
    accepted his mission knowing he
        would endure suffering, 61
    advice on straining towards what is
        ahead, 165
    advised Timothy to use wine, 203
    assured of the crown of
        righteousness, 168
    on awaking to righteousness and
        sinning not, 83
    became dead to the reigning power
        of sin, 63
    on being carnally minded is death,
        66
    on being perfect, 100
    boasted in his infirmities, 168
    on bringing his body under
        subjection, 167
    on characteristics of God's chosen
        people, 140
    chastised the church for profaning
        the Lord's Supper, 26
    on Christians
        crucifying God afresh, 87
        departing from iniquity, 96
    on the church as a body with
        Christ as the head, 212
    on the circumcision made without
        hands, 68
    on cleansing from all filthiness of
        the flesh and spirit, 64, 72

SUBJECT INDEX

commanding the church to "be perfect," 94
on competing according to the rules, 167
on conversion, 58–59
conversion of, 60–61
on crucifying the flesh, 66
on the depth of the wisdom and knowledge of God, 214
did not reject Jesus, 114
encouraging Christians to present their bodies as a living sacrifice, 192–93
on entering the kingdom of God, 42
exhortation to Timothy on the rich, 140
on existence without Christ as worthless, 39
on exulting in tribulations, 138–39
on faith in God, 63
on fleeing from illicit sexual activity, 77
on forgiveness, 139, 145
on God
    blessing us, 213
    choosing foolish things of the world to confound the wise, 114
    grafting us back into the True Vine again, 89
    as God's ambassador of patience, 138
on God's power, 82
hardships endured by, 193–94
on the Holy Spirit, 35
on immorality, 195
kingdom of God as the message of, 41
on the law of God according to the inward man, 11
on laying all on God's altar, 162
on life without sin, 90
listing offenders who will not inherit the kingdom of God, 198–99
on living through the Spirit, 194
on making us perfect, 85–86
mission to evangelize the Gentiles, 61
on moving on to perfection, 81
on Noah, 98–99
on not being godless like Esau, 119–20
obtained warrants to continue persecution of the church, 193
on our bodies
    as a living sacrifice, 211
    as members of Christ, 76–77
    as the temple of the living God and the home of the Holy Spirit, 56
on overcoming evil with good, 80
overshadowed by a light from heaven that blinded him, 72
passionate dying declaration, 99–100
on perfecting in the flesh, 87–88
on predestination to be holy, 80
prepared
    himself for enduring suffering, 167–68
    to survive on the basic necessities of life, 136
on the punishment of those who do not know God, 15–16
on putting on the new man, 67
recognized as perfect, 99–100
rejected the gospel news of salvation until humbled by God, 113
responsible for the murder of many Christians, 114
on sanctification
    of our bodies, 75
    of spirit and soul and body, 73
as Saul was a sinner of the worst kind, 61
on separating Christians from God's love, 91
on sin breaking the seal of redemption, 87
on the sinful nature of man, 65–66, 97
sins of, 51

Paul (continued)
  on specific Christian experiences, 101
  on striving to win the prize at the end of the Christian's physical life's journey, 166
  testified at the end of his Christian experience here on earth, 193
  on the value of treasures of the kingdom of God, 39
  as a very faithful soldier of the cross, 168
  warning to the rich, 214
Pentecost, events on the day of, 35–36, 71
perdition (destruction), 92
perfect being, God created Adam as, 93
perfect churches, 98, 101, 102
perfect moral being, man created as, 4
perfect wisdom, coming from God, 111
perfection, 81, 101
Pergamos, compromising church at, 101
perpetual truths, 187
person, God as, 189–90
Peter
  astonished at a large catch of fish resulting from obedience, 156
  on becoming holy, 63–64
  on the church as God's living, spiritual house, 212
  on conversion, 59
  on escaping the corruption of sinful desires, 86
  in the garden of Gethsemane, 27
  on God making one strong, firm and steadfast, 144
  healed a man lame from birth, 37
  on holiness, 69
  on inheritance incorruptible and undefiled, 166
  on the kingdom of God, 42
  on the lives of all married persons, 195
  preached on repentance, 37
  preached on the day of Pentecost, 36
  on purifying souls, 79
  putting the cares of the world before the things of God, 46
  raised Dorcas from the dead, 85
  on repentance, 34–35
  on sanctification of our spirit, 74
  testified about Jesus to Cornelius and his household, 36
  on the unfading crown of glory, 169
  witnessing the glory of Christ on the Mount of Transfiguration, 169
Pharaoh, 126, 127
Pharisee, meaning "one who is separated," 48
Pharisee and the sinner, praying in the temple, 48–49
Pharisees, 43, 47, 48, 50
Philadelphia, faithful church at, 102–3
physical death, 13, 19
physical existence, surrendering our, 13
physical sins, destroying our relationship with Christ, 77
Pilate. See Pontius Pilate
pleasure, temptation for, 5
police work, preparing for, 186
political leaders, xii, 215
political speeches, of Stuart at rallies, 141
politicians, defects of, 152
Pontius Pilate, 28, 31, 38
the poor, active response to, 84
possessions, man's life not ultimately fulfilled by, 227
Potiphar, 124–25
Potiphar's wife, 125
Potiphera, father of Asenath, 127
poverty, as piety, ix
power
  to choose, 4, 7–9
  desire for, 6
  of evil, 42
  of fasting, 49
  of the flesh, 66
  of God, 82
  of the gospel, 114
  of the Holy Spirit, 35
  of Jesus, 47
  merchants worshipping, 215

SUBJECT INDEX

of the old nature, 64
of sin, 63
temptation for, 6
praises to God, sacrifices of, 191
prayer of intercession, of Jesus to our Father in heaven, 90
praying, that God will forgive our trespasses and sins, 49–50, 145
predatory thought, leading to predatory action, 226
predetermined plan, to achieve a predetermined result, 110
pretenders, to wisdom and education, 113
pride, 5, 6, 47, 48–49
priestesses, of Aphrodite, 198
priests. *See also* kings and priests
    accepting imperfect sacrifices, 191
prime minister of Barbados, Freundel Stuart's vision to become, 134
principles of Christianity, viii
prison warden, put Joseph in charge, 125–26
prisoners, working in the fields in exchange for freedom, 128
prize winners, of a perishable prize, 166
prodigal son, wasted all his financial resources, 204
prosperity
    defining God's pathway to, viii
    depending on our relationship with God, ix
    envying that of others, 227
    Jacob's pathway to, 118–19
    obedience ensuring, 157–58
    as a special blessing from God, xi
    through obedience, 155–79
    through tithes and offerings, 180–212
    through wisdom, 109–54
proud person, boasting of the cravings of his heart, 6
purification, redemption required for, 55–56
purity, as God's passport for entry in the kingdom of God, 94

Rachel, Joseph's mother, 124
Rahab, 114, 225
rain, sending on the just and unjust, 218
Rebekah, became pregnant with twins, 119
recession, overcoming, 138
redemption, 52–57
rejoicing, reward of a crown of, 171–72
religious leaders, Jesus as a threat to, 26
repentance
    defined, 34
    Esau found no place for, 208
    importance of, 34–40
    for the kingdom of heaven is at hand, 38–40
    leading to life, 37–38
    none beyond the grave, 55
    required if a Christian sins, 104
    of sins, 34–57, 96
    of Zacchaeus, 51
restoration through the church, if a Christian sins, 212
resurrection, 31–33
retirement, planning for as wise, 218
Revelation, perfect churches of, 101
reward, being prepared to share, 223
rewards, waiting for us in heaven, 165–73
the rich, 148, 214
rich fool, parable of, 217–19
rich young man, 46, 82–83
rich young ruler, parable of, 217
riches, 136, 214
right living, not substituting tithing for, 188
righteousness
    coming from God, 39
    described, x
    life of, 63
    not remembered because of iniquity, 104
    reward of a crown of, 167–68
    of the scribes and the Pharisees, 48
robbery, as a serious offence, 189
robbing, God, 189–94
Roosevelt, Theodore, on character, 153
root of evil, love of money as, 46

Royal Barbados Police Force, basic
    training, 186
royal priesthood, 188

sacrifice, ix, 28
sacrifices, 39, 191, 212
saints of God, 16, 40
Salome, 31
salvation, 7, 50, 113–14, 165
Samaritan woman at the well, 35, 171
same-sex unions, 201
Sampson, 203
sanctification, 62, 64–65, 73, 81
Sanhedrin council, mock trial before,
    28
Sardis, dead church at, 101–2
Satan
    accused Job of being faithful to
        God only because he was rich,
        150
    as the author of sin, 8
    battling with God for our souls, 77
    burdened Paul with a thorn in his
        flesh, 168
    cast into hell eventually, 16–17
    cast out of heaven because of his
        pride, 6, 49
    deceived Adam, 77
    exiting control of our lives, 42
    interrogated about Job's perfection,
        98
    putting Job's faithfulness to God to
        the test, 158
    rich and powerful countries of
        the world uniting under the
        influence of, 215
    sinneth from the beginning, 83
    thought he had won a resounding
        victory after the death of Jesus,
        31
Saul of Tarsus, 60, 61. *See also* Paul
Savior, need for, 10–19
scribes, 47, 48, 50, 54, 171
Seale, Orlando, 3
second death, 18–19, 89, 102
seed, multiplied back several times, 182
seeds, of the good news of the gospel
    of Jesus, 44–47

seeking, God first, x
self-centered life, enjoying, 218
self-control, strengthening our inner
    being, 75
self-imposed penalty (curse), for
    violating the spiritual principle
    of tithing, 184
selfishness, 66, 67, 83
sexual diseases, 198, 200
sexual immorality, 6, 72, 77
sexual infidelity, 198
sexual intercourse, 196
sexual partners, becoming one flesh,
    77
sexual sins, 194
Shadrach, 172–73, 208–9
shedding of blood, as the method for
    the redemption of mankind, 22
shepherd of the sheep, Jesus as, 91
shrewd manager, parable of, 219–22
silent man, Stuart scorned as, 149–51
sin(s)
    blotted out by repentance, 37
    causing the Holy Spirit to lose
        control of our being, 96
    Christ died for our, 20–33
    commenced with Satan's revolt
        against God, 8
    conceived in the heart, 12
    consequences of, 226
    corrupting
        our relationship with Christ, 90
        our souls, 78
    defined
        as disobedience to God's laws,
            155
        as lawlessness, 10–11
    of disobedience to God by Adam,
        15
    eating away at our relationship
        with God, 15
    entered the world because of
        disobedience, 5
    of envy, 223
    eternal death and, 54
    facing the consequences of, 55
    God forgetting, 85–86
    making us imperfect, 96

SUBJECT INDEX

as an offense to the Holy Spirit, 87
repentance of, 34–57
separating us from God, 88, 89, 91
shedding of blood as God's method of covering, 22
sin offering, Israel making to God, 22–23
sinful flesh, putting to death, 66
sinful mind, as hostile to God, 75
sinful nature, 64, 65–66, 97
sinfulness, inherited from Adam, 65
sinners
    avoiding contact with, 171
    born as, 95
    Jesus as the guest of, 51
    receiving God's forgiveness, 201
    recognizing the need for a Savior, 3
    seeking to escape hell's fury, 16
smoke, from the burnt offering, 23
smoking, dangers of, 211
Sodom and Gomorrah, 21, 155–56
soils, parable of, 44–47
Solomon
    on choosing wisdom, 109
    endowed with wisdom, 111
    promised riches, 213
    promised wisdom and prosperity, 112
    on restraining lips as prudent, 149–50
Son of man
    coming in his Father's glory with his angels, 164, 165
    as God himself in a human body, 25
    having power on earth to forgive sins, 47
    returning in all his glory with all his angels, 16
sons of perdition, 90, 92
sons of the world, 220
soul(s)
    described, 77
    giving over to the control of Christ, 165
    living forever, 119
    purified through obedience, 79
    sanctification of our, 77–80
    value of, 119
soul winners, crown of rejoicing for, 172
sower, parable of, 44–47
sowing and reaping, described, 182–83
speaking in other tongues, allowed by the Holy Spirit, 36
Spirit. *See* Holy Spirit
spirit, being in control of, 75
Spirit of Christ, having, 75
spiritual adultery, against God, 117
spiritual birth, as a birth of righteousness, 95–96
spiritual death
    described, 14–15
    resulting in eternal death, 200
    sanctification of, 74–75
    suffering the consequences of, 104
spiritual growth, helping with, viii
spiritual sacrifices, offering, 212
standard, for entrance in the kingdom of God, 47–50
Standard & Poor's, downgraded the credit rating of Barbados, 146
Stephen, 61, 89, 169–70
stewards, 219–20
stewardship of money, 221
stigma of association, with sinners, 171
stony ground, seeds falling on, 45–46
Stuart, Freundel Jerome
    accepted all blame for his party's loss, 153–54
    called by God as prime minister of Barbados during its recessionary crisis, 142
    core values that effected the life of, 134–42, 145–46
    delegating duties to his cabinet, 149
    deposed, 152–54
    education of, 132
    endured the suffering and pain of recession, 138
    gave land for the erection of an evangelical church, 140
    handling of a perceived coup, 142–45
    legacy of moral uprightness, 154

Stuart, Freundel Jerome (continued)
  patient in spirit, 138
  practiced God's wisdom, 135
  represented clients unable to pay the legal fees, 136
  scorned as the silent man, 149–51
  succeeded Thompson as prime minister, 141–42
  success of, 132–54
  as a teacher and lawyer, 133–34
stumbling block, not putting in our brother's way, 207
subconscious mind, the will living in, 78
success
  of Freundel Jerome Stuart, 132–54
  of Jacob, 118–24
  of Joseph (Jacob's son), 124–32
  of Joshua, 8–9, 118
  of leaders, 152
  obedience ensuring, 157–58
  wisdom giving, 117
suffering
  of the church at Symrna, 102
  enduring for the sake of the gospel of Christ, 167
  of Freundel Jerome Stuart, 138
  of Job, 138
  of Paul, 61, 167–68
  taking up our crosses of, 67
suicide, committed by Judas Iscariot, 92
superiority, of the Pharisees, 48
Symrna, persecuted and suffering church at, 102
Synagogue of the Freemen, 61

Tabitha Dorcas, raised from the dead, 85
tares, as children of the devil, 46
tasks, wisdom instructing us how to handle, 117
tax collector, humbled himself before God, 49
temptation
  of Adam and Eve called the lust of the flesh, 5
  on the Christian journey, 172–73
  endured by Jesus, 5

  God knowing how to deliver Christians out of, 104–5
  of power, 6
  suffered by Jesus Christ, 125
Ten Commandments, given by God, 22
ten percent, giving, 186, 187
tenth and final commandment, given to Moses on Mount Sinai, 224–25
thanking God, for bringing us through every situation, 162
theft, robbery as an aggravated form of, 189
"there," meaning of in Hebrews 7:8, 185
Thompson, David John Howard, 141
thorns, seeds sown among, 46
Thyatira, worldly church at, 101
Timothy, 90, 140, 167, 203
tithe, 180–81, 184–85
tithes and offerings, prosperity through, 180–212
tithing
  as an act of worship, 180
  biblical plan of, 184
  in the early church, 185–86
  establishing a new relationship with God, 181
  history of, 183–87
  instituted under Abraham, 187
  under the new covenant, 187–89
  as obeying God's command, 186
  obligation of reaching across dispensations, 183
  as a perpetual truth, 187
tobacco, as a primary health concern, 211–12
tomb, of Jesus was not sealed by God, 31
touching, Paul on abstaining from, 197–98
tragedies, in this world today, 38
training, of athletes, 166
treasures in heaven, laying up eternal, 221
tree of knowledge of good and evil, 4, 206
tribulations, glorying in, 138
true vine, remaining attached to, 87

SUBJECT INDEX

true wisdom, producing peace and goodness, 110–11
trusting, in God for security, 214

unbelief, 88, 89
ungodly people, knowing how to secure the most from the ungodly things of this world, 220
unity with Christ, destroying the power of the old nature, 64
unjust steward, 220, 221
unquenchable fire, place of, 17–18
unrighteous dead, white throne of judgment for, 53
unrighteous mammon, not being faithful in, 221
unsaved person, as a slave to the things of the flesh, 66
Uriah, 6, 117

valley of dry bones, Ezekiel prophesying to, 159
value
　of the kingdom of God, 39
　of life, 227
vegetables, eating only, as being weak in the faith, 206
victor's crown, for our heavenly reward, 166
vineyard of God, parable of, 222–24

wages of sin, as eternal death, 15, 88
weak things, of the world confounding mighty things, 114
wealth
　Christian perspective of, 213–27
　coming from God, 109–10
　as a negative influence on spirituality, 214
　as not evil, 216
　not Job's priority, 158
　not mattering in this present world, 165
　possession of, 46, 213

the wealthy, 44, 217, 218
whore of Babylon, 117
wickedness of man, 20
widow of Zarephath, 174, 178
will, of God, 75, 91–93, 94
wine, 202, 203
wisdom
　benefits of, 115–17
　characteristics of true, 110
　core value of for Stuart, 134–35
　defined, 110–11
　drunkards lacking, 204
　God created the world by, 112–13
　making a person successful, 117
　prosperity through, 109–54
　resisting the temptation of the devil, 125
　saving us from immorality, 116–17
wisdom of God, 111–12, 113, 114–15
wise man, 143
wise person, 110, 150
withholding the tithe, as robbing God, 180
woman
　becoming one flesh with her husband, 200
　caught in the sin of adultery, 47–48
workers, responded to the call and received their reward, 224
workforce, sustaining an overpopulated, 148
world conspiracy, involving merchants or superrich magnates, 215
worship of idols, Israelites returned to, 8
worth, of the kingdom of God, 39
wrath to come, redemption saving us from, 53
wrongdoing, procedures for handling, 145–46

Zacchaeus, 51–52, 85
Zacharias and his wife Elizabeth, 100
Ziba, advised King David on the use of wine, 203

Scripture Index

OLD TESTAMENT

Genesis

1:31	4
2:7	78
2:16–17	4
2:24	77
3:1–7	77
3:6	5
3:21	22
4:20	187
6	20
6:9	98
6:19–20	204
12:1–3	20, 21
14	185
14:19	186
17:1	98
17–20	213
19:20–27	204
25	207
25:30	208
25:34	207
27:27–29 NIV	120
27:28	202
28:1–5 NIV	121
28:3–4 NIV	120
28:16 NIV	122
30–31	213
39	195
39:1–6	124
39:9	125
39:21–23	125–26
40:8	126
41	213
41:16	126
41:38–45	127
41:51	131
45:4–5 NIV	131
47:5–6	132
47:13 NIV	128
47:14 NIV	128
47:15–26 NIV	128–29

Exodus

18	149
19	21
19:5	xiii
19:5–6	21–22, 69
19:9–10	22
20	21
20:17	224
29:40	203
31	111
34:6–7 NIV	139
34:28–30	170

Leviticus

1:3	191
1:9 NIV	23
3:1	192

Leviticus (continued)

4:1–5	22
5:14–19	23
5:15	23
6:7	23
6:24–30	22
7:1–16	23
8:14–17	22
10:20	116
11	206
16:3–22	22
18:22	198
20	195
20:10	195
20:13	198
23:13	203
27	184
27:30	184
27:30–32	180
27:30–33	184

Numbers

6:3	203
18:21–24	181
25:1–9	195
32:23	225

Deuteronomy

5	175
8:17–18	110
10:17 NIV	12
14:2	68
14:22–27	181
17:1	192
22:22	195
26:2	181
26:10	181
26:12	181
28	175
29:5–6	203
30:19	8

Joshua

1:8	ix, 118, 157
7	118
7:1–5	225
7:11	157
7:18–26	225
24:14–15	9

Judges

9:1–5	226
13	203

1 Samuel

2:12	208
2:17	208

2 Samuel

11:1–27	226
11:2–4	6
16:2	203
22:21–24	99

1 Kings

3:11–12	213
14:8	99
15:5	99
17:1	174
17:2–5	174
17:17 NIV	175
18	177
18:21 NIV	176
18:36–37 NIV	176
18:38–39 NIV	176
19:4	179
21:1–19	226

2 Kings

2:11	178

1 Chronicles

22:9–10	112
22:12–13	112
29:12	213

2 Chronicles

9:22	213
17:5	213
19:6–7 NIV	12

30:9 NIV	60	127:1	31
		130:4	139
Job		139:13–15	199
2:3	98	145:13	39–40
12:13	111		
14:1–2	13	**Proverbs**	
15:2–3	151	2	115
19:25	158	2:16–19 NIV	116
35:5	111	3	115
36:10–11	157	3:1–2	156
36:11	155	3:8	115
42:12–15	151	4:6–8	110
		4:7	109, 134
Psalms		10:19	149
1	ix	10:22	ix
1:3	156	14:12	209
9:17	16	17:27–28	150
14:3	11	18:10	144
18:18	143	18–21	ix
23	156	20:1	204
24:1–2	186	21:20	148
24:4 NIV	96	21:22	143
32:1–2	98	23:2	208
32:5	51	23:20–21	208
32:8 NLT	118	24:5	143
33:12	xii	25:16	208
34:4	ix	25:28	75, 209
34:14	59	28:13	225
34:16	103	28:16	226
37:37	98	31	204
50:12	186		
51	117	**Ecclesiastes**	
51:2–4	117	3:2	13
51:5	4	7:11–12 NIV	109
69:33	126	7:19	143
75:6–7	142	7:20	11
86:5	139	7:29	4
89:11	186	10:10	117
89:48	13	12:14	220
90:8	220, 225		
103:10–14	146	**Isaiah**	
103:12	85	1	155
103:19–20	40	1:19	156
104	112	5:22	204
104:24–27	112	6:3–7	159
121:4–8	144	9:19	131

Isaiah (continued)

14:13–14	6
25:6	205
28	204
28:7–8	204
35:8–9 NIV	69
40:26, 28 NIV	111
42:5	186
43:25	85
52:1 NIV	105
53	192
53:3–5, 7	28
53:4–5 NIV	29
53:7	28, 151
53:10	23
54:17	143
55:7	58
58:6	49
59:2	14

Jeremiah

1:10	159
9:4–9	131
12:6	131
17:9–10	11
29:7 NIV	vii
29:10	vii
29:11	137
29:11 NIV	vii

Ezekiel

16:49	208
18:4	12
18:7	84
18:24 NIV	103
18:26	103
18:30–32	104
22:29–30	158
33:12–13	104
36:25–27	92
36:25–27 NIV	67–68
36:26 NIV	74

Daniel

1:15–16	209
5	185

7:13–17	40
7:17–18	40

Hosea

2:8–9	202–3

Micah

7:6	130

Habakkuk

1:13	105

Malachi

1:7–8	191
3:1	159
3:8–10	180
3:9	184, 190
3:10	182
3:10–11	182

NEW TESTAMENT

Matthew

1:19	100
1:21	24
3:1–2	40
3:12	17
4:23	40
5:18	187
5:19–20	44
5:20	47
5:45	218
5:48	93
6:1–20	222
6:12	139
6:14–15	145
6:16–18	49
6:25	136
6:25 NIV	x
6:31–33 NIV	135
6:33	44
6:33 NIV	x
6:34 NIV	x

SCRIPTURE INDEX

7:6–8	161
7:13–14	96
7:21–23	92–93, 224
8:11–12	18
9:37	222
10:26	220
12:28	42
12:36	220
13:41–42	17
13:49–50	17
14:3–12	195
15:11–19	216
16:21	26, 32
16:23	46
16:26–27	165
16:27	172
17:14–21	49
17:22–23	32
18:15–17 NIV	145–46
19:9	196
19:21	82
19:23–24	150
19:27–30	39
20:10–12	223
20:13–16	223
20:16	224
20:19	32
21:21–22	160
22:1–14	18
22:37–40	8
23	48
23:23	187
24:13	173
24:13–14 NIV	44
25:14–30	18
25:30	18
25:31–46	16, 18
25:31–46 NIV	84
25:41	16
26:2	25
26:42 NIV	27
26:57–68	28
27:66	31
28:2	31
28:6	32

Mark

1:14	41
2:1–12	47
2:6	47
2:16	47
3:22	47
3:27	144
6:20	100
7:18–23	206
7:21–23 NIV	88
8:35–37 NIV	119
9:14–29	49
10:17–31	217
11:18	48
14:16–25	41
16:16	89

Luke

1:5–6	100
1:34–35	95
1:35	24
2:25	100
5:5	156
5:31–32	34
6:7	47
6:11	47
6:27–35	79–80
6:38	140, 182, 190
7	160
7:7–8	160
7:28	159
7:33–34	202
8:1	41
9:1–2	41
9:22–24	167
9:23	67
9:56	112
10	203
12:1	227
12:13	226
12:13–34	217
12:16–21	226–27
12:20	218
12:21	218
12:33–34 NIV	ix
12:51–53 NIV	130
13:1–5	37, 38

Luke (continued)

15	204
15:1–7 NIV	171
16:1–13	221
16:1–16	219
16:8	220
16:9	221
16:10–12	221
16:16	40
16:25–26	16
17:21	43
18:9–14	49
18:22–25	217
19:1	25
19:9–10	50
23:1–25	28
23:10	48
24:6–7	32

John

1:1, 14	25
3:1–5	39
3:5–6 NIV	94
3:6–10	83
3:16	54, 192
4:14	35
4:34–35	222
5:24	37
5:28–29	53
6:5–12	188
6:37–39	91
8:1–11	47
8:34	52
10:27–29	90
11:18–19	202
14:1–3	164
15:2–6 NIV	87
15:7	160
17	90
17:12	92
17:19–23	83
18:13	28
18:36	38

Acts

2:38	34–35, 36
3:19	37
4:32–35	180
6	169
7:51	89
7:55–56	170
10	206
10:1	100
10:43 NIV	36
11:18 NIV	37
11:27–30	181
19:6–8	42
20:28 NIV	56

Romans

1:24–27	199
2:4	214
3:10	11
3:22	101
3:23	4, 11
3:25	30
5:3–5 NASB	138–39
5:4	137
5:8–9	53
5:12	5
5:14 NIV	7
6:1–7	97
6:5, 11	32
6:6–7	66
6:11	32
6:12, 13	212
6:12–14	75
6:19	77
6:23	12
7:7–25	11
7:14–25	65–66
7:24–25	11
8:3–8	201
8:5–9 NIV	75
8:6	66
8:7–8	66
8:8–9 NIV	90
8:12–13	194
8:13	65
8:25	137
8:28	143
9:23	214
11:20–23 NIV	87–88

11:33	214	15:54–57	14
12:1	190, 192	16:1–2	180
12:1–2	64		
12:1–2 NIV	211	## 2 Corinthians	
12:2	58, 78		
12:12	137	1:21–22	89
12:20–21	80	5:21	23
13:13–14	209–10	6:14–18	216
14:1–23	206	7:1	64, 65, 72, 211
14:6b, 10–15	207	9:6 NIV	183
14:11–13	220	9:7 NIV	183
14:17	38, 205	9:8	xi
14:23	11	9:8 NIV	183
15:26	180	11:22–33	168
16:17	143	12:7–10	168
		13:11	94

1 Corinthians

Galatians

1:21	113	2:20 NIV	30
1:24	114	3	xiii
1:26	113	3:3	63
1:26–30	151	3:9	18
1:27	114	3:13	29
2:11	189	3:16–25	187
3:11–15	164	3:29	183, 187
4:1–2	219	4:3–7	54
4:5	220	5:1	59
5:1	195	5:16	65
6:9, 10	194, 200	5:16–17	66
6:15–20	76–77	5:19–21	5
6:16	211	5:24	66
6:18–20	197	6:1	212
6:19–20 NIV	56	6:2	65
6:20	29	6:6	180
7	195, 197	6:7	182
7:1–2	197		
7:7–12	196	## Ephesians	
9:14	180		
9:24–27	166	1:4	7
9:27	193	1:4–5	80
10:8	196	1:7	29, 214
10:14	65	1:7–8	52
10:21	66	1:13–14 NIV	86
10:21 NIV	94	1:18	213
10:26	186	1:18–23	32
11:27 NIV	27	2:1–3	14
11:28	27	2:4–6	15
15:34	83	2:5–7	32

Ephesians (continued)

2:6–7	214
2:8	19
2:13	31
2:13 NIV	29
3:16	214
4:11–13	100
4:15, 16	212
4:22–24	67
4:30 NIV	87
4:32	139, 145
5:3	77
5:25–27	72
5:26–27	97
6:1–3	157

Philippians

2:13–14	165
3:7–11 NIV	59
3:8–10 NIV	39
3:15	100
4:11–13	136
4:13	216
4:18	191
4:19	214
5:7	25

Colossians

1:12–14	42
1:16–17 NIV	25
1:20	31
2:11–12	68
2:13	32
2:14	29
3:1–4	32
3:12–14 NIV	140
4:11	42

1 Thessalonians

2:19	172
4	72
4:3–8	62
4:14–17	177–78
5:23	193
5:23–24	73

2 Thessalonians

1:8–10 NIV	16

1 Timothy

1:9–10	201
4:1–5	206
4:7	65
4:12–15	65
5:17	180
5:23	203
6:3–5	135
6:6–8 NIV	135
6:9	136
6:10	216
6:17	214
6:17–18	ix
6:17–19 ESV	140

2 Timothy

1:10	54
1:11–12	82
2:3	168
2:5	167
2:19	90, 96
2:22	65
2:24	137
3:10–12	167
4:6–8	99–100, 193
4:7–8	168

Titus

2:11–14	55
3:7	97
3:9–11 NKJV	145

Hebrews

2:9 NIV	28
2:10	138
2:11–14	64
2:14 NIV	29
3:8–12	88
6:1	81, 94
6:4	86–87
7:1–11	183
7:4–5	186–87

7:8	185	1:23	95
7:26–28	192	2:5	212
8:6	189	2:9	69, 188–89
8:12	85	2:19–23 ESV	137
9:12 NIV	23	2:24	29
9:22	30	3:9	140
9:27	13	3:11 NIV	59
10:12	188	3:21–22	33
10:14–18	85	4:1–2	195
10:16	187	4:10	219
10:19	31	5:1–5	169
10:19–22 NIV	29	5:2–4	169
10:39	92	5:10	144
11:5	100		
11:6–7	99	## 2 Peter	
11:8–10	162	1:10–11	42
11:13–16	163	2:4–9	105
12:1	138	2:6–10	200
12:1–2 NIV	59		
12:2	138	## 1 John	
12:14	64, 96	1:7	30, 31
12:16–17	207	1:8–10	34, 51
13	195	1:9	93, 225
13:5	135	2:1–2	30
13:15	191	2:1–3	93
13:16	191	2:29	96
13:20–21	85–86	3:3–9	94
		3:4	10
## James		3:4–5 NIV	10
1:12	138, 172	3:16	30
1:19	137	3:21–22	161
1:27	181	4:9–10	30
2:1	12	5:1	95
2:8–9 NIV	12	5:13–15	161
3:13–17	110–11	5:18	96
4:7	63		
4:17	11	## Jude	
5:1–3	214	24–25	82
5:17–18	174		
		## Revelation	
## 1 Peter		2:8–11	102
1:2–5	74	2:9–10	173
1:3–5	33	2:10 NIV	102
1:14–16	64, 69	3:1–6	101
1:20	7	3:7–13	102
1:22	79		

Revelation (continued)

3:8, 10 NIV	102–3	20:10	17
3:12 NIV	103	20:11–15	19
5:9	30	20:12–15	53
5:9–10	57	20:15	173
13:8	7	21:1–4	70
14:9–11	17	21:1–7	163
18	215	21:8	18, 89
18:17	215	21:22–27 NIV	70
19:20–21	17	22:12	164
20:1–3	17	22:14	94
		22:14 NIV	105

www.ingramcontent.com/pod-product-compliance
Lightning Source LLC
Chambersburg PA
CBHW070243230426
43664CB00014B/2395